From Black Power to Hip Hop

In the series *Politics, History, and Social Change,*
edited by John C. Torpey

From Black Power to Hip Hop

RACISM, NATIONALISM,

AND FEMINISM

Patricia Hill Collins

 Temple University Press

PHILADELPHIA

PATRICIA HILL COLLINS is Professor of Sociology at the University of Maryland, College Park, and author of *Black Feminist Thought: Knowledge, Consciousness, and the Politics of Empowerment* and *Black Sexual Politics: African Americans, Gender and the New Racism.*

Temple University Press
1601 North Broad Street
Philadelphia PA 19122
www.temple.edu/tempress

∞ The paper used in this publication meets the requirements of the American National Standard for Information Sciences—Permanence of Paper for Printed Library Materials. ANSI Z39.48–1992

Library of Congress Cataloging-in-Publication Data

Collins, Patricia Hill.
From Black power to hip hop : racism, nationalism, and feminism /
Patricia Hill Collins.
     p. cm. — (Politics, history, and social change)
Includes bibliographical references and index.
ISBN 1-59213-091-7 (alk. paper) — ISBN 1-59213-092-5 (pbk. : alk. paper)
1. African Americans—Race identity.   2. African Americans—Social
conditions—1975–   3. African Americans—Politics and government.
4. Afrocentrism—United States.   5. Ethnicity—United States.
6. Racism—United States.7. United States—Race relations.   8. Nationalism—
United States.   9. African American women—Social conditions.
10. Feminism—United States.   I. Title.   II. Series.

E185.625.C646 2006
305.896'073–dc22

                                                      2005049885

ISBN 13: 978-1-59213-091-7 (cloth : alk. paper)

111507P

Contents

vi   Contents

Acknowledgments

B ecause this project consists of a series of essays that were written and published over a period of some years, the list of people who contributed is long. Many have been acknowledged elsewhere, so here I wish to recognize those who supported the final stages of this project.

I thank Vallarie Henderson, Tamika Odum, and Julie Hilvers, three graduate students in sociology at the University of Cincinnati who served as graduate research assistants for various parts of this project. Their professionalism, diligence, and great ideas made a significant difference.

The University of Cincinnati helped defray costs associated with this manuscript. The support provided by the Taft Fund within the McMicken College of Arts and Sciences for costs associated with manuscript preparation has been invaluable. I also thank Provost Anthony Perzigian for his tireless support of my scholarship during lean financial times. I also appreciate the support of Karen Gould, dean of the College of Arts and Sciences, and members of her administrative team. Josephine Wynne, the administrative secretary in African American studies for the duration of this project, also provided important support.

This project would not have come to fruition without the support of the team at Temple University Press. Micah Kleit, my editor, has been with me through this entire project. I am also grateful to the entire editorial team who worked on the manuscript, with special thanks to Jennifer French and Gary Kramer for their contributions during the production process. Expert copyediting was done by Susan Deeks.

Finally, I thank my family for their continued backing. My spouse, Roger; my daughter, Valerie; and my father, Albert Hill, have been among my strongest and most consistent supporters.

Introduction

From Black Power to Hip Hop

My life was totally consumed by all aspects of gang
life.... My clothes, walk, talk, and attitude all reflected
my love for and allegiance to my set. Nobody was more
important than my homeboys—nobody.... I was six
years old when the Crips were started. No one antici-
pated its sweep. The youth of South Central were being
gobbled up by an alien power threatening to attach itself
to a multitude of other problems already plaguing them.
An almost "enemy" subculture had arisen, and no one
knew from where it came. No one took its conceptions
seriously. But slowly it crept, saturating entire households, city blocks, neighborhoods, and eventually the
nation-state of California.

—Sanyika Shakur, AKA "Monster" Kody Scott

Many in hip-hop are simply carefully navigating the
waters of their sexuality. These guys I refer to as homie-
sexual are, clinically speaking, homosexual. But they very
much take on a machismo that separates them from as-
sociations with words like gay, queer, and most especially fag. I would guess that this has a lot to do with
safety, and with a culture that hates you because you're a
fag and most definitely hates you because you're black.

—Village Voice

My father got at least twenty years of good high living
out of the [drug] business.... That's power. To be able
to set up your own empire in your neighborhood, or
even somebody else's neighborhood for that matter. To
buy cars, Jeeps, trucks. To sport the flyest shit made by
top designers everyday.... To be able to shit on people
before they get a chance to shit on you. That's power.
Who could argue with that? A regular nigga worked all
week for change to get to work plus a beer to forget
about how hard he work.... Let's compare it, ten years

1

of good living and twenty years of high living versus sixty years of scraping to get by. Enough said.

—*Winter Santiaga, fictional character*

I don't act the way society dictates that a woman "should." I am not dainty. I do not hold back my opinions. I don't stay behind a man. But I'm not here to live by somebody else's standards. I'm defining what a woman is for myself. Simply put, I am not interested in subscribing to what society has decided for half of humankind. I am an individual.

—*Queen Latifah*

Gang member Sanyika Shakur and rap star Queen Latifah refuse to "live by somebody else's standards," yet the standards they choose seem diametrically opposed to one another. How should we understand young African American men whose loyalties to their gang surpass their commitment to their families? How will they get along with women who refuse to be "dainty" and who define "what a woman is" for themselves? What are we to make of young gay men who craft "homie-sexual" identities within the hypermasculine trappings of some elements of hip-hop culture, yet eschew self-definitions as "queer" or "fag"? Winter Santiaga, the protagonist in rapper Sister Souljah's novel *The Coldest Winter Ever*, bluntly embraces a materialism that seems at odds with traditions of the Black freedom struggle: "To be able to shit on people before they get a chance to shit on you. That's power." Santiaga's philosophy seemingly contradicts an ethos of Black solidarity that takes ironic forms in Shakur's words, "nobody was more important than my homeboys—nobody."

During the 1990s, Bakari Kitwana, head editor of *The Source: The Magazine of Hip-Hop, Music Culture and Politics*, began to use the term "hip-hop generation" to define this population of Black youth who were born between 1965 and 1984 and who shared a value system that was often at odds with the generation that preceded them.[1] Describing this same cohort of Black American youth, Mark Anthony Neal uses the term "post-soul" to describe the political, social, and cultural experiences of African Americans since the end of the Civil Rights and Black Power movements. Neal argues that the "soul babies" of this period have produced a "post-soul aesthetic" whereby the hip-hop generation and the generational consciousness attached to it are now much broader than its origins in Black American and Latino neighborhoods.[2] Hip-hop culture is a global phenomenon, yet Black American youth remain its most visible ambassadors. Because they occupy such a visible position within American society, and more recently within global mass media, African American youth stand at ground zero for issues of race, nation, gender, age, and sexuality.

In the United States, the paradoxical beliefs expressed by African American members of this group reflect the contradictions of a new racism. Coming to adulthood after the decline of the Civil Rights and Black Power movements of the 1950s and 1960s, contemporary Black youth grew up during a period of initial promise, profound change, and, for far too many, heart-wrenching disappointment. During this period marked by the end of the Black Power Movement and the ascendancy of hip hop, they lived the shift from a color-conscious racism that relied on strict racial segregation to a seemingly colorblind racism that promised equal opportunities yet provided no lasting avenues for African American advancement. Despite protestations to the contrary, this new colorblind racism claimed not to see race yet managed to replicate racial hierarchy as effectively as the racial segregation of old.

The lives of poor and working-class Black youth who symbolize the contradictions of this new racism are especially telling. Ironically, this is a generation whose actual members remain written off, marginalized, and largely invisible in everyday life. Isolated and ghettoized within American society, "domestic" African American youth—namely, those who are neither foreign migrants nor the children of migrants from countries of the Caribbean, continental Africa, or Europe—represent a highly stigmatized yet important population. In 2002, 33 percent of all African Americans were under age 18, compared with 23 percent of non–Hispanic Whites. A larger proportion of Black males than non–Hispanic White males were under age 18 (36 percent compared with 24 percent), a statistic that reflects the shorter life expectancy for African American men. The poverty status of African American youth is especially revealing. In 2001, among all American children under age 18, the poverty rate was 16 percent, but it was three times as high for Black children (30 percent).[3]

At the same time that Black American youth experience these social problems, their mass-media images tell a different story. In the 1990s, images of poor and working-class Black American youth as athletes and entertainers flooded global popular culture. The actual ghettoization of poor and working-class African Americans may render them virtually invisible within suburban malls, on soccer fields, and in good public schools, yet mass media created a seemingly authentic Black American culture that glamorized poverty, drugs, violence, and hypersexuality. As a result, representations of these same Black youth became hypervisible throughout far expanses of the globe.[4] The music, fashion, dance, styles, and post-soul aesthetic of Neal's soul babies seemingly catalyzed a multibillion-dollar hip-hop industry. "To buy cars, Jeeps, trucks," in the words of Sister Souljah's Winter Santiaga, "to sport the flyest shit made by top designers everyday" appealed to huge audiences that were hungry for these images of Blackness. Apparently, singing and dancing about Black pain and wearing the latest styles while doing it could generate cold, hard cash.[5]

What are the effects on Black American youth of being simultaneously so ignored and so visible? Recently, sociologists have begun to define cohort effects in a more specific way that may shed light on the Black hip-hop generation's curious position of invisibility and hypervisibility. This work stresses the impact of specific historical events on the character of generations. Public events experienced at a critical period in the life course, usually defined as the years of adolescence and early adulthood, may produce a specific set of attitudes in an entire generation that persists throughout its lifetime. Sharing great events may create a distinct generational consciousness. Within this framework, American youth of varying social classes, races, genders, ethnicities, and sexual orientations who came of age after the victories of the Civil Rights era and became adults during the dual processes of economic decline and the failure of racial integration may share a generational consciousness.

Beyond their actual numbers, the questions that confront African American youth have implications that reach far beyond this particular population. The status of Black youth who came of age during the period marked by the end of the Black Power Movement and the ascendancy of hip hop tests the veracity of core themes of American democracy. The vision of American democracy is remarkable—namely, a belief in the equal treatment of each individual citizen over differential group treatment; the guarantee of basic fairness in jobs, education, housing, and consumer marketplaces; and the promise that, if one works hard, one can have a promising future. For many Americans, these ideas shape their understandings of themselves as Americans and describe their realities. Others take a less sanguine view. For Black Americans, Latinos, indigenous peoples, poor people, racial/ethnic immigrant groups, and many others, these ideals remain an illusive dream. Despite the currently unrealized potential of this American Dream, its vision remains attractive. If Black American youth as a group achieve success, then African American civil society and American democracy both become stronger. Unfortunately, as the one-third of Black American youth under age 18 who live in poverty suggests, this has not yet happened.

How will Black youth negotiate their generational consciousness, especially regarding issues of race, gender, class, sexuality, and American democracy? How will their diverse patterns of participation in the privileges and penalties associated with the new racism shape their political consciousness? How might coming of age during the period from Black Power to hip hop shape the political responses of this generation toward racism, nationalism, and feminism?

The quotes that opened this introduction demonstrate the contradictions of the value system of the Black hip-hop generation. This cohort embraces the beliefs of American society concerning individualism, personal expression, and material well-being, yet it also sees how social issues such as incarceration, poor schooling, no jobs, drugs, and the erosion of family structures arise not just from individual failures but from racially disparate, group-based treatment. Stated differently, this population has benefited from the Civil Rights Movement to make democracy work for African Americans; from union movements that pressured all levels of government to protect the interests of the most economically vulnerable workers; from Black nationalist–influenced social movements that maintained churches, schools, and other community institutions dedicated to nurturing the next generation of African American leaders; from a women's movement that demanded rights for women and girls equal to those afforded to men; and from movements for sexual liberation that created political space for new identities for lesbian, gay, bisexual, and transgendered (LGBT) people. Yet as a group, Black American youth have also routinely been denied structural opportunities to exercise their citizenship rights and to achieve personal goals. In this sense, the status of Black American youth serves as a barometer for the status of American democracy itself.

Black Political Responses to the New Racism

No longer are state troops used to block entry to schools and other public institutions—segregation's strong arm, states' rights, has found a new home in an economic

> gestalt that has simply privatized everything. Whites
> have moved to the suburbs and politicians have with-
> drawn funds from black to white areas in unsubtle re-
> districting plans. No longer is the law expressly
> discriminatory...yet the phenomenon of laissez-faire
> exclusion has resulted in as complete a pattern of eco-
> nomic and residential segregation as has ever existed in
> this country.
>
> —*Patricia Williams*[6]

Pointing to the "phenomenon of laissez-faire exclusion," the critical race theorist and legal scholar Patricia Williams describes the contradictions of the new colorblind racism. On the one hand, the new racism relies on a longstanding logic of segregation, one where Whites move to the suburbs and Black youth remain within increasingly impoverished city limits. As Williams points out, the result is a pattern of economic and residential segregation that constitutes little change from the Jim Crow patterns of the past. Beliefs in the racial purity of segregated neighborhoods have been discredited (except, perhaps, among readers of White-supremacist literature), leaving a new multicultural America that is ruled not by big government, but by fair and open marketplaces. Because racially pure spaces can no longer be mandated by legislation, they re-emerge through custom. On the other hand, the ideologies that uphold these now customary segregated spaces have changed. Trumpeting a belief that American society is a meritocracy, mass media masks the actual segregation in everyday life by pushing an ideology of color-blindness. Lani Guinier and Gerald Torres explain how this ideology uses ideas about individual effort to explain the success of Black middle-class people and identifies a deficient Black culture that is riddled with bad values as the ball and chain of poor and working-class Black failure:

> The stock story of colorblindness is that the only motive of the civil rights
> movement was to free individual black people from state-sponsored dis-
> crimination. This depiction of the civil rights movement put assimilation
> (an option available primarily to middle- and upper-class blacks) as the
> engine that drove the civil rights movement. After formal, state-sanctioned
> barriers to individual mobility are removed, any continuing inequality must
> result from the personal failure of individuals or, in its modern iteration, the
> dysfunction of black culture.[7]

In this context, one can not only celebrate racial and ethnic mixtures of all sorts. One can even develop positive feelings about the music and dance styles of impoverished Black American youth. Privatization masks these relations. By making the marketplace the final arbiter of all social relations, the segregation and racial hierarchy that does remain can be attributed to the good and bad qualities of people who compete in the marketplace.

This new colorblind racism is also highly nationalistic. A greatly changed global political economy has left America as the sole remaining superpower. In this transnational context, American national identity and nation-state policies (both domestic and foreign) have grown in significance. Within American politics, a series of conservative Republican administrations have redefined American national identity as a de facto (White) nationalism that masks its own success. Since the 1980s, the American nation-state has increasingly defined ideas about what it means to be American through ideas of Whiteness, Christianity, wealth, masculinity, and heterosexuality. As a result, social inequality of race, class, gender, ethnicity, and religion, among others, appear to be natural and normal and certainly not socially constructed by public policies and everyday customs. Despite its claims of being a meritocracy, the United States has become highly nationalistic, with the boisterous "We're Number 1" of sports fans and soldiers drowning out other perspectives where might does not make right. The events of September 11, 2001, served as a tragic reminder that many people in the world hate the United States—or, at least, the version of American nationalism that far too often backs the wrong side of democratic movements.

The simultaneous invisibility and hypervisibility of Black American youth is situated in this broader context. This contradiction of the invisibility of actual racial segregation and the hypervisibility of a new, mass-media–constructed, multicultural America reflects three important features of the new racism. These features in turn have great implications for African Americans generally, and for Black American youth in particular. First, the effects of globalization have had an especially harsh impact on African Americans, with disparate effects on young Black men, Black women, and Black children. African Americans have not been alone in suffering the economic penalties associated with Blackness. People of African descent and those who are socially constructed as "Black" within their societies (for example, indigenous people in Canada, Afro-Brazilians under policies of racial democracy, and darker-skinned people within the caste system of India) are routinely disadvantaged in this global economy. Under globalization, corporations make the decisions, and "the company is free to move; but the consequences of the move are bound to stay."[8] Globalization is not new, yet the increasing concentration of capital in the hands of fewer and fewer corporations distinguishes contemporary global capitalism from its nineteenth-century counterpart. Moreover, the weakening of democratically elected governments in response to the growing strength of global organizations that set policy and often operate in secrecy effectively elevates marketplace forces over democracy itself. Today, relatively few transnational corporations are driving the world economy, and their decisions affect the global distribution of wealth and poverty. Ironies abound. American commitments to expand democracy through policies such as the war in Iraq seem undermined by the growing ineffectiveness of existing democratically elected governments to improve the economic lives of their citizenry.

Within a global context, because they live in poor countries or because they are "socially Black" within multicultural societies, Black people and people of color are more likely to lose jobs in local labor markets. They are the ones who lack control over oil, mineral wealth, and other natural resources on their land; who lose their land to global agribusiness; and who are denied basic services of electricity and clean water, let alone the luxury goods of the new information age. For African Americans, jobs have disappeared; funding for urban public housing, education, transportation, and health care has eroded; and the American public increasingly blames African Americans for their own fate.[9]

Second, mass media is vitally important within the global social relations of the new, seemingly colorblind racism. Multiculturalism, privatization, and other ideologies that justify inequalities not just of race, but also of class, gender, religion, sexuality, age, and ethnicity, are increasingly reproduced by an influential, global popular-culture industry that needs a continuing supply of new cultural material for its growing entertainment, advertising, and news divisions. Because of its authority to shape perceptions of the world, this popular-culture industry circulates representations of women and men of African descent in domestic and transnational contexts. African American culture can be photographed, recorded, and digitalized and can now travel to all parts of the globe. For many world citizens, news footage of the American presence in the war in Iraq is supplemented by images of Black American basketball players and rap artists. This is the face of America.

The established African American leadership seems incapable of addressing social issues that have disproportionate impact on African American youth. This is a third defining feature of the new colorblind racism—namely, the ineffectiveness of political strategies that strive to resist it. Here African American politics provides a lens into the contradictions of trying to meet new social challenges with old political responses. For a variety of reasons, no one of the four major philosophies that have long guided African American politics has been successful in meeting the challenges of the new racism, especially concerning Black American youth.

Racial integration, the primary strategy pursued by the Civil Rights Movement, has produced unprecedented gains for a sizable segment of the African American population. But it also has failed large numbers of working-class and poor African Americans who continue to deal with higher unemployment rates than Whites, poorer housing, bad schools, and disparate health outcomes. Moreover, despite their accomplishments, many middle-class African Americans express frustration with what they see as the continued barriers that confront them. Through strategies such as offering successful middle-class African Americans as role models for poor Black youth, and affirmative action to force police forces, colleges, suburban neighborhoods, public schools, and other social institutions to accept African Americans, integrationist projects advise young African Americans to assimilate into a social system that repeatedly signals that they are not welcome. Traditionally not deeply concerned with altering the basic values of society or initiating fundamental institutional changes, integrationist and assimilationist movements hoped that collective action by African Americans would increase the opportunities for African Americans as individuals within existing social institutions.[10] No doubt, the new Black middle class owes its success to racial integration. But the one-at-a-time strategy of racial uplift has failed to deliver meaningful change for the majority of African Americans.

Nowhere is this more apparent than in an examination of the life chances of the Black hip-hop generation. Joblessness, illiteracy, unplanned pregnancy, criminal activity, drugs, and alarmingly high rates of HIV infection spark the same response: Black youth are told to "speak proper English, pull up your pants, and take off that miniskirt." This failure stems in part from the success of the conservative Republican backlash against the gains of progressive social movements. But it also reflects the established Black American leadership's continued commitment to racial integration, the crown jewel of the Civil Rights agenda. Working hand in hand with multiculturalism, racial integration is now the official policy of the United States. Yet when it comes to actual social change, more attention has been paid to this ideology than to hard-hitting social policies that might integrate suburban housing or American public schools. The large numbers of African Americans who remain confined to racially segregated, poor neighborhoods, coupled with the staunch resistance on the part of White people to racial integration of housing, schools, employment, and public facilities, leave integrationists apparently out of touch with the concerns of contemporary working-class and low-income African Americans.

The federal government's retreat from enforcing civil-rights legislation has effectively repositioned the state not as a champion of the rights of the dispossessed, but as a defender of elite interests. The global context reflects a similar failure of integration, this time refracted through a global marketplace that seemingly controls everything but in which no one is responsible for the poverty, homelessness, poor health, and hunger that persists among a large proportion of the world's population. Nation-states become the new toothless political units that bear a striking resemblance to American cities that build brand-new sports stadiums for losing teams yet seem unable to fund roads, police forces, and effective public-school systems. When open elections and the vote deliver so little to the dispossessed, democracy no longer seems to matter. Given this reality, many African Americans no longer believe that racial integration constitutes a realistic strategy for Black empowerment. Racial integration may be alive in public rhetoric, but how realistic is it to argue that racial integration will solve the social problems facing Black youth in a domestic and global context?

Black nationalist projects may offer some answers, but they, too, proved to be no match for the new colorblind racism. The broad range of political projects stimulated by the three orienting strategies of Black nationalist ideology—namely, self-definition (cultural), self-determination (political), and self-reliance (economic)—shrank in the context of the new racism.[11] In their place, a new politics of representation emerged whereby Black people were integrated into existing social structures one by one. Getting Black individuals jobs or elected to political office supposedly constituted a victory for the entire group. The limitations of this approach soon became apparent. The 1992 appointment of Clarence Thomas to the Supreme Court signaled a shift in Black nationalist politics. Despite Thomas's record, Black Americans supported his candidacy because they still espoused norms of racial solidarity associated with Black nationalism. As a result of these types of decisions, African Americans found themselves increasingly represented by "Black" appointees who, often hand-picked by conservatives, failed to represent African American interests. Black nationalism as a political ideology was greatly watered down, leaving a politics of group representation that became increasingly fragmented along social-class lines and subject to manipulation and abuse by individual opportunists.

Ironically, in the context of the new racism, politics has seemingly shifted into the terrain of identity and culture. Projects for self-definition, the portion of Black nationalist projects devoted to values, culture, and new Black identities not only survived the challenges of the new racism but seemingly flourished within the increasingly conservative racial climate in the United States, where cultural arguments that explained class inequalities rose in importance. The Nation of Islam and Black studies programs in higher education that overtly espoused Afrocentric philosophies constitute two nationally visible organizational sites for Black cultural nationalism. With their emphasis on Black identity and culture, these projects maintained their strength via the seeming failure of racial integration. In the absence of a richly textured Black nationalist debate, the ideas and actions of a few organizations became the new archetypes of Black nationalism. A good deal of recent Black intellectual criticism of Black nationalism, much of it apparently quite convincing to others in the academy, seems directed toward a relatively small segment of Black nationalist thought, especially its misogynistic elements.[12] After all, if the Nation of Islam and Afrocentric Black studies programs become the straw men who stand for all Black nationalism, then it becomes relatively straightforward to dismiss Black nationalism in total by criticizing the limitations of these expressions of Black cultural nationalism.[13]

Socialism and similar class-based initiatives, the third major ideology shaping Black politics, also floundered in responding to the new racism. In contrast to the European acceptance of socialism, African Americans advancing socialism since the 1950s have had a hard time being heard in America.[14] Several themes have suppressed socialist ideology within African American communities, among them the McCarthy era of the 1950s and its attack on communism; the assassination of Martin Luther King Jr. in 1968 (when he began to advance

a class-based, global agenda for human rights); and government per-
secution in the 1970s of Black radical organizations such as the Black
Panther Party for Self-Defense that offered critiques of capitalism.
Moreover, the 1990 collapse of the Soviet Union as a major communist
world power simultaneously elevated capitalism's status as the dominant global economic system and nationalist ideologies in which
groups competed with one another in the new global marketplace. As a
result, socialism has rarely been tested within African American politics, and when it has, its language has been co-opted.

Black feminism, a fourth major ideology shaping African American
politics, experienced a renaissance in the 1970s and 1980s but also
proved unable to sustain its radical potential in the face of the new
racism. Historically, because African American women lived racially
segregated lives, Black feminism found expression within the confines
of Black community politics. This meant that African American feminism had a dialectical and synergistic relationship with Black nationalism as a "Black feminist nationalism" or "Black nationalist feminism."
Black women participated in community politics, and the models that
developed there moved into modern Black feminism of the 1970s and
1980s. Individual African American women also participated in and
continued to work within U.S. mainstream feminism during this period, a fact that is lost on those who argue that feminism is for White
women. African American women have been in feminism since its inception, and during the 1970s and 1980s they launched a distinctive,
albeit less well known, Black feminist movement.[15] Like mainstream
feminism, conservative forces that set out to dismantle women's rights
also affected Black feminist politics in the 1980s and 1990s. Black
feminism garnered increasing recognition within the academy, yet it
also began to succumb to the pressures of the new racism to eschew
group-based politics of all sorts. Currently, the shift away from its roots
in Black political activism has led some to ask: What has Black feminism built *within* African American communities?

From Black Power to Hip Hop: Overview of the Volume

Collectively, the six essays in *From Black Power to Hip Hop: Racism,
Nationalism, and Feminism* explore the political realities of this period
marked by the end of Black Power to the ascendancy of hip hop. I
focus on the experiences of African Americans, yet the issues raised

concerning American national identity, public policy, oppositional ideologies and social movements, and reformulated structures of social inequality are broader than this population. The essays focus neither on African American youth nor on hip-hop culture. Rather, they aim to map patterns of converging and cross-cutting racism, nationalism, and feminism that are vitally important to the Black hip-hop generation.

The essays have several defining features. First, they focus on the relationship between new racial formations and on political responses to them. Part I examines the American nation-state and sketches a framework for thinking through how race, gender, and class affect American national identity, especially its impetus toward democracy. Nationalism and feminism, the focus of the essays in Parts II and III, respectively, constitute two powerful ideologies that have catalyzed major social movements and that have shown resilience where other ideas have floundered. I am especially interested in these two belief systems because individually and collectively, these ideologies have been more likely to engage politically active Black youth than ideologies of racial integration and socialism. As ideologies, nationalism and feminism both signal new types of social relations. The group-based, social-justice framework associated with nationalist ideologies has been used by many oppressed groups, not simply by racial/ethnic minorities. At the same time, the individual-rights framework advocated by Western feminism has been central in the global women's movement. Despite their importance within African American politics, integrationist and class-based ideologies are not the focus of the essays, but they do reappear as themes throughout the volume.

Second, the essays rely on a paradigm of intersectionality to explore the connections among race, nation, gender, class, ethnicity, sexuality, and age. Intersectional paradigms view race, class, gender, sexuality, ethnicity, and age, among others, as mutually constructing systems of power. Whereas all of these systems are always present, grappling with their theoretical contours is far more difficult than merely mentioning them. The essays in *From Black Power to Hip Hop* should be read in the context of my consistent efforts to theorize intersectionality. The focus here is on intersections of race, nation, and gender, but selected essays also examine how these constructs intersect with other equally important systems of power. For example, while not a major focus of this volume, social class is an important sub-theme. In particular, an increasingly heterogeneous Black social-class structure has brought a greater degree of civil-rights protection to middle-class African

Americans. What are the new contours of race and class-consciousness that accompany these new social relations? Historically, African Americans have shown a strong degree of racial solidarity, largely because they had common problems and saw their fate as intricately linked. Despite significant changes in the post–Civil Rights era, African American voting behavior still shows a noteworthy degree of racial solidarity, one indicator that Black Americans choose race over class.[16] But the race-versus-class argument may oversimplify the complexities of contemporary political consciousness among African Americans across social-class differences. Rather than choosing race or class, a more provocative question concerns the patterns of race/class political consciousness across Black social-class structures.[17] For example, are middle-class African Americans as a group more likely to endorse racial integration as a political strategy simply because they are the group that is most favorably positioned to benefit from it? Will poor and working-class African Americans embrace Black nationalist ideologies because they have greater resonance with the group-based racial discrimination that accompanies racial segregation? The essays do not directly engage these questions, yet these issues run throughout the volume nonetheless.

A third distinguishing feature of this volume is that the essays explore a longstanding theoretical interest of mine—namely, how it is that the more things change, the more they stay the same. Today's new colorblind racism in the United States characterizes this curious combination of the old with the new. Such racism is old in that Black Americans and people of African descent in a global context remain disproportionately stuck on the bottom of the racial hierarchy, and White Americans and Whites from former colonial powers continue to enjoy the privileges associated with being on top. Despite massive changes in law, economy, politics, customs, and social norms, the basic racial hierarchy that characterized the founding of the United States, as well as the one that characterized the global colonial period, persists. However, such racism is new in its economic, political, and ideological organization. Specifically, the deeply entrenched legal and customary racial segregation that historically permeated American social institutions has given way to unevenly desegregated schools, job categories, workplaces, neighborhoods, and public spaces. Whiteness is not celebrated to the same degree, although it remains the implicit normative yardstick against which everything else is measured. The essays struggle to understand this process of stasis and change, with an eye toward conserving those elements of society that are worth keeping and changing those that are not.

Finally, the essays collected here all constitute critical social theory.[18] Critical social theory consists of bodies of knowledge and sets of institutional practices that actively grapple with the central questions facing groups of people who are differently placed in specific political, social, and historic contexts characterized by injustice. African Americans constitute the group that focuses the theory developed in these essays. As works of critical social theory, the essays presented here use a conceptual framework concerning the intersections of race, gender, and nation to raise questions that may help African Americans, especially Black youth in the hip-hop generation, and their supporters craft more effective responses to the new colorblind racism.

Part I: Race, Family, and the U.S. Nation-State

When it comes to contemporary America, the very meaning of democracy is at stake. Given its current place in global politics, can the United States bring about a democracy that delivers on its promises? Can a nation-state that is composed of so many different kinds of people from all over the world find a way to use that diversity to craft a unified whole that protects and nurtures every single individual? National identity, a form of ethnic identity writ large, is a powerful template for telling us who we are, why we are here, what our responsibilities (or lack thereof) are to one another, and what we can expect for ourselves as unique individuals. Rather than seeing nationalism as a backward, essentialist ideology, I view nationalism as a powerful set of ideas that can be used for a variety of purposes. Elsewhere I suggest that the power of nationalism, like that of religion, lies in its ability to annex expressive needs to political ends. Certainly, conservative Republican politicians who manipulated American patriotism for their own ends—the war in Iraq comes to mind—understand this process. In defining the contours of the nation-state, ideas about patriotism that draw on notions of race, gender, sexuality, class, and age are vitally important. Patriotism asks who is deemed worthy to serve and who should be protected from harm. American nationalism draws on the power of nationalist ideology and is unlikely to disappear in the near future. Thus, questions of what kind of American national identity will emerge from these troubled times of the new millennium are crucial.

The struggles in the 1980s and 1990s over the meaning of American national identity may have been depicted as "culture wars" between those who saw themselves as defending the best of America's past and those whose race, class, gender, ethnicity, and sexual orientation reflected America's present and future. Such debates forget that the archetypal American citizen may be seen as White, male, heterosexual, and wealthy, yet the United States has been a multiracial, multiethnic, and multicultural nation-state since its beginning. Arguments about what it means to be American also tap deep-seated anxieties and aspirations about the very definition of America—they were and are nationalist debates about the meaning of American national identity and the significance of America.

As the essays in Part I explore, notions of family are central to widely held understandings of American national identity. This is why the religious right and the conservative Republican politicians that it has supported from the 1980s to the present have been so effective. Both groups recognize the significance of family to the American population and to the idea of what it means to be American. Together, they have developed a position on "family values" that places family rhetoric in service to their definitions of American nationalism.

The two essays in Part I examine how intersecting ideologies of nation, race, class, and gender operate in shaping American national identity in general and public policies in particular. Ideas about nation, race, and gender gain meaning from one another, and these interpretive frameworks infuse nation-state policies in the United States as well as nationalist and feminist social movements that have arisen to challenge them. Together, these two essays provide a theoretical and historical context for the more specific analyses of nationalism and feminism in the remainder of the volume.

Chapter 1, "Like One of the Family: Race, Ethnicity, and the Paradox of American National Identity," examines how American politicians, academics, leaders, and ordinary citizens draw on a family ideology to construct ideas about American national identity and citizenship. Western feminists have long identified the family as an important site of women's oppression. They point to the association of women and domestic space. Yet broadening these understandings of the family to see families as actual sites of social reproduction as well as ideological sites where individuals and groups are socialized into their appropriate places in the social order makes family a crucial template for conceptualizing nation. Nationalism as an ideology and set of social practices draws meaning from Western conceptions of family and race. Moreover, racism refracted through an ideology of family occurs within specific national and international contexts. Taking different forms in Europe, Latin America, Asia, and Africa, much of the new racism that appropriates this rhetoric of family is organized through nation-state policies and resisted by antiracist movements that, whether intentionally or not, draw on nationalist ideologies. The question remains as to ways in which the American nation-state has incorporated these contradictions into notions of American national identity, citizenship, patriotism, and into its public policies. Because race and nation have been mutually constructing categories, nationalism and racism also are linked.

To develop the implications of this rhetoric of family for public policy, chapter 2, "Will the 'Real' Mother Please Stand Up? Race, Class, and American National Family Planning," investigates how ideas about motherhood frame contemporary population policies. Nationalism and gender are not only linked in shaping American national identity. These ideas also influence the social policies of the nation-state itself. Women remain central to nationalist ideologies, to the concept of nation on which nationalist ideologies are built, to reproducing the populations of nations on both sides of power, and to resistance movements organized around nationalist ideologies. Feminist analyses of gender and nationalism have been very helpful in rethinking ideas about the concepts of nation, nation-state, nationalism, and national identity.[19] Fundamentally, feminist analyses see nationalism as deeply gendered, with women fulfilling specific functions for all sorts of nationalisms, whether ethnic or civic, nation-state or oppositional. These functions are (1) women as reproducing the nation's population—for example, their actual activities as mothers; (2) women as keepers of traditional culture and their actions in passing it on; and (3) women as symbols of the nation to be protected—for example, as such mother figures as "Mother Africa," "Mother Ireland," and "Mother India." All three of these ideas operate in determining which women are deemed fit to be mothers of the American nation.

In chapters 1 and 2, I discuss women, but this does not mean that issues of gender and nationalism are the exclusive purview of women. Men's relationship to the nation-state creates competing discourses of masculinity, now highly visible around ideas of patriotism. Patriotism also derives from a public discourse about family. Men are encouraged to view and defend the nation-state as if they are defending their own families. For men in the military, sacrificing one's life for one's country is equivalent to protecting the homeplace of family and homeland of

America. Defending democracy may be presented as the ideological face of patriotism, yet ensuring homeland security is the purpose of the military mission. Despite women's entry into U.S. military service, patriotism remains coded as a masculine activity. One need only view the names of those killed in the war in Iraq to see the disproportionate percentage of young men who die in warfare. Military service enhances masculinity so that the ideal American citizen becomes a male who has served honorably in combat. Violence and the use of force also become important elements of masculinity and, in turn, yardsticks for evaluating patriotism. Violence is not only an appropriate mechanism for defending American interests; it also is implicated in reproducing hierarchies of masculinity grounded in race, class, and sexual orientation.

Part II: Ethnicity, Culture, and Black Nationalist Politics

With hindsight, it is easier to see how the transitional decades of the 1960s and the 1970s marked the end of the effectiveness of traditional Civil Rights agendas and the need for something new. When it came to the contours of racial oppression and the paths that African Americans might follow to resist it, few could have foreseen how factors such as the ascendancy and suppression of the Black Power Movement, the success of Black conservatives in gaining visible places in government and industry, the shift of Black feminism from its origins as a social movement to its acceptance within academic settings, and the generational divide between the Civil Rights and hip-hop generations would all shape African American politics. How did African Americans respond to this greatly changed economic, political, and ideological context that managed to reproduce longstanding racial hierarchies in a context of seemingly liberal ideology and favorable laws?

The essays in Part II examine a small portion of Black nationalist politics. My emphasis on Black nationalism is designed neither to defend nor to condemn it. Rather, because Black nationalism is both routinely criticized and embraced by African American academics and Black youth alike, I think that it merits further analysis. African Americans have experienced the highest degree of racial segregation over an extended period of time; as a result, this population has long embraced some variation of Black nationalism. Yet African American intellectuals have long been ambivalent about, if not dismissive of, Black nationalist projects, typically defining Black nationalism mainly as the obverse of racial integration and primarily in the context of domestic American politics. Pan-Africanism has deep historical roots, yet contemporary Black intellectual discourse basically ignores those roots. As a result, racial integration and Black nationalism have been presented as *competing* strategies for addressing racial inequality. Within this context, Black nationalism's tenets of seeking group-based remedies for racial inequality and promoting group-based social action have often been seen as antithetical to American ideals because they violate tenets of liberal individualism that underpin U.S. laws and social customs.

The two essays in Part II investigate how Black nationalism's tenet of Black solidarity constitutes a core theme within African American politics. Despite a longstanding commitment to Black solidarity, definitions of what solidarity is and how Black people would recognize it remain open to debate. Currently, criticisms of Black solidarity arise from surprising and quite diverse places. For example, Black feminists, LGBT Black people, biracial and multiracial people of African descent, and others who feel pressured to submerge their specific interests for the good of Black unity have increasingly challenged unquestioned assumptions that racial solidarity is achieved by suppressing differences.[20] This view of unity through uniformity may have been necessary in situations where a lack of a united front constituted danger for all. However, this vision of a Black community speaking in one voice becomes increasingly difficult to achieve under current conditions, if in fact it is desirable. Black solidarity far too often leads to the interests of Black women, LGBT Black people, biracial and multiracial people, and other distinctive segments of Black civil society being routinely submerged for the alleged good of the group.

Others point to the increasing manipulation of an unquestioned Black solidarity within the new colorblind racism, arguing that, when it is strategically used against African Americans, Black solidarity can become a problem. For example, Kimberlé Crenshaw claims that an unquestioned racial solidarity worked against African American interests in the confirmation hearings of Supreme Court Justice Clarence Thomas. She notes that "the vilification of Anita Hill and the embracing of Clarence Thomas reveal that a black woman breaking ranks to complain of sexual harassment is seen by many African Americans as a much greater threat to our group interests than a black man who breaks ranks with our race policy."[21] In a similar vein, creating African American electoral districts to ensure that Black candidates can be elected seemingly promises Black representation. However, when these Black elected officials find themselves outnumbered by White officials elected by White electoral districts, racial solidarity dilutes the ability of Blacks to elect officials who represent them.

Still others suggest that Black solidarity is more illusion than reality and call for more fluid and encompassing identities for individuals. Eschewing group identities of all sorts, especially those imposed from without, they deconstruct the category "Black." Just who is "Black," they ask? On one level, efforts within the 2000 U.S. Census to develop biracial and multiracial categories strive to include the growing numbers of individuals who do not fit neatly within racial boxes. On another level, without having some sort of alternative way of responding to group-based racial discrimination, dissolving the formal group status of groups that currently benefit from some sort of protected status based on historical racial discrimination is worrisome.

One might ask: If political interests in the United States are no longer formally expressed through groups, then how can group-based social injustice be remedied? Without some imagined group of Blacks, women, or youth in the hip-hop generation, the question of any group that is treated differently because of its race, ethnicity, gender, sexuality, or citizenship status having common interests becomes moot. Given these challenges, should Black solidarity be discarded? Or must it be rethought in light of current challenges facing African Americans? As the British cultural critic Kobena Mercer suggests, "Solidarity does not mean that everyone thinks in the same way; it begins when people have the confidence to disagree over issues of fundamental importance precisely because they 'care' about constructing common ground."[22]

Using the contested politics of Afrocentrism as a lens, the two essays in Part II examine how contradictions of Black solidarity, ethnicity, and Black culture shape contemporary Black nationalist politics. Nationalisms have come under increasing scrutiny regarding their connections to other systems of power—namely, those of race, gender, sexuality, and social class. At the same time, the ascendancy of the conservative right in the United States and its logic of colorblindness raise new challenges for Black nationalist politics. Because Black nationalist thinkers have historically been highly vocal in identifying the importance of Black identity and Black culture for political struggle, the two essays in Part II use contemporary Black nationalism to explore the challenges that confront African Americans in the post–Civil Rights era.

Chapter 3, "Black Nationalism and African American Ethnicity: Afrocentrism as Civil Religion," cuts into the contradictions of the

interconnections of race and ethnicity for African Americans by sur-
veying efforts to recast Afrocentrism as a civil religion for purposes of
ethnic mobilization. Ethnic politics have a long history in the United
States. Yet when African Americans pursue strategies of *ethnic* mobilization, such strategies are routinely recast within the *racial* frame of
the United States and derogated as anti-American, special-interest,
separatist politics. Certainly, some Black ethnic projects do fit this
description, but many do not. This continual pressure to deny an ethnic
history and a valued ethnic culture to African Americans narrows political space and suggests that African American ethnicity is acceptable
just as long as African Americans make no appreciable demands on the
nation-state.

Chapter 4, "When Fighting Words Are Not Enough: The Gendered Content of Afrocentrism," provides a close reading of how the
main ideas of Black cultural nationalism were imported into the halls
of academe. Here, Afrocentrism's aspirations to become a science of
Blackness foundered on the shoals of scholarly norms of science. The
essay contrasts the gender politics of the Black cultural nationalist
movement of the Black Power Movement with those of Black cultural
nationalism within American higher education as a lens to assess the
political viability of Afrocentrism. The essay concludes that Afrocentrism's problems within the academy were not solely the result of
White resistance (although this was an important factor). Problems
within the very paradigms of Afrocentrism were equally culpable.

Part III: Feminism, Nationalism, and African American Women

Theorizing women's political activism has always been a slippery
theme in the two predominant approaches within the literatures of
power and resistance.[23] Power-as-domination models typically define
power as an entity possessed by an individual or a group who may or
may not choose to use it. Under racism, sexism, class exploitation,
heterosexism, and similar systems of oppression, elite groups use their
power to uphold privilege through the economic, political, or ideological domination of Blacks, women, poor people, and LGBT people.
This perspective sees power relations as a zero-sum game—one in
which less powerful people gain power when it is redistributed to them
from more powerful groups. Within this power-as-domination model,
social change occurs through negotiation and rational planning: The
dispossessed plead their case to those in power, and if they are successful, they receive a greater share of the pie. When rational planning

fails or appears to go too slowly, resistance also can mean taking power away from others, often by force, revolt, or revolution.

In contrast to this power-as-domination approach, other views of power embrace a resource-mobilization framework. In this second approach, power consists of the use of resources of whatever kind to secure outcomes. Because power relations are continually enacted, actions for empowerment are ongoing. Here resistance can be everywhere, in any action, as social actors mobilize to challenge the powers that be. Rather than taking a structural, top-down approach, the resource-mobilization framework sees power struggles in the micropolitics of everyday life. Whether negotiations of heterosexual partners within a love relationship; the use of hair, clothing, and fashion to challenge norms of femininity; or the grassroots activism of blockwatch programs in local neighborhoods, resource mobilization seems to be the bedrock of social change.

Because both of these meta-theories of power and resistance were developed using men's behavior as the norm, neither approach adequately conceptualizes women as political actors or accounts for forms of women's resistance. Because most women eschew tactics of force, revolt, or revolution and are routinely deferential to men, women are typically perceived under the power-as-domination model to be inherently less political than men. Women do appear more often in the resource-mobilization framework, primarily as social actors in interpersonal and small-group settings. But because resource-mobilization strategies are typically situated within the power-as-domination model, resource-mobilization strategies by default become second-class strategies of political resistance.[24] Thus, when they are combined, these two models assign women to less effective or ineffective forms of political resistance, when they acknowledge that women resist at all.

African American women, a group that has rarely been considered in either of the prevailing meta-theories of power and resistance, provide an excellent starting point for rethinking the broader question of women's resistance. How does one conceptualize political resistance among Black women in the United States, both in the context of America's colorblind racism and in ways that take into account heterogeneity among African American women? In the aftermath of the turn toward highlighting differences among women, it is easy to overlook the many commonalities that women of African descent, wherever they are situated, encounter with various dimensions of the new racism. They typically confront sexism, racism, heterosexism, and class exploitation simultaneously. As a result, the political resistance of Black women must grapple with intersecting systems of oppression.[25] In the global context, women of African descent in continental Africa, the Caribbean, and Latin American nation-states such as Ecuador and Brazil, and as racial minorities within Great Britain, France, Germany, the Netherlands, and other European nation-states constitute an important segment of the global women's movement. Ignoring the treatment of women who are noticeably of African descent or who are socially constructed as Black elides the power of racism to continue to affect women's lives.

I use the term "Black women" deliberately, because I feel that there is a pressing need for a unifying language that women of African descent and women who are rendered socially Black can use to describe their needs as racial/ethnic women.[26] I suspect that the common political, economic, and social conditions of Black women do foster a shared recognition of common problems that take different forms in a Black transnational context. Brazil, South Africa, Great Britain, France, and the United States are very different societies with quite different histories with colonialism and capitalism, yet Black women (however identified) confront very similar issues in all of these locations. As the stellar accomplishments of Condoleezza Rice, Oprah Winfrey, and Winnie Mandela suggest, individual Black women may achieve great prominence, yet Black women as a collectivity remain on the bottom of the social hierarchy. In nation-states that are racially homogeneous and Black-run—for example, those of the Caribbean and of continental Africa—racism may be less obvious. There racism operates by holding the entire nation-state hostage to structural-adjustment policies and crushing debt. Within these societies, the status of women (who by default are overwhelmingly of African descent) becomes even more degraded by gender policies that keep them at the bottom. In this way, Black women's placement within the global social relations created by globalization, a transnationalism that has weakened African and Caribbean nation-states and fostered major population shifts, and a persistent racism that denies first-class citizenship to Black women within advanced industrial societies converge to frame a common set of challenges for Black women.

The content of Black women's political activism is also important—especially how Black women remain positioned between often competing politics of nationalism and feminism. Black feminism constitutes one strong challenge to norms of Black solidarity, the influence of those norms on Black women's politics, and historically entrenched forms of inequality within African American communities. But here the record of success is mixed. Black women have united with Black men around issues of class and race: Employment, education, health, and education issues required a united front. Yet Black women and men often found themselves at cross-purposes around issues of domestic violence, sexual violence, and homophobia. The political theorist Cathy Cohen refers to these contradictory relationships as the consensus issues provided by race and the cross-cutting issues provided by gender.[27] The friction between nationalist-inspired norms of Black solidarity and community service (primarily around issues of race and class) and the personal politics advanced within American feminism (primarily around issues of gender and sexuality) frame modern Black feminism.

To explore this theme of Black women's political activism, especially the contours of modern Black feminism, the two essays in Part III, "Feminism, Nationalism, and African American Women," use the experiences of Black women in the United States as a jumping-off point for examining broader questions concerning Black women's political resistance. When read together, both essays explore how women who are differentially placed within the same social structure may advance diverse views of what counts as women's political activism. Differences among women that reflect their disparate group locations in hierarchical power relations of race, class, nationality, religion, and sexuality often catalyze group standpoints on feminist political activism that demonstrate comparable heterogeneity.[28] African American women in particular aim to reject what many perceive to be a Western feminism that has incorporated, often uncritically, assumptions of individualism, materialism, and personal choice without accountability, hallmarks of American society. Moreover, the high degree of racial segregation within American society means that Black American women often find their politics refracted through a nascent Black nationalist framework. At the same time, because Black American women are American, they simultaneously accept many ideas that stem from a common understanding of American national identity. Extracting these and other expressions of women's political activism from ideologies of race and class that shape American national identity not only creates new frameworks for analyzing Black women's political activism in particular, but it also creates new opportunities to revitalize American feminism.

Chapter 5, "Why Collective Identity Politics Matter: Feminism, Nationalism, and Black Women's Community Work," takes up the question of Black women's resistance traditions, but it does so by investigating Black American women's community work as an important site of their political activism. Using a materialist framework, this essay examines what African American women actually do, what they think about what they do, and how these material and ideological conditions simultaneously catalyze and suppress their political consciousness and behavior. The essay introduces the concept of Black women's community work as a traditional form of political activism that articulated with African American community structures during the Jim Crow era. I also analyze nationalist and feminist interpretations of Black women's community work that have been advanced within Western societies and argue that neither adequately understands the political implications of community work.

I suggest that a better approach recontextualizes Black women's community work within an emerging framework of global feminist nationalism—namely, women's political ideas and actions to come to a "global consensus on reconstructing both feminism and nationalism with the concerns and interests of women at the center of discourse and action."[29] This recontextualization reveals the ways in which Black women's community work might become more, not less, "feminist." It also places issues of gender more squarely in the center of the African American struggle for freedom where neither race (nationalism) nor gender (feminism) can gain primacy without harming overall political efficacy. If young African American women are at the forefront of political struggle, a clear implication of the incarceration of young Black men and the high number of Black families headed by women, then gender needs to be at the *center* of Black political agendas. Moreover, this framework of feminist nationalism may not only shape African American women's political behavior in the context of racially desegregating conditions of the new racism in the U.S. context. This dynamic relation of nationalism and feminism may be present among women of African descent and other groups of women of color in a transnational context.

Chapter 6, "Is the Personal Still Political? The Women's Movement, Feminism, and Black Women in the Hip-Hop Generation," explores the feminist politics expressed by African American women in the hip-hop generation. One important focus of this politics seems to be a renewed focus on "The Personal Is Political." Yet their version of both the "personal" and what constitutes the "political" resembles yet differs dramatically from that expressed by feminists of the 1960s and

1970s. Contemporary women of color seemingly follow a different personal path to find feminism than that taken by African American, Chicana, Puerto Rican, and other women in the 1960s and 1970s; they also seem to face a different political reality when they find it. During this earlier period, a rich social-movement context played an important role in shaping all segments of the women's movement. In contrast, conservative, right-wing Republican governments of the 1980s to the present have led the way in criticizing and ridiculing not just the women's movement, but also the aspirations of unions, civil-rights groups, sexual minorities, immigrant groups, and poor people.

I investigate the ways in which the feminist politics of women in the hip-hop generation signal a significant break from or continuation of earlier expressions of feminism by African American, Latina, and other groups of racial/ethnic women. On the one hand, women of color in the hip-hop generation embrace a version of "The Personal Is Political" that enables them to raise Black women's issues within women's studies classrooms, popular culture, and grassroots organizations. This signals a continuation of prior struggles. On the other hand, the version of feminism expressed by women of color also exudes the ideas of the hip-hop generation cited at the beginning of this essay. Recall Queen Latifah's claim, "I'm not here to live by somebody else's standards. I'm defining what a woman is for myself. Simply put, I am not interested in subscribing to what society has decided for half of humankind. I am an individual."[30] This insistence on a personal, unique, individual identity unencumbered by "somebody else's standards" recurs in the music, style, and behavior of those in the hip-hop generation.

My overarching goal in these final two essays is to make a case for anti-racist, group-based political struggles that respect individual rights and human rights; that embrace a global analysis of how our lives are all interconnected; and that are informed by the best of feminism and nationalism and not their troubling elements. In this sense, Anna Julia Cooper's words "when and where I enter" still ring true. When and where Black girls enter into freedom, there, too, will others also find hope for the future.

I

Race, Family, and
the U.S. Nation-State

1

Like One of the Family

Race, Ethnicity, and the Paradox of American National Identity

Hi Marge! I have had me one hectic day.... Well, I had to take out my crystal ball and give Mrs. C... a thorough reading.... Well, she's a pretty nice woman as they go and I have never had too much trouble with her, but from time to time she really gripes me with her ways.... Today she had a girl friend of hers over to lunch and I was real busy afterwards clearing the things away and she called me over and introduced me to the woman.... Oh no, Marge! I didn't object to that at all. I greeted the lady and then went back to my work... And then it started! I could hear her talkin' just as loud... and she says to her friend, "We *just* love her! She's *like* one of the family and she *just adores* our little Carol! We don't know *what* we'd do without her! We don't think of her as a servant!" And on and on she went.... and every time I came in to move a plate off the table both of them would grin at me like chessy cats.

—*Mildred, fictional character*

I
n this passage from *Like One of the Family*, one of sixty-two fictional monologues penned by the African American writer Alice Childress, we meet Mildred, a working-class, African American domestic worker, and her good friend Marge. First appearing in Paul Robeson's newspaper *Freedom* under the title "Conversations from Life," the short conversations between Mildred and Marge continued to be published in the *Baltimore Afro-American* as "Here's Mildred." Many of the African American readers of these newspapers were themselves domestic workers, and Mildred's bold assertions resonated with their silenced voices.[1] Thus, Mildred's identity as an African American working-class domestic worker and the initial publishing venue of these fictionalized accounts illustrates an increasingly rare practice in the intellectual

29

production of African Americans—an African American author writing to an African American, working-class audience, using a medium controlled by people of African descent.[2]

This passage from *Like One of the Family* suggests two important themes concerning the connections among race, ethnicity, and American national identity.[3] The first is how racial/ethnic groups can hold markedly different perceptions of the social inequalities that surround them.[4] This particular vignette suggests two views of the meaning of race and citizenship in American society, one advanced by more powerful groups who minimize its importance and the other by less powerful groups who have limited venues to advance alternative arguments. The superficial dialogue between Mrs. C and Mildred is just as Mrs. C wants it. Pinioning Mildred within the framework of a beloved yet second-class family member allows Mrs. C to ignore the power relations linking the two women. Moreover, Mrs. C's reliance on seemingly natural authority structures within her perceptions of family allows her to mask the real power involved. The qualifier "like" is crucial here, for it signals the power of Mrs. C to define what family means and position Mildred within her definition of a normal family. As long as Mildred knows her place in the family as a subordinated worker, she can stay. Understandings of American national identity, with citizenship marking categories of belonging, resonate with similar themes. Mrs. C's perception that she treated Mildred "like" she was one of her family mirrors widespread beliefs among White Americans that African Americans, Native Americans, Chicanos, Puerto Ricans, and other historically oppressed racial/ethnic groups are treated equally enough within American society. Marked with the status of subordinated workers, such groups are tolerated as long as they remain in their prescribed places. This is not a politics of exclusion, but one of containment. American non–Whites are *like* us, they are *connected* to us, but they are *not* us, such views suggest. In this context, as Mrs. C's verbosity and Mildred's forced silences reveal, White Americans rarely get to hear uncensored views expressed by African Americans on their seemingly shared American experiences.

Mrs. C's words in this passage from *Like One of the Family* also signal a second important theme concerning the connections among race, ethnicity, and American national identity—namely, the significance of family rhetoric in normalizing and naturalizing this entire process.[5] Unlike feminist analyses that blame White men for racial oppression yet remain strangely silent concerning White women's culpability,

Childress's passage reveals how racial power operates among women. By this move, she implicates both men and women in constructing racial inequality and introduces an important gender analysis into discussions of American citizenship. Within prevailing logic, because family relations are often seen as private matters, both families and the women associated with them are thought to fall outside the public-sphere activities that legislate racial, ethnic, and citizenship status. Yet treating women as the only group for which gender matters, and re-legating them to the seemingly private sphere of the family, effectively removes gender from important political questions concerning race, ethnicity, and American citizenship. By depicting how racial hierarchy is constructed and naturalized *within* a family setting, Childress's vignette dissolves this public–private binary. Instead, Childress's fiction encourages us to examine the dual function of family. For one, family operates as an ideological tool that both constructs and masks power relations. Mrs. C's perception that Mildred was like one of the family constructed and masked the power dynamics of race and class that shaped their everyday interactions. At the same time, family constitutes a fundamental principle of social organization. Mrs. C and Mildred are members of different biological and racial families. In American soci-ety, where family and racial lineage has long been used to distribute social rights and obligations, being born into a White American or Black American family remains vitally important.

Using the experiences of African American women such as Mildred as a touchstone, I explore in this chapter how this construct of African American women as "like one of the family"—that is, as legally part of the American nation-state but holding second-class citizenship within it—fosters our understanding of the connections among race, ethnicity, and American national identity. Mildred's predicament illustrates a fundamental paradox of American national identity—namely, how the promise of individual rights guaranteed to her via American law re-mains juxtaposed to the reality of the differential group treatment she receives in the United States due to her race, gender, and class. Mil-dred's situation also provides important clues to how these relations become seen as normal and natural, as well as to the significance of family rhetoric and practices to this intertwined normalization and naturalization process.

Investigating these relationships reveals a seemingly peculiar feature of American society: the curious combination of change and continuity characterizing social institutions in the United States. How is it that

American society has undergone such massive social reorganization since its origins as a settler society in the 1600s yet remains characterized by a deeply entrenched racial hierarchy? Surely the many changes in the American political economy have provided ample opportunity to dismantle racial hierarchy that characterized the founding of the United States. Why does race continue to matter?

On Change and Continuity: Race, Ethnicity, and American National Identity

The philosopher Etienne Balibar identifies external and internal racisms as two interrelated phenomena that appear across diverse societies.[6] External racisms occur when powerful racial groups aim to remove less powerful groups from schools, jobs, neighborhoods, regions, nation-states, or social spaces that more powerful groups perceive as being their property or birthright. As racisms of elimination or extermination, external racisms foster ideas and practices that exclude outsiders or "others" from these spaces. Designed to maintain the racial homogeneity of the neighborhood, school, occupational category, or nation-state, such racisms aim to purify geographic or social space of the threat that inferior races seemingly represent. Expressed via practices such as xenophobia, genocide, or so-called ethnic cleansing, external racisms aim to remove undesirable races from what is seen as privileged home space.

In contrast, internal racisms occur when powerful racial groups subordinate less powerful racial groups within one society, typically because they need such groups to maintain their standard of living. Practices associated with internal racisms typically exploit less powerful racial groups to benefit more powerful racial groups. As racisms of oppression and exploitation, internal racisms foster ideas and practices that partition society into distinctive racial groups and that maintain social hierarchies through racialized group identities. Expressed via practices such as colonialism, apartheid, and racial segregation, internal racisms include and control less powerful racial groups within what is seen as privileged home space.

While the two forms are analytically distinct, neither typically appears by itself, and because they remain deeply intertwined, external and internal racisms often reinforce each other within the boundaries of pre-existing nation-states. The virulent anti-Semitism in 1930s Germany and Austria that influenced Nazi nation-state policies illustrates how the internal racism that ghettoized Jewish populations for purposes of exploitation and control transformed into an external racism of genocide. Both forms of racism were annexed to a national racial agenda, with tragic consequences. Similarly, the rise to power of modern European nation-states such as Great Britain, Germany, Italy, France, Spain, and Portugal relied in large part on colonial conquests in Africa, North America, and Latin America, as well as imperial relations with Asian peoples. The seeming purity within European nation-state boundaries prior to anticolonial struggles required the external racisms of excluding foreigners from European home spaces as well as removing selected native peoples from the lands that were conquered. More recently, however, with the increased migration of people from Africa, Asia, and the Caribbean to these same nation-states, mechanisms of internal racism have become increasingly important.

What happens when these dual racisms become integral to the *founding* moments of a nation-state? National identity itself can become so compromised by such deeply embedded racial processes that it becomes difficult to conceive of national identity in terms other than racial. The formation of the United States as a nation-state as well as American national identity sadly reflect this tightly bundled nexus of external and internal racisms. In forming a settler society that privileged Whiteness, European American settlers saw their search for land and resources as their right as a new people or nation. During the American colonial period, Whiteness, whether propertied Whites or White indentured servants, became defined in opposition to and elevated above the non–White status assigned to indigenous peoples and enslaved Africans. This core racial triangle among White settlers, indigenous peoples, and enslaved Africans became foundational to the new American nation-state.

Indigenous peoples encountered the external racism of being treated as foreign interlopers or "nations" in their own homelands. Initially conquered and often killed in warfare during the settler era and during the first 100 years of the nation-state, indigenous populations became "Indians" or natives confronting a plethora of broken treaties and public policies dedicated to their extermination.[7] In contrast, during the settler era, enslaved Africans encountered the internal racism of being commodified and exchanged on the marketplace, then exploited for their manual labor in Southern agriculture as well as the reproductive labor of African American women. The mechanisms of internal racism certainly changed over time—from slavery, to Jim Crow, to deeply entrenched racial discrimination in housing, education, and employment—but the need for the exploitation of Black labor persisted. The external racism targeted toward indigenous peoples reflected White settlers' need to eliminate Native Americans from White settler home space, whereas the internal racism directed at African Americans marked the dependence of the new nation on African labor. Moreover, these interconnections among European settlers, indigenous peoples and people of African descent not only formed the template for constructing categories of American citizenship—the first-class White citizen, the foreign Indian who stands outside citizenship, and the second-class Black citizen—the relationship *among* these three groups became fixed as essential ingredients for a fundamentally racialized American national identity.

Accomplishing this racialized national identity required reducing the myriad of ethnicities that characterized European, American Indian, and African populations into three core racial categories. English, French, and Norwegians became White Americans whose power eventually allowed them to erase the assumed Whiteness associated with being a full-blooded "American" as a visible identity category. Yet whereas Whiteness itself was erased, class differences among Whites persisted as visible markers of U.S. identity. Cherokee, Mohicans, and Navajo became natives who were removed from the body politic and ghettoized in quasi-autonomous colonies or "reservations." Despite the irony of the term "Native American," Native Americans have more often been seen as foreigners than as bona fide Americans. Igbo, Yoruba, and Ashanti became Blacks who, upon migration to cities encountered a form of urban colonization that resembles that reserved for rural Native Americans. Always subordinated within the nation-state, people of African descent carried the automatic stigma of second-class citizenship. Both natives and Blacks were marked with race that stood as proxy for class. Overall, creating this foundational racial triangle of Whites, natives, and Blacks enshrined in American law and custom required collapsing the multiple ethnicities within each racial category to create the very racial categories themselves. White, native, and Black were constructed both in relation to one another and from the stuff of pre-existing ethnicities.

As markers of citizenship rights, racial categories frame different ways of belonging to the nation-state itself—namely, variations of first-class citizenship for White Americans of varying class status, an ambiguous and contested citizenship status for indigenous peoples, and permanent second-class citizenship for people of African descent. The relationships among these three racial groups not only were integral to the inception of American national identity and its codification in the founding of the nation-state, but the racial triangle has repeatedly been reworked in response to the exigencies of subsequent historical periods. Historically, because the racial triangle of White, native, and Black lay at the core of American national identity, it neither disappeared nor radically transformed. Instead, the flexibility of racial meanings allowed it to shift shape but not essence. For existing and immigrant ethnic groups alike, the process of being or becoming "American" required jockeying for a position in relation to the racial reference points of White, native, and Black. As long as the national compass provided by the racial triangle remained intact—namely, the external racism of extermination characterizing the White–indigenous relationship—and the internal racism of slavery, Jim Crow segregation, and genteel de facto segregation characterizing the White–Black relationship, then American national identity had meaning. All else could change, but the racial triangle provided an important continuity to American national identity.

It is important to remember that this racial triangle describes a template for conceptualizing American national identity. Actual population groups have never fit smoothly into these categories. For example, the Latino population constitutes varying mixtures of all three "racial" categories and thus from its inception has constituted an important challenge to the racial triangle described here. Rather, the triangle constitutes benchmarks against which individuals and groups measure racial categorization and the political power it engenders.

The tenacity of this racial triangle explains in part how American society can undergo massive reorganization of its basic social institutions and ethnic populations in response to phases of capitalist development, yet somehow manage to replicate a seemingly permanent racial hierarchy. Whites were on top at the founding of a nation-state reliant on agrarian capitalism; they remain so today. Native Americans and African Americans were on the bottom, and these groups remain so today. Despite massive reorganization of social institutions in the United States during transitions from industrial capitalism to a global capitalism reliant on the service industry, the basic contours of the racial triangle persist. Definitions of White, native, and Black; the size, physical appearance, and cultural attributes of populations included within each category; and the actual terminology used to describe these categories—for example, whether to capitalize terms such as "white," "negro," and "black"—do change over time. Ethnicities come and go, yet the *need* for the racial categories themselves persists.[8]

This racial/ethnic logic frames understandings of American national identity. The United States is often seen as an important example of civic nationalism, a form of nationalism that arose in modern nation-states and that is characterized by features such as democratic institutions, the protection of individual rights, and the belief in law as a way to mediate claims of special-interest groups.[9] Formally, the United States is a civic nation; the democratic principles of the U.S. Constitution promise equality for all American citizens, because regardless of race, national origin, former condition of servitude, and color, all citizens stand equal before the law. Via these principles, the United States aims to craft one nation out of many different ethnic groups and foster interethnic cooperation among citizens.

But as the argument linking race, ethnicity, and American national identity advanced here suggests, the actual workings of U.S. society might remain closer to ideas associated with ethnic nationalism. Within assumptions of ethnic nationalism, a "nation" consists of a group of people who share an ethnicity grounded in blood ties. In the case of the United States, Whites constitute such a "nation," with Whiteness itself grounded in blood ties of racial purity. For an ethnic nation, cultural expressions of their sense of being a "people"—their music, art, language, and customs—constitute their unique national identity. Again, many White Americans argue for English-only social institutions and routinely castigate speakers of non-standard American English and those whose social institutions do not match an assumed White culture. Under this ethnic-nationalism model, ideally, each ethnic group should have its own nation-state, a political entity where the ethnic group can be self-governing. While this understanding of nation has a long history within European cultures, it is less often applied to questions of American national identity.[10] Ironically, nation-states where ethnic or tribal membership confers citizenship rights are often seen as being premodern or "backward," but when it comes to the United States, civic nationalism seemingly erases the highly visible ethnic foundations of American national identity. The paradox of American national identity that juxtaposes the democratic freedoms associated with individual rights to the reality of differential group treatment of Whites, indigenous peoples, and people of African descent thus reflects a complicated tension between the ideas of civic and ethnic nationalism.

Immigrant groups have long faced the challenge of negotiating an American racial/ethnic identity within the racial triangle that is so essential to American national identity. The massive European immigration to the United States and of Caribbean immigration to the United States, as well as important internal migrations of African Americans within the United States in the early twentieth century, illustrate one important period in which American national identity was renegotiated. On arriving in the United States, European groups whose Irish, Italian, or Jewish ethnicity may have set them apart as other "races" in their nation-states of origin became redefined as ethnic immigrants, often non–White foreigners. These new Irish American, Italian American, and Jewish American immigrants possessed the biological qualifications for achieving a White identity but lacked experiential history with the racial triangle. Members of these groups could move from second-class to first-class citizenship via assimilation into new American identities. But which American identities showed the most promise? Should European ethnic immigrants throw in their lot with the historically disadvantaged African Americans and Native Americans, whose subordination within forms of internal racism seemed eerily familiar? Or should they claim the White-skin privilege required for first-class American citizenship?

As Noel Ignatiev reminds us in *How the Irish Became White*, the answers to these questions were far from clear-cut.[11] For groups that had been treated as subordinated "races" in Europe, redefining themselves as a privileged "race" in the American context did not occur uncontested. The anthropologist Karen Sacks advances a similar argument via her query, "How Did Jews Become White Folks?"[12] Despite the divergent paths followed by White ethnic groups to assimilation, claiming and then erasing Whiteness apparently was a small price to pay for the benefits attached to first-class American citizenship.

African Americans forced to watch this European assimilation process often found it a bitter pill to swallow. In a "rap on race" with the anthropologist Margaret Mead, the African American author James Baldwin described the significance of race in definitions of "American":

> I had my fill of seeing people come down the gangplank on Wednesday, let us say, speaking not a word of English, and by Friday discovering that I was working for them and they were calling me nigger like everybody else. So that the Italian adventure or even the Jewish adventure, however grim, is distinguished from my own adventure . . . by one thing. Not only am I black, but I am one of our niggers. Americans can treat me in a certain way

because I am an American. They would never treat an African the way they treat me.[13]

In this passage, Baldwin points to the links among assimilation, Whiteness, and first-class citizenship, as well as to how the internal racism of racial discrimination worked to keep African Americans subordinated as second-class citizens.

Afro-Caribbean immigrants in the early twentieth century quickly found that they faced a challenge that was similar to, yet different from, that faced by their European counterparts. They, too, longed for the benefits of first-class American citizenship but found that, when they "came down the gangplank on Wednesday," their Friday experience differed from the Italian or the Jewish "adventure." Distancing themselves from Black Americans by highlighting a Caribbean ethnic identity may have yielded some relief from the second-class treatment given to African American "niggers," but it did not guarantee first-class treatment. Recognizing these contradictions, large numbers of Afro-Caribbean immigrants joined the Garvey Movement. Choosing to throw in their lot with African Americans and help redefine African American ethnicity, members of Garvey Movement and similar political organizations realized that they would remain second-class citizens as long as the silent "White" accompanied the term "American." Their experiences suggest that the myth of assimilation as the route to upward social mobility held out to all new immigrants had different meaning for those immigrants with identifiably African features.

The seeming permanence of this process of using multiple ethnicities to construct a racialized American national identity (but not the form that racialized citizenship categories will assume in any given historical era) raises the question of how this racialization process happens? Surely there must be other fundamentals that interlock with this racial template. In this regard, gender matters greatly, but how?

The American Family Ideal: Normalizing and Naturalizing Racial Hierarchy

One important contribution of Western feminism has been its analysis of how the American family ideal contributes to women's oppression.[14] This ideal has several components. Defined as a natural or biological arrangement based on heterosexual attraction, idealized families consist of married, heterosexual couples that produce their own biological children. A well-functioning family protects and balances the interests of all its members—mothers and fathers care for children, adults care for their elderly parents, and husbands care for wives. Everyone contributes to and benefits from family membership in proportion to his or her capacities. Despite this seeming unity of interests among family members, hierarchies not only exist within families but also are deemed to be natural, normal, and necessary for family survival. Normal families have a natural authority structure—namely, a father-head earning an adequate family wage, a stay-at-home wife, and children. Those who idealize this family form as a private haven from a public world see family as held together by primary emotional bonds of love and caring across this natural authority structure. Assuming a relatively fixed sexual division of labor, wherein women's roles are defined as primarily in the home and men's in the public world of work, the American family ideal also assumes the separation of work and family.

As feminist scholarship points out, this ideal fosters gender inequities. In particular, notions of male family headship simultaneously privilege and naturalize masculine authority as a fundamental premise of American society overall.[15] Just as fathers are heads of households in the private sphere of family, men are heads of social institutions in the public sphere. Moreover, the notion of appropriate spheres of influence for men and women fosters gendered understandings of public and private space. Because women are so often associated with family, home space becomes the private, feminine space that is distinct from the public, masculine space that lies outside its borders. Family space is for members only: Only family members can invite in outsiders or else they are intruders. Within these gendered spheres of private and public space, women and men again assume distinctive roles. Women are expected to remain in their home place. Avoiding the dangerous space of public streets allows women to care for children, the sick, and the elderly, and other dependent family members. Men are expected to support and defend the private, feminine space that houses their families. Overall, notions of naturalized gender hierarchies advanced by the American family ideal—the differential treatment of sons and daughters regarding economic autonomy and free access to public space— intertwine with practices such as the sex-typing of occupations in the paid labor market and male control of government, professional sports, the streets, and other public spaces.

The significance of the American family ideal for gender hierarchies suggests that this ideal might function in a similar fashion for other social hierarchies. For example, via its centrality as a mechanism for regulating property, family reappears as an important social institution in normalizing social-class hierarchies.[16] Inheritance laws in the United States have been devoted to the intergenerational transfer of wealth, not exclusively from individual to individual, but through family lines. At birth, individuals inherit the accumulated wealth or debt of their families that in turn frames the social and actual capital that defines their childhood. This intergenerational transfer from parents to children of actual property and the benefits that accrue to those with property suggest that family constitutes an important social institution in regulating unequal concentrations of wealth and poverty, especially from one generation to the next.[17]

Family rhetoric thus works to naturalize and normalize social practices that distribute wealth and poverty among U.S. families. The intergenerational transfer of wealth and debt constitutes one important site where social class hierarchies are reproduced. Labor-market practices that distribute individuals across labor-market segments that in turn result in markedly different income for women and men in different jobs require rules that portray this process as fundamentally fair. Labor-market practices require a legitimate authority structure that routinely relies on the American family ideal for meaning. For example, within the logic of the American family ideal, age or seniority constitutes a normal form of social hierarchy where adults have natural authority over children and older siblings are naturally responsible for younger ones. Those with greater seniority garner greater responsibility and benefits. Ideas such as these seem to be benign and fair notions for creating an equitable, normal authority structure. Yet when mapped onto labor-market practices, these seemingly natural ideas become important in manufacturing economic opportunity and disadvantage. Beliefs that "last hired, first fired" rules fairly discriminate among workers ignore exclusionary practices of the past that discriminated against women and racial/ethnic groups. Similarly, the intergenerational transfer of wealth, ironically via the mechanism of family inheritance, remains grounded in a similar belief that slaveowners, homesteaders, and others who made fortunes in prior eras had a legitimate head start in accumulating property.

In this fashion, social hierarchies of social class and gender rely on the rhetoric and practices associated with the American family ideal. At the same time, these hierarchies do not invoke family in the same way. On the one hand, class hierarchies rely heavily on exclusionary practices that seem designed to keep families separated from one another.

Exclusionary practices appeal to notions of group purity. Reminiscent of external racisms, the goal is to remove the offending social group, in this case poor and working-class families, from competition for college admissions, desirable neighborhoods, and professional jobs seen as the property of more affluent middle- and upper-income American families. In contrast, gender hierarchies rely more heavily on practices designed to subordinate members who are permanently included within individual family units. For women with spouses who batter and children with abusive parents, domination becomes intertwined with love. Suggestive of Mrs. C's perceptions of Mildred—"We *just* love her!"— the seemingly natural authority of husbands over wives, parents over children, and benevolent employers over their Black servants masks the power involved. Reminiscent of the practices associated with internal racisms, gender hierarchies work with the theme of a proximate difference where it becomes important to maintain power differentials among individuals included in the same system. Whereas class and gender clearly work together, family practices that subordinate and exploit within the family can be less visible as oppression, as well as more difficult to resist, in part because they are learned in a context of family and all that family should be.

Take, for example, little Carol's growing understanding of class privilege, gender subordination, and racism as portrayed in Childress's vignette. Carol learns both forms of hierarchy via interactions with her two mothers, Mrs. C and Mildred. Despite Mrs. C's protestations that Mildred was like one of the family—"she *just adores* our little Carol!"— Carol clearly knew that her White mother was superior to her Black one. As a miniature Mrs. C in training, Carol was learning a gendered understanding of White women's place in a racialized class hierarchy. In a similar fashion, legions of middle-class and affluent White American boys and girls live in virtually all–White neighborhoods, attend virtually all–White schools, and play on virtually all–White soccer teams. When children like little Carol do encounter members of racial/ethnic groups, such individuals routinely are in subordinate roles or, more recently, are handpicked friends with similar social-class backgrounds. These children learn the meaning of a racialized social-class hierarchy in gender-specific ways from within the safety purchased by their propertied families. Hierarchy in this sense becomes normalized because it occurs within seemingly natural family processes associated with their family households, neighborhoods, schools, churches, recreational facilities, and local shopping malls.

Using a series of interrelated practices resembling those of external and internal racisms, the rhetoric and practices associated with the American family ideal naturalize and normalize racial hierarchy. Family ideology is especially important in the construction of ideas about race. For example, one important component of the naturalization process concerns how presumptions of "blood ties" frame the perceived links among blood, family, kin, and race. In the United States, concepts of family and kinship draw strength from the flow of blood as a substance that regulates the spread of rights.[18] Families are mechanisms for perpetuating blood ties via maintaining bloodlines through reproduction. Whereas the legal system is deeply implicated in legitimizing marriages for heterosexual partners, the importance given to the seemingly natural bonds between mothers and children, brothers and sisters, grandmothers and grandchildren signal the importance of blood in crafting biological and therefore naturalized definitions of family as well as those of race. To appreciate the depth of blood ties as the basis of family, one need only review the deep-seated resistance to gay and lesbian marriages. Because such unions are seen as nonprocreative, they disrupt the seeming naturalness of lineage by blood idealized by heterosexual sexuality and marriage. Representing the genetic links among related individuals, the belief in blood ties naturalizes the bonds among members of kinship networks.

Given the significance attached to biology, women of different racial/ethnic groups have varying responsibilities in maintaining these seemingly natural blood ties.[19] For example, White women of different social classes play special roles in keeping family and racial bloodlines pure. Prior to contemporary reproductive technologies, maintaining propertied White families required controlling White women's sexuality, largely through social norms that advocated premarital virginity. By marrying White men and engaging in heterosexual relations only with their husbands, propertied White women ensured the racial purity of White families. Thus, through social taboos that eschewed premarital sexuality and interracial marriage for all White women, pure White families could thereby avoid racial degeneration into hybridity.[20] When reinserted into naturalized hierarchies of gender, class, and race and institutionally enforced via mechanisms such as racially segregated space and state-sanctioned violence, efforts to regulate sexuality and marriage reinforced beliefs in the sanctity of blood ties.

Historically, through their reliance on a racist biology, definitions of race in U.S. society normalized the importance of blood ties via laws, customs, and an infrastructure of racialized social institutions. Biological families and racial families rely on similar notions.[21] Definitions of race as family in the United States traditionally rested on biological classifications legitimated by science and sanctioned by law. By grouping people through notions of physical similarity, such as skin color, facial features, or hair texture, and supported by law and custom, White Americans used scientific racism to define themselves, indigenous peoples and Black Americans as distinctive social groups.[22] Just as members of "real" families linked by blood ties were expected to resemble one another, so were members of racial groups descended from a common bloodline seen as sharing physical, intellectual, and moral attributes. Within this logic, those lacking biological similarities became defined as family outsiders, while racially different groups became strangers to one another.

In addition to the rhetoric provided by the American family ideal, practices concerning actual American families work to naturalize and normalize racial hierarchy. The multiple meanings attached to the concept of *home*—home as family household and home as neighborhood—also speak to the significance of family in regulating the property relations that are so central to racial hierarchy. Within the logic of the American family ideal, the ideal home is a single-family dwelling in a nice neighborhood where property values will appreciate over time. The family home is the family investment. However, when combined with ideas about family that view White, native, and Black families as the building blocks of different races, what appears to be a relatively benign idea about the family home emerges as a fundamental mechanism for reproducing race and class hierarchies.

The history of race- and class-segregated housing that in turn constitute the core identity of race- and class-segregated neighborhoods forms one important pillar of racial hierarchy in the United States. Just as the value attached to actual families reflects their placement in racial and social-class hierarchies, the property values characterizing the neighborhoods where these families live demonstrate comparable inequalities. The practice of encouraging families to purchase single-family homes over other housing options works to mask how the property values of the housing occupied by different racial/ethnic groups is central to racial hierarchy. For example, residential housing and racially segregated neighborhoods in the United States, one referred to as "American apartheid," virtually insures that families like Mildred's will never move next door to families such as

Mrs. C's.[23] Assumptions of race-, ethnic-, and class-segregated space mandate that American families and the neighborhoods where they reside be kept separate.

Just as crafting a family from individuals from diverse racial, ethnic, religious, or class backgrounds is frowned on, mixing different races within one neighborhood is discouraged. Neighborhoods allegedly operate best when racial or class homogeneity prevails. Class-segregated and racially segregated neighborhoods suggest that families and racial groups both require their own unique places where they can feel "at home." Assigning Whites, African Americans, Latinos, and new racial/ethnic immigrant groups their own separate spaces reflects efforts to maintain a geographic, racial purity. As the dominant group, White Americans continue to support legal and extralegal measures that segregate African Americans, Native Americans, Mexican Americans, Puerto Ricans, and other similar groups, thereby perpetuating cultural norms about desirability of racial/ethnic purity in schools, neighborhoods, and public facilities. In this regard, the continual White flight out of inner cities has been buttressed by an arsenal of public policies such as tax benefits for home ownership, subsidized roads and infrastructure for fast-growing suburban areas, zoning in suburban communities that restricts low-income housing, the denial of loans and insurance to racial/ethnic groups who want to move to all–White areas, and resisting suburban incorporation into metropolitan school districts that would place middle-class White children in school with working-class racial/ethnic students. These public policies are supplemented by what appear to be more individualized, private choices that effectively maintain racially segregated home spaces for White men, women, and children. For example, the increasing privatization of U.S. public schools, health care, recreational facilities, and security forces speaks to the ability of White people with money to purchase racially homogeneous experiences for themselves and their offspring. What remains noteworthy about these practices is that they are typically defended as being non-racial because they allegedly occur in defense of family.

The gendered nature of the American family ideal means that the production of racial hierarchy via racially segregated geographic and social space is also deeply gendered. Because racialized home spaces of all sorts are coded as private spaces, homes serve as sanctuaries for family members. Surrounded by individuals who seemingly have similar objectives, these homes represent idealized, privatized spaces where members can feel at ease. Women become important in maintaining this sense of home as sanctuary and place of renewal. The family home contains the women who are responsible for reproducing the family as well as the children who represent its future. Both are in need of protection from outsiders. On both sides of racial power, White, native, and Black women thus occupy an ironic position: They must be subordinated within the family yet protected from threats that lie outside the family home. Moreover, in a system where family rhetoric and practices become the building blocks of racial hierarchy, whether the women who become symbolic of actual families or the racial "families" that are constructed as private, feminine entities in need of protection from intruders, defending the family becomes important.

In this sense, constructing racial hierarchy is a gendered process that works with and through social class, age, and heterosexism as comparable hierarchies. Gender proves to be a malleable category that often is not matched to the biological sex assigned to individuals. The gendered infrastructure of the traditional family ideal works with multiple hierarchies. But how might these ideas concerning family work with a racialized American national identity?

Constructing and Reconstructing American National Identity

If the nation-state in the United States is conceptualized as a large American national family understood via the rhetoric of the American family ideal, then this ideal may provide a template for assessing group placement within and contributions to American national well-being. Within this logic, Native Americans, African Americans, Puerto Ricans, and Chicanos become the "domestic others"; they become included within the body politic *like* one of the American family. In contrast, racial/ethnic immigrants from Mexico, Central America, Latin America, the Caribbean, and Africa become the "foreign Blacks" and "Latino immigrants" who become targets of exclusionary policies. A curious reversal takes place. Native-born, domestic Blacks and Native Americans become quasi-women. Just as women are required for the idealized family yet subordinated within it, native-born racial/ethnic groups become constructed as insiders. They clearly belong to the U.S. body politic yet remain subordinated within it. As a proximate danger to the nation-state that threatens its well-being from within its borders, such groups encounter a politics of exploitation and containment. In contrast, people of African descent or Hispanic heritage or indigenous backgrounds who are born outside the United States become constructed as outsiders. The nature of their threat lies in their desire to enter and thereby pollute the privileged home space reserved for the American national family.

Mead's response to Baldwin's analysis of the Americanization process highlights the gendered dimension of how being "like" family fosters differential treatment. Drawing a parallel between race and gender, she notes: "Getting back to treating your own worse than other people: Many men won't put up with from their wives what they will put up with from other women, because their wives are theirs and they are going to stay home and do what their husbands want."[24] Within Mead's family property model, domestic negroes and native peoples become equated with wives or children within families. Thus, the "childlike wife" and "innocent women and children" become templates for constructing racial and gendered meanings. Racial ideologies that portray racial/ethnic groups as intellectually underdeveloped, uncivilized children require parallel ideas that construct Whites as intellectually mature, civilized adults. When applied to race, family rhetoric that deems adults more developed than children, and thus entitled to greater power, uses naturalized ideas about age and authority to legitimate racial hierarchy and to distribute national rights, entitlements, and responsibilities. Ironically, because Native Americans, African Americans, Puerto Ricans, and Chicanos are "natural" albeit subordinate members of the national family, the potential threat posed by these so-called domestic, or insider, minorities can be seen as more dangerous than that posed by "foreign" racial/ethnic immigrant groups.

Notions of American national identity grounded in this gendered family rhetoric conceptualize the United States as a large national family. Moreover, this imagined national family finds hierarchy within unity by invoking principles of civic nationalism claiming a unity of interests that supersedes the special interests affiliated with class, ethnic, racial, or gender groups.[25] At the same time, ideas of ethnic nationalism compartmentalize the population in the United States into racial/ethnic "families" that are hierarchically arranged within the nation-state. In this context of naturalized hierarchy within American national unity, members of some racial/ethnic families receive full benefits of membership in the American nation-state while others encounter inferior treatment associated with second-class citizenship. Interestingly, contemporary constructions of Whiteness allow for variations that encompass ethnicity. Eschewing the empty Whiteness of an assimilation process that erases ethnicity to become White, many White Americans now claim multiple ethnicities. Mary Waters refers to this process as "optional ethnicity" and describes how ethnicity operates as an option only for White Americans.[26] Yet this optional ethnicity masks the power of Whiteness to define citizenship. Only White Americans can shed their racial and ethnic identities to stand for the generalized national citizen. Only White Americans can be full, "red-blooded" Americans. Representing the epitome of racial purity that is also associated with American national interests, Whites constitute the most valuable citizens. In contrast, racial/ethnic groups remain tainted with the stigma of representing particularism, backwardness, childishness, and special interests.

In this racialized nation-state, racial/ethnic groups negotiate a fluid landscape of ethnic meanings that are tightly bundled to American understandings of race. Foreign-born and domestic-born both matter, with race, gender, class, and ethnicity all gaining meaning from one another. Indigenous people, African Americans, Chicanos, native Hawaiians, Puerto Ricans, and other domestic minorities become second-class citizens. In contrast, immigrants from the Caribbean, Asia, Latin America, and Africa who cannot pass as White encounter more difficulty gaining citizenship than immigrants from European nations. Because racial/ethnic immigrant groups cannot become biologically White and therefore lack the appropriate blood ties, such groups confront the contradictions raised by a deeply entrenched racial triangle that seemingly contradicts the principles of civic nationalism. Moreover, once domesticated and included within the American family via gaining citizenship, they encounter the challenges of being treated as second-class citizens. Unlike prior waves of European immigrants who could in fact become White, recent racial/ethnic immigrant groups can at best become "honorary Whites."

When placed in the context of a racialized ethnic nationalism, ideas about naturalized hierarchies provided via family rhetoric and actual family practices shape the meanings of American citizenship. Common-sense understandings of family suggest that individuals feel that they owe something to and are responsible for members of their families. For example, individuals routinely help their family members by providing child care, lending money, locating employment and housing, or nursing the sick. Family members linked by blood acquire these benefits merely by belonging. Even when family members lack merit, they are entitled to benefits simply because they belong. Beyond this issue of access to entitlements, individuals incur differential responsibilities that depend on their placement in family hierarchies. For example, women are expected to perform much of the reproductive labor, whereas men's duties lie in providing financial support.

In a similar fashion, under the tenets of civic nationalism, U.S. citizens by birth or naturalization acquire certain rights and responsibilities that accrue from membership. All American citizens are promised entitlements such as equal protection under the law, access to unemployment insurance, old-age pensions, free public education, and other social-welfare benefits. Citizens are also expected to fulfill certain obligations to the nation-state, such as paying taxes, observing the law, and engaging in military service when required. In contrast to the rights and responsibilities provided to insiders, outsiders lack the entitlements given to group members and the obligations attached to belonging. Similar to non-family members, non–U.S. citizens are neither entitled to citizenship benefits nor responsible for national duties.

In the United States, where race is constructed via assumed blood ties, the differential distribution of citizenship rights and responsibilities creates categories of first- and second-class citizenship that remain unduly influenced by the foundational racial triangle. Citizenship status is conferred at birth, regardless of individual merit. To be convinced of this discrepancy, all one need do is compare the differential distribution of citizenship rights to American children based on the race, ethnicity, and class of the families into which they are born. The widely varying quality of public education provides a sobering case study of how much family origins matter. Contrast, for example, the quality of public education routinely provided to the largely African American, Chicano, Puerto Rican, and working-class children in inner-city schools with that granted their middle-class and overwhelmingly White counterparts in suburban districts. Despite the 1954 *Brown v. Board of Education* decision outlawing racial segregation in public schools, large numbers of working-class and poor African American children remain warehoused in poorly funded, deteriorating, racially segregated inner-city schools. Regardless of *individual* merit, these children as a *class* of children are seen as lacking merit and unworthy of public support and are treated as second-class citizens. Contrasting their lot with the often lavish school facilities and services provided to children attending overwhelmingly White suburban schools, especially in affluent districts, reveals the significance of possessing first-class citizenship. Even though many *individual* suburban children lack merit, the property values of their parents' homes, the location of these homes in homogeneous neighborhoods with appreciating value, the dominance of their parents in professional and managerial jobs, and the accumulated family wealth that may have been passed down from previous generations automatically entitles this *class* of children to first-class treatment.

By relying on the belief that children and their families have assigned places where they truly belong, images of place, space, and territory link gendered notions of family with constructs of race and nation.[27] In this logic where everything has its place, maintaining borders of all sorts becomes vitally important. Preserving the logic of segregated home spaces requires strict rules that distinguish insiders from outsiders. As was the case linking racially homogeneous American families and the property values of their racially segregated neighborhoods, American national identity also relies on protecting the borders of the United States as a strategy of ensuring citizenship entitlements for American citizens. Securing a people's "homeland" or national territory has long been important to nationalist aspirations.[28] Just as households and neighborhoods are seen as needing protection from outsiders, maintaining the integrity of national borders persists as a pillar of American foreign policy. Because the United States has operated as a dominant world power since World War II, shielding its own home soil from military assault has been less emphasized than protecting so-called American interests abroad. American citizens and American businesses that are on foreign soil represent extensions of U.S. territory, citizens of the national family who must be defended at all costs.

As is the case with all situations of hierarchy, actual, or implicit use of force, sanctions and violence may be needed to maintain unequal power relations. However, in securing a racialized American national identity, violence can be so pervasive that it is rendered virtually invisible. For example, feminist efforts to have violence against women in the home taken seriously as a bona fide form of violence and not just a private family matter have long met with resistance. In a similar fashion, the extent of the violence against Native Americans, Puerto Ricans, Chicanos, African Americans, native Hawaiians, and other groups who were incorporated into the United States through conquest and slavery remains routinely ignored or distorted. Even current violence against such groups remains underreported unless captured in a dramatic fashion, such as the videotaped beating of the motorist Rodney King by Los Angeles police officers. Despite their severity and increase in the

1990s, hate crimes against racial/ethnic minorities, women, children, and against gays, lesbians, and bisexuals remain largely invisible. Through these silences, these forms of violence are not only neglected; they become legitimated. Family rhetoric can also work to minimize understandings of violence in groups that define themselves in family terms. In the same way that wife battering and childhood physical and sexual abuse become part of the "family secrets" of far too many families, so does the routine nature of violence targeted against women, LGBT people, children, and racial/ethnic groups become the dirty family secret of American national identity.

In the United States, the period since 1965 has been marked by new contradictions of change and continuity. The phrase "the browning of America" seemingly describes the changing multiethnic and multiracial character of the population in the United States. When coupled with changing ideas about family, these trends collectively produce new opportunities to reconfigure the significance of both the foundational racial triangle and the American family ideal in shaping American national identity. Whether old racial meanings will reorganize under the rubric of new racial terminology, or whether the United States will be able to craft a multiethnic, multiracial democracy that in actuality reflects the principles of civic nationalism, remains to be seen. However, recent demographic changes do raise several interesting issues for investigation.

One of these issues concerns the impact of the growing numbers of new racial/ethnic immigrant groups from Asia, Latin America, and Africa that have swelled the numbers of Chicanos, Puerto Ricans, Chinese Americans, and Japanese Americans and other historically subordinated racial/ethnic groups. New immigrant populations see the United States as a land where economic opportunities outweigh the drawbacks associated with being non–White. Because most leave negative economic or political situations, America still represents a land of opportunity. New relationships between color and power become renegotiated in the face of these massive demographic changes. Within this browning of America, Latino populations play a pivotal role in reinforcing and challenging longstanding racial meanings. Latino populations have an established history in the United States. What is new is the size of this population and the diversity of groups who now fall under the rubric "Latino." On the one hand, Latino populations may choose to replicate racial triangles *within* the category of Latino, giving benefits to those who are biologically White and discriminating against those who appear to be native or Black. On the other hand, because Latino populations encompass multiple racial categories, such populations can dissolve power dynamics of the foundational racial triangle by embracing the multiracial character of their own population. Moreover, because no fixed boundary exists between Latino and other groups—there are "White" Latinos, "Black" Latinos, and myriad variations of all combinations—the Latino population has the ability to constitute a new center of American national identity that is deeply enmeshed with other populations.

The relaxation of longstanding rules against interracial marriage, as well as the growing acceptability of White families' pursuing transracial adoption, raises another set of questions concerning the future of the foundational racial triangle. A changed legal climate has created new visibility for the children of mixed-race relationships. Historically, because the majority of these non–White children were born outside of marriage to racial/ethnic women, most mixed-race children were absorbed into existing racial/ethnic communities. Currently, however, such children are increasingly born to White mothers. Marital and child-support laws allow such children to claim the property rights that accrue to them as children of White mothers or fathers. These biracial children do not fit neatly into any existing racial/ethnic category, nor should they. In a similar fashion, racial/ethnic children adopted and raised by White families do not fit precisely into any racial category. Many are "honorary Whites" and as such are uniquely positioned to challenge a racialized American national identity as never before. Collectively, both groups challenge longstanding understandings of family purity and bloodlines advanced by the American family ideal.

The kaleidoscope of color that increasingly characterizes the U.S. population does not mean that the foundational racial triangle has disappeared. Rather, new racial/ethnic immigrant groups, mixed-race U.S. citizens, and racial/ethnic children raised in White homes confront a question similar to that faced by their early-twentieth-century European and Afro-Caribbean counterparts. In this sense, the changing demographics of American society provide yet another opportunity to confront the basic paradox of American national identity. Collectively, such groups demonstrate that the boundaries demarcating Whites, native peoples, and Blacks are far from fixed and inviolable. Instead, the situation resembles a shifting mosaic of continual renegotiation of group position within a relatively fixed racial triangle. These groups renegotiate their identities against and within the still fixed reference points of White, native, and Black. Whether their claims to American identity will take the form of dissolving the racial triangle itself remains to be seen.

Concluding Remarks

The paradox of American national identity pivots on multiple contra-dictions—namely, those of the citizenship rights promised to U.S. citizens juxtaposed to differential group discrimination; those of ex-ternal and internal racisms that work with and through one another by excluding and containing selected categories of citizens; those of civic and ethnic nationalisms that provide an unstable, Janus-faced American national identity; those of the curious combination of change and continuity that has allowed American society repeatedly to transform while maintaining a deeply entrenched racial hierarchy; and those of a deeply gendered American family ideal that simultaneously constructs and masks these contradictions.

Addressing these contradictions requires listening to those with different interpretations of what it means to be treated "like" one of the American national family or to be excluded from the American national family altogether. In this regard, Mildred's reactions to the two women who grinned at her "like chessy cats" differed markedly from those of her employer. After hearing Mrs. C claim that Mildred was like one of the family, Mildred comments, "After I couldn't stand it any more, I went in and took the platter off the table and gave 'em both a look that would have frizzled a egg. . . . Well, you might have heard a pin drop and then they started talkin' about something else. When the guest leaves, I go in the living room and says, 'Mrs. C . . . , I want to have a talk with you.'" [29] What follows Mildred's request to "have a talk" with Mrs. C provides important guidelines for exploring the contradictions that characterize American national identity.

First and foremost, Mildred rejects her subordination within the family. She is not seduced by the promise of better treatment afforded her because, unlike her African American women counterparts who are not allowed in Mrs. C's house, she is "like one of the family":

> Mrs. C . . . , you are a pretty nice person to work for, but I wish you would please stop talkin' about me like I was a *cocker spaniel* or . . . a *kitten*. . . . Now you just sit there and hear me out.
>
> In the first place, you do not *love* me; you may be fond of me, but that is all. . . . In the second place, I am *not* just like one of the family at all! The

family eats in the dining room and I eat in the kitchen. Your mama borrows your lace tablecloth for her company and your son entertains his friends in your parlor, your daughter takes her afternoon nap on the living room couch and the puppy sleeps on your satin spread. . . . So you can see I am not *just* like one of the family.

In this passage, Mildred clearly describes the distinctions between first- and second-class citizenship in the C family, and points out that the benefits of full membership are denied to her. Instead, from her specific location as an African American woman, Mildred identifies two dimensions of second-class citizenship applied to the multiple racial/ethnic groups now unfolding in U.S. society. Within this logic of the American family ideal, African American women have been subordinated either as pets to serve at the whim of more powerful Whites or as mules, beasts of burden to perform the labor that makes the assumed family norm possible at all. These remain the categories available to racial/ethnic groups who fail to confront the racial triangle itself but who aim merely to coexist within it.

Mildred then moves on to describe how many of the ideas attributed to her concerning her acceptance of her subordinate status are just that: ideas attributed to her by more powerful groups who need ideologies such as that surrounding the American family ideal to mask existing power hierarchies. Take, for example, her explicit rejection of the mammy role, one that portrays African American women as possessing unlimited love and affection for the White children under their care.[30] Sharing her true feelings about little Carol, Mildred clearly refutes this particular family relationship between White and African American women:

> Now for another thing, I do not *just* adore your little Carol. I think she is a likable child, but she is also fresh and sassy. I know you call it "uninhibited" and that is the way you want your child to be, but *luckily* my mother taught me some inhibitions or else I would smack little Carol once in a while when she's talkin' to you like you're a dog, but as it is I just laugh it off the way you do because she is *your* child and I am *not* like one of the family.

Speaking from a particular social location that reveals a distinctive angle of vision on race, gender, and class, Mildred rejects dominant feminist ideologies that women have a common feminist consciousness stemming from their relations with motherhood.[31] Mildred clearly is not impressed by Mrs. C's beliefs concerning how children should be raised. Instead, Mildred draws a line in the sand concerning middle-class White girls such as little Carol who get first-class treatment and her own working-class African American children left at home and relegated to second-class treatment. That line demarcating the history of race, class, and gender relations in the United States becomes especially visible in the quoted passage: Mrs. C stands on one side, and Mildred stands on the other.

Mildred also challenges how Mrs. C's use of family language obscures class inequalities. In this case, Mrs. C wants to believe that Mildred is so happy to serve the C family that Mildred would be flattered to find out that Mrs. C would miss her. Again, Mildred rejects this idea that exploited people are happy in their place:

> Now when you say, "We don't know what we'd do without her" this is a polite lie...because I know that if I dropped dead or had a stroke, you would get somebody to replace me.
>
> You think it is a compliment when you say, "We don't think of her as a servant..." but after I have worked myself into a sweat cleaning the bathroom and the kitchen...making the beds...cooking the lunch...washing the dishes...I do not feel like no weekend house guest. I feel like a servant, and in the face of that I have been meaning to ask you for a slight raise which will make me feel much better toward everyone here and make me know my work is appreciated.[32]

In the space of their conversation Mildred challenged not only *ideas* about race and gender that constructed her as lesser, but *actual practices* that fostered her economic subordination. Mildred not only refuted ideas that she was "like one of the family"; she asked for a raise while doing so! No matter how much Mrs. C commiserated with Mildred's situation, finding more money and granting Mildred a raise meant more to her than Mrs. C's well-meaning albeit impotent race talk.

Addressing the paradox of American national identity requires finding a way to reconfigure the longstanding relations among race, ethnicity, and American national identity and to reclaim the language of family in doing so. In this enterprise, the words and actions of women like Mildred matter greatly because they reveal questions and perspectives that often go unheard. As Mildred reminds us, when it comes to the promises of citizenship, being *like* one of the family simply is not good enough.

2 Will the "Real" Mother Please Stand Up?

Race, Class, and American National Family Planning

I n the United States, motherhood as a constellation of social practices, a social institution, and an American cultural icon remains central to multiple systems of oppression. Just as mothers are viewed as important to family well-being, the status of motherhood as an institution remains essential to American health and prosperity. But in a nation-state like the United States, where social class, race, ethnicity, gender, sexuality, and nationality comprise intersecting dimensions of oppression, not all mothers are created equal.

In the politicized climate of late–twentieth-century America, the issue of which women are "real" mothers best suited for the tasks of reproducing both the American population and the alleged values of the U.S. nation-state takes on added importance. "Real" has many meanings, such as authentic, genuine, indisputable, and true. "Real" also has physical connotations, meaning concrete, tangible, and material. Another constellation of meanings of "real" refers to sincerity—earnest, honest, truthful, trustworthy, and reliable. Within these intersecting meanings of "real," binary thinking constructs certain groups of women of the right social class, race, and citizenship status as "real" mothers who are worthy and fit for the job. Affluent, married, White, and holding American citizenship, "real" mothers are those who fit cultural criteria for idealized motherhood. Against these idealized "real" mothers, other categories of women of the wrong social class, marital status, race, and citizenship status are judged to be less fit and less worthy to be mothers. Within this intellectual framework, women deemed fit to be "real" mothers encounter state-supported family-planning options that support their contributions as mothers to national well-being. In contrast, those deemed unfit to be "real" mothers experience reproductive policies that are markedly different.

In this chapter, I explore the relationship among motherhood, American national identity, and population policies. First, I examine how the traditional family ideal functions to structure notions of "real" motherhood and how this family ideal in turn frames American national identity. I suggest that not only does the metaphor of the biological, nuclear family operate to shape notions of an American nation whose health is assessed using family rhetoric, but that this American national family draws on race for much of its meaning.

Second, I investigate how a logic of eugenics provides an intellectual context for assessing contemporary family and reproductive policies by which the nation-state evaluates its health. Societies that embrace eugenic philosophies typically aim to transform social problems such as unemployment, increasing crime rates, childbearing by unmarried adolescents, and poverty into technical problems amenable to biological solutions. Via social engineering, societies shaped by eugenic thinking see "race and heredity—the birth rates of the fit and the unfit—as the forces that shape...political and social developments."[1] Moreover, eugenics movements that seek biological solutions to what are fundamentally social problems often arise when other mechanisms of controlling subordinate populations seem no longer adequate. The late–twentieth-century United States may be experiencing such a period, and American understandings of population policies aimed at regulating the mothering experiences of women from diverse racial, social class, and citizenship groups might benefit by viewing such policies within the context of a logic of eugenics.

Finally, to highlight the centrality of motherhood in these relations, I survey family and reproductive policies targeted toward middle-class White women, working-class White women, and working-class African American women. These three groups of women each occupy different social locations in their ability to be "real" mothers of the nation. As a result, population policies applied to each group demonstrate how the American nation-state seeks to regulate experiences with motherhood of women from different racial, ethnic, social-class, and citizenship groups in defense of nation-state interests.

"Real" Mothers in Family, Race, and Nation

As the sociologist Paul Gilroy observes, " 'race' differences are displayed in culture that is reproduced in educational institutions and, above all, in family life. Not only are families the nation in microcosm, its key components, but they also act as the means to turn social processes into natural, instinctive ones."[2] In the United States, families constitute primary sites of belonging: the family as an assumed biological entity, the racial family or community reinforced via geographically identifiable and racially segregated neighborhoods, and the national family symbolized via images of mom, dad, baseball, and apple pie.

The particular model of family is germane here, for a specific family ideal frames family rhetoric in the United States. According to the American traditional family ideal, a normative and ideal family consists of a heterosexual couple that produces its own biological children. A state-sanctioned marriage confers legitimacy not only on the family structure itself but on children born in this family. This metaphor functions as a deep taproot in American social policy. Individuals acquire varying degrees of authority, rights, and wealth based on their mode of entry into their biological families; a nation-state's population reflects similar power relations. The nation gains meaning via family metaphors. Moreover, this family metaphor articulates both with structures of institutionalized racism and with the labor needs of capitalism, such that the American national family is defined in race- and class-specific terms in the United States.[3]

Several features characterize the links between the biological, nuclear family and the American national family. First, presumptions of blood ties underlie both constructs. Just as women's bodies produce children that are part of a socially constructed family grounded in notions of biological kinship, women's bodies produce the population for the national family or nation-state, conceptualized as having some sort of biological oneness. In nuclear families, the legitimate sons and daughters of a heterosexual marriage, related by blood to biological parents, are contrasted to illegitimate children who, while they may also be related by blood, stand outside state-sanctioned marital relationships. In a similar fashion, those lacking the appropriate blood ties to the American nation-state are seen as outsiders, non–family members, and are treated accordingly. "Real" mothers remain central to reproducing these genuine blood ties.

Second, family metaphors and those of nation rely on distinctive notions of place, space, and territory. This dimension of the link can be seen through multiple meanings that people attach to the concept of home, meanings that range through levels of family household, neighborhood as family, home as the place of one's birth, and one's country as home. For example, the theme of the home as a sanctuary from outsiders and the turmoil of the public sphere creates boundaries for the biological family along lines of privacy and security. The notion of homeland or national territory that must be defended against marauding aliens or foreigners operates in a similar fashion. Both spaces are seen as needing protection from outsiders. "Real" mothers are those who take care of the home, who provide that sanctuary that must be protected.[4]

Third, in the same way that those born into a biologically defined family acquire certain lifelong rights and obligations to other family members, those born into the American national family as so-called natural or real citizens acquire certain rights attached to that citizenship. Citizens are also expected to fulfill certain obligations to one another. For example, people within family units routinely help members of their own families by babysitting, lending money, assisting relatives in locating employment and housing, or caring for economically unproductive family members such as the very young or the elderly. Family members are entitled to these benefits merely by belonging. In contrast, those who lie outside the family orbit are not entitled to such benefits, but individuals may earn them by being redefined as fictive kin or by being particularly worthy. Since citizenship is often conferred through birth or attachment to the mother, determining the "real" mother of a child can serve as a test of citizenship and belonging.[5]

Fourth, within biological families a pecking order or naturalized hierarchy emerges with, for example, good sons and daughters compared with their less ambitious or less fortunate siblings. This internal hierarchy parallels notions of first-class and second-class citizenship in the national family. Hierarchy may be determined by order of arrival: either birth order or immigration order. Claims that White Anglo-Saxon Protestants who migrated to the United States earlier are entitled to more benefits than more recent immigrants reflect this notion. Or hierarchy accompanies gender. In many families, girls and boys are treated differently regarding economic autonomy and freedom to move in public space. This differential treatment serves as a foundation for sex-typing occupations in the paid labor market and male domination of public arenas such as politics and professional sports. As is the case with all situations of hierarchy, actual or implicit use of force, sanctions, and violence may be needed to maintain unequal power relations.

Finally, families contain policies or rules regulating their own reproduction. Family planning comprises a constellation of reproductive options that range from coercion to choice, from permanence to reversibility. Within individual families, decision making lies with family members—technically, it is they who decide whether to have children, how many children to have, and how those children will be spaced. But can this analogy from family to nation be extended to public policies on the national level? In what ways do social policies designed to foster the health of the American nation-state, especially those concerning motherhood, follow a similar family-planning logic?

Planning for the National Family: The Logic of Eugenics Thinking

Eugenics movements or movements for "racial hygiene" of the early twentieth century compellingly illustrate the thinking underlying family and reproductive policies designed to control the motherhood of different groups of women for reasons of nationality or race. Eugenics philosophies and the population policies they support emerge within political economies with distinctive needs and within societies with particular social-class relations.

Common to eugenics movements throughout the world has been the view that biology is central to solving social problems. Societies that embrace eugenics philosophies typically attempt to transform social problems into technical problems amenable to biological solutions brought about through social engineering. Eugenics approaches thus combine a "philosophy of biological determinism with a belief that science might provide a technical fix for social problems."[6] Two sides typically exist to eugenic thinking. So-called positive eugenics consists of efforts to increase reproduction among the "aristogenic" or "fit" who allegedly carry the outstanding qualities of their group in their genes. So-called negative eugenics aims to prevent reproduction by the "cacogenic" or "unfit," those likely to have undesirable or defective offspring.[7]

The case of population policies enforced by the Nazi government offers an unsettling example of a nation-state that was able to follow to its rational conclusion the logic of eugenics thinking grounded in national family-planning rhetoric. Because German scientists borrowed from eugenics philosophies developed elsewhere in Europe and in the United States, German nation-state policies during the Nazi era of 1933–45 provide a particularly compelling case for understanding the connections among the logic of eugenics, institutionalized racism, institutionalized sexism, and social policy. The intellectual climate characterizing the Nazi German nation-state was not unique. Rather, it emerged from a common intellectual heritage framing Western in-dustrialized countries, including the United States.[8] Unlike other countries that held similar beliefs about eugenics or "racial hygiene" but were unable to implement them as fully, the Nazi German nation-state actually enforced eugenics philosophies.

Under the Nazis, eugenics thinking followed three main paths. First, the German population was racialized, with Jews and Aryans, among others, constructed as categories of immutable difference. Second, these putative racial differences were linked to issues of national identity and prosperity. Stigmatized as hindering German national prosperity, Jews were blamed for failed economic and political policies and char-acterized as outsiders in the homeland of the German national family. Finally, specific population policies were designed for the worthy and unworthy segments of the general population. For example, the Jewish population encountered a continuum of policies designed to control their numbers. Stripping Jewish citizens of their property rights, legal protections, and employment opportunities; relegating the Jewish pop-ulation to ghettos; deploying specific reproductive policies such as sterilization; and the so-called final solution of genocide targeted against the already born population collectively constitute eugenics as public policies that were framed within a logic of eugenics.[9]

Historically, U.S. public policy has relied on all three elements of eugenics thinking. First, because the United States has operated as a racialized state since its inception, race operates as a core concept in constructing American national identity. Despite promises of political and religious freedom for all American citizens in the U.S. Constitu-tion, by excluding sizable segments of the population from citizenship, this same constitution simultaneously codified race, gender, and class into the founding laws of the country.[10] Enslaving African Americans to exploit their labor and reproductive capacities and conducting mil-itary actions against Native Americans to acquire their land constituted population policies targeted explicitly for these racialized groups. Moreover, race remains important in framing the basic institutions that make up political, economic, and social institutions in the United States.[11] While the categories of race may shift in response to changing political and economic conditions, the fundamental belief in race as a guiding principle for defining segments of the American population remains remarkably hardy.[12]

The second element of eugenics-inspired public policies consists of associating diverse racial groups with perceived national interests. This element also has a long history in the United States. At various times, this has taken the form of restrictive immigration legislation targeted toward non–European racial and ethnic groups, a response to what was seen as the non–White threat from outside national boundaries. Slavery, de facto segregation, and other repressive policies applied to African Americans, Latinos, and other non–White populations within American borders also operated in response to perceived threats from non–White populations. Recent interconnections of racism and national policy may be more covert than in the past, operating, as the sociologists Michael Omi and Howard Winant suggest, in a hegemonic fashion, yet such ties continue. Racialized discourses exist around themes that serve as proxies for race: themes such as poverty, crime, immigration, affirmative action, and urban policy. None of these terms directly refers to people of color, yet all have been used as codes to indicate how the presence of people of color is problematic for national unity or national aspirations.[13]

The third feature of eugenics-inspired population policies, the direct control of different segments of the population through different population control measures, also characterizes American public policies.[14] Ironically, social and natural sciences in England and the United States pioneered the eugenics thinking that so influenced public policies implemented by the Nazi nation-state. Francis Galton, the founder of the eugenics movement in England, claimed, "Anglo-Saxons far outranked the Negroes of Africa, who in turn outranked the Australian aborigines, who outranked nobody."[15] Because Galton believed that large innate differences between races existed, he supported programs to raise the inherent abilities of mankind by replacing inferior races with superior ones.

Galton's ideas proved popular in the racially segregated United States. Preceding the sterilization laws of other countries by twenty years, American eugenics laws were seen as pioneering ventures by eugenicists of other countries. The U.S. Supreme Court's 1927 *Buck v. Bell* decision held that sterilization fell within the police power of the state. Reflecting the majority opinion, Oliver Wendell Holmes contended,

> It would be strange if it could not call upon those who already sap the strength of the state for these lesser sacrifices, often not felt to be such by those concerned, in order to prevent our being swamped by incompetence. It is better for all the world, if instead of waiting for their imbecility, society can prevent those who are manifestly unfit from continuing their kind. The

principle that sustains compulsory vaccination is broad enough to cover cutting the Fallopian tubes.... Three generations of imbeciles is enough.[16]

Given this intellectual context, it seems reasonable to conclude that differential population policies developed for different segments of the American population, especially those identifiable by race, citizenship status, and social class, have long existed in direct relation to any group's perceived value within the United States. Rather than the more familiar definition of population policies that emphasizes reproductive policies, I define population policies more broadly. Population policies comprise the constellation of social policies, institutional arrangements, and ideological constructions that shape reproductive histories of different groups of women within different racial/ethnic groups, social-class formations, and citizenship statuses. Examining population policies through this lens reveals the fallacy of viewing race-based policies and gender-based policies as basically regulating different forms of social relations. Current assumptions view Black men as having race, White women as having gender, and African American women as experiencing both race and gender, with White men lacking both race and gender. Such assumptions dissipate when confronted with actual population policies aimed at regulating the mothering experiences of different groups of women. Since the 1970s, major changes in the American political economy brought about by globalization have fostered job loss and declining standards of living for American workers. Moreover, a series of conservative administrations ushered in with the 1980 election to the presidency of Ronald Reagan has aimed to install differential population policies for different groups of women in the United States. Given this context, how does the logic of eugenics thinking frame the population policies targeted to different groups of women?

Policies for "Fit" Mothers: Middle-Class White Women

According to the logic of eugenics, falling birthrates of the dominant group constitute "race suicide." In this situation, women of the dominant group are routinely encouraged to increase their reproductive capacities. In the United States, White women's reproduction remains central to American national aspirations. Currently, efforts to encourage White women to produce more White babies, a so-called positive eugenics goal, occur for several reasons. First, only White women possess the genetic material necessary for creating White babies. Thus, all White women hold the biological key to notions of racial purity central to systems of White supremacy. Second, middle-class White women remain central in socializing young White people into a system of institutionalized racism. Their activities as mothers receive praise in light of this goal. Finally, middle-class White women allegedly fulfill the symbolic function of mothers of the national family. White women have been central as symbols of the nation that must be protected and defended and as the group responsible for transmitting national culture to the young.

Overall, access to new reproductive technologies, dominant ideologies about motherhood promulgated in the media, and social institutions work to keep middle-class White women firmly entrenched in popular culture and scholarship as the essence of desirable motherhood that is worth protecting. Health-care policies in particular reflect a fascination with increasing middle-class White women's fertility, often to the detriment of other pressing maternal and child health needs. Specifically, the construction of infertility as a national tragedy and the huge amounts of media attention paid to this condition reflect this preoccupation with increasing reproduction among women of the dominant group. Infertility is typically presented either as a human tragedy, the case of the unfortunate woman who cannot bear the child she so desperately wants, or, increasingly, as a personal failing—women who pursued careers, waited too long to have babies, and now find themselves childless because they turned their backs on their rightful roles as women.[17] Middle-class women found to be infertile are assisted with a dazzling array of medical advances to cure this socially constructed tragedy. Usually insured by private carriers, these women are able to defray part of the enormous costs of infertility procedures. New reproductive technologies such as in vitro fertilization, sex predetermination, and surrogate embryo transfer are routinely differentially distributed depending on the race, class, and sexual orientation of women.[18]

Popular culture and media representations play a part in both identifying middle-class White motherhood as ideal and creating a climate in which acquiring and raising a healthy White baby takes on such importance. Beginning in the 1980s, the mothering capacities of working mothers came under particular scrutiny. For example, the film *Baby Boom* (1987), a portrait of a successful career woman who suddenly discovers how unfulfilled her life had been when she inherits a baby, seems designed to tell middle-class White women that working mothers are acceptable just as long as motherhood comes first. Similarly, *The Hand That Rocks the Cradle* (1992), whose plot centers on an affluent White woman who innocently hires a crazed nanny who tries to steal her baby, trumpets the social message that children belong at home with their "real" mothers.

Social institutions also encourage middle-class White women to aspire for the idealized "real" mothering experience. Despite the increase in the numbers of working mothers, schoolday schedules that can begin as early as 7:30 A.M. and dismiss children as early as 1:30 P.M. continue to privilege stay-at-home mothers. Modest reforms designed to make the workplace accommodate the family needs of women remain more a reaction to the stated needs of middle-class White female professionals to juggle family and career than they do any sustained national commitment to child care. While working-class mothers do benefit from corporate day care, because so many working-class women do not work for large corporations, the children of White middle-class women remain the primary beneficiaries of this upper-tier child care.

Racial segregation, and to a lesser extent social-class segmentation, in American housing, education, and public services also support middle-class White mothering. The growth of gated communities and planned suburban developments designed to keep out unwelcome others speaks to the need to protect White children and their mothers. Privatizing educational and recreational experiences of White middle-class children reflects efforts to insulate this group from the perceived harm of attending school with working-class Whites and working-class children of color. The signs of racial segregation have been taken down, yet the results that these signs were designed to produce have not changed as rapidly. Middle-class White children still receive markedly better treatment than all other children in areas such as education, health care, housing, recreational facilities, nutrition, and public facilities such as libraries and police protection. Through public policy, ideological mechanisms, and institutional policies, their mothers receive strong messages to reproduce.

Policies for "Less Fit" Mothers: Working-Class White Women

The position of working-class White women, especially those living in poverty, differs dramatically from that of middle-class White women.

On the one hand, working-class White women's ability to produce White babies renders this group "fit" to produce the biological or population base of the nation. But on the other hand, when it comes to passing on national culture, raising academically and economically productive citizens, and being symbols of the nation, working-class White women remain less "fit" for motherhood. Public policies, popular ideology, and the structure of social institutions all work to encourage White middle-class women to fulfill their expected place as mothers of the nation by encouraging them to have and raise children. In contrast, working-class White women are encouraged to bear children but receive much less support for their ability to raise them.

Social policies reflect this basic contradiction. With the passage of *Roe v. Wade* in 1973, working-class and poor White women gained legal access to safe abortions. As a result, many young White women chose not to carry their babies to term. At the same time, the decreasing stigma attached to single motherhood, coupled with changes in eligibility for social-welfare benefits, lessened the social and economic barriers confronting all single mothers. Many young, unmarried White women who formerly would have given their children up for adoption chose to raise their children themselves, often alone. Together, these factors, among others, resulted in a sharp decrease in healthy White babies who would have been available for adoption into White middle-class families.

In the 1980s and 1990s, conservative Republican politicians and the members of the religious right successfully moved to decrease social-welfare benefits, to weaken antidiscrimination legislation against women in the workplace, and to limit access to abortion and other selected family-planning services for working-class and poor women. As a result, working-class White women's reproductive "choices" have changed. If working-class White women carry babies to term, the result will be an increase in the number of healthy White babies. This changing political climate suggests that young White mothers will find it more difficult to raise their children in poverty and, denied access to the choice of whether to choose to carry a child to term, will be increasingly pushed toward adoption as the best "choice."

Ideological portrayals of working-class White women as mothers must be careful to validate motherhood as a biological function yet support the notion that working-class White women do not make particularly fit mothers. In some cases, working-class White women become fit mothers by giving up their children. In her study comparing unmarried White and African American mothers in the 1950s, Rickie Solinger reveals how working-class African American women were actively discouraged from placing their babies up for adoption, while working-class White women encountered serious pressure to become fit mothers by releasing their children for adoption. They were told that they became good women by doing what was best for the child. Through these policies, working-class White women could gain respectability.[19] Representations of working-class White women in the mass media must also walk this fine line between constructing them as simultaneously fit for some dimensions of motherhood and unfit for others. Take, for example, *Roseanne* and *Grace under Fire*, two popular American television shows of the 1990s that depicted working-class White mothers. Roseanne clearly violates many of the rules of fit motherhood, yet because she remains married she gains legitimacy. In contrast, Grace, a single mother with three children, is portrayed with dignity, yet her checkered past of illicit sexuality, wife battering, and alcoholism speaks to her former transgressions. As the series continued, Grace also was revealed to have had an illegitimate child that she relinquished for adoption. Both Roseanne and Grace gain respectability within the parameters set for working- class White women.

Social institutions such as housing, schools, employment, and health care also collectively frame the mothering experiences of working-class White women. Many working-class White women are in the labor market, often in part-time work or in service jobs that offer less desirable salaries and benefits, especially health-care benefits. Working-class White women thus encounter a specific constellation of population policies, ideological constructions, and social institutions. They are denied comprehensive family-planning and abortion services. They are denied opportunities to support their children financially. They encounter increased exposure to cultural messages that encourage them to have their biologically White babies but to give them up for adoption to "good" homes. Because they receive insufficient economic support in raising their children from the disadvantaged position of working-class White men, from their own position in the labor market, and from the insufficient government support for poor families, working-class White women are increasingly encouraged to give up their babies to infertile middle-class White women.

Policies for "Unfit" Mothers: Working-Class African American Women

Working-class African American women, especially those who live in poverty, encounter markedly different treatment. In this section, I emphasize working-class African American women's experiences not because I see these experiences as reflecting some sort of essential Blackness, but because Whites typically perceive this group's experiences as normative for all African Americans. Working-class White women's fitness for motherhood is measured against the assumed norms of middle-class White women. African American women experience a reversal of this process. Specifically, working-class African American women's experiences are stereotyped and labeled as deviant from those of middle-class White women and are simultaneously considered normative for African American women as a collectivity. In policy discussions of reproduction, middle-class African American women are compared not with middle-class White women, but with working-class African American women, when they are rendered visible at all.

Controlling both the biological reproduction and the mothering experiences of working-class African American women has long been essential to maintaining a racialized American nationalism. In prior eras, a combination of a need for cheap, unskilled labor and the political powerlessness of Black populations worked to produce population policies that encouraged African American women to have many children. Because Black youth did not require costly training and could easily be fired, such children cost employers little. In Southern states, for example, school years for African American children were often shorter than those for White children and adjusted to allow Black youth to work in agriculture. Because they were denied education and social-welfare benefits routinely extended to other groups, they cost the state little. Black children were viewed as expendable.

The post–World War II political economy changed all this. The mechanization of agriculture, industrial relocation out of inner-city areas, and other economic trends fostered a decreasing demand for low-skilled labor.[20] Instead, the so-called postindustrial economy sought more highly skilled labor that required expensive investments in schooling and health care. During this same period, African Americans gained political rights that had been unavailable prior to the passage of the 1964 Civil Rights Act and 1963 Voting Rights Act, which allowed them to benefit from entitlement programs long enjoyed by Whites.[21] From the perspective of employers, a large African American population who were now legally entitled to the benefits of first-class citizenship became both economically unfeasible and politically dangerous. Since fewer African Americans were needed, population policies, ideological constructions of African American women, and the structure of social institutions combined to discourage working-class and poor African American women from having children.

Providing lavish services to combat infertility for White middle-class women while withholding family-planning services except sterilization from poor African American women reflects how the logic of eugenics thinking frames late–twentieth-century population policies. Currently, poor women and women of color are often discouraged from having children and are rewarded by government policy if they do so. In *Killing the Black Body: Race, Reproduction, and the Meaning of Liberty*, Dorothy Roberts details the range of public policies that strive to limit Black women's reproductive freedom and treat them as unfit mothers. These policies include the coercive sterilization of Black women under government welfare programs of the 1970s; the distribution of risky, long-lasting contraceptives such as Norplant through Medicaid; and the rendering of reproduction a crime by prosecuting women who expose their fetuses to drugs; as well as the controversies over transracial adoption. As Roberts claims, "Poor Black mothers are blamed for perpetuating social problems by transmitting defective genes, irreparable crack damage, and a deviant lifestyle to their children."[22] In the context of lack of abortion services, government-funded permanent sterilization often becomes one of the few viable methods of birth control.

Ideological constructions of African American women also foster a climate in which it is claimed that they make bad mothers and thus are irresponsible if they reproduce. Media images of African American women as matriarchs or "unfit" mothers are now joined by new images that portray them as sexually irresponsible, as abusive mothers, and/or as welfare queens. Building on stereotypes of people of African descent and women as being less intellectual, more impulsive, and more emotional than Whites, the image of the welfare queen in particular provides a context for quasi-sterilization methods such as Norplant and Depo-Provera. Ironically, mass-media depictions of middle-class African American women, especially high-achieving professionals, can also perpetuate views of African American women as unfit mothers. By choosing to remain childless, such women are seen as being selfish, hoarding resources, being overly aggressive and unfeminine, and thinking only of themselves. Moreover, these new "black lady" overachievers, as Wahneema Lubiano describes them, are simultaneously constructed as affirmative-action hires, the middle-class, unworthy recipients of government favors that parallel their less affluent welfare-queen sisters. Within this nexus of images, middle-class and working-class African American women can both be constructed as the enemy within whose reproduction, or lack of it, threatens American national interests. Yet working-class and poor African American women remain most vulnerable to attacks that result from this logic.[23]

In this climate, where African American women are constructed as unfit mothers, social institutions that they encounter take on a particularly punitive cast. Black working-class and poor mothers are often employed yet are severely disadvantaged. Child care remains hard to find; health benefits are limited for those in part-time or seasonal employment; and lack of job security makes it difficult to plan. A history of racial segregation means that working-class African American women encounter limited opportunities in their own education, housing, employment, access to health care, and access to high-quality schools and recreational facilities for their children.[24]

New Realities

If the nation-state is conceptualized as a national family, with the traditional family ideal structuring normative family values, then standards used to assess the contributions of family members in heterosexual, married-couple households with children become foundational for assessing group contributions to national well-being overall. The United States may be in an important historical moment in which the logic of eugenics is being appropriated by interest groups who aim to reconstruct the American national family to its former glory. In understanding these new realities, several themes have special significance.

First, the range of reproductive choices available to White women could not have been offered without the exploitation of the labor of African American women and of other women of color. As women of the desirable group, middle-class White women have long depended on the labor of poor women and women of color to fulfill their responsibilities as mothers. Historically, for example, African American women served as child-care workers and performed the domestic labor that allowed middle-class White women to maintain their social position as fit mothers. These traditional functions are more recently being taken over by new "employable mothers"—namely, undocumented immigrant women of color. In her analysis of undocumented Latinas, Grace Chang notes that in the past, analyses of immigration focused on male laborers who allegedly stole jobs from "native" American workers. Since the mid-1980s, this concern has shifted to an emphasis on how immigrants impose a heavy welfare burden on American "natives." As Chang observes, "Men as job stealers are no longer seen as the immigrant problem. Instead, immigrant women as idle, welfare-dependent mothers and inordinate breeders of dependents are seen as the great menace."[25] In this context, the treatment of undocumented Latina mothers and other women who lack the benefits of American citizenship closely resembles historical patterns of regulation of African American mothers. In these cases, the notion of non–White mothers as employable exists alongside prevailing views that maternal employment harms children's development.

Second, the connection between welfare-state capitalism and perceived national interests remains significant, especially regarding women of varying race, social class, and citizenship groups. The welfare state mediates the conflicting demands placed on all women. On the one hand, social norms encourage women to remain in the home to care for their children and thus reproduce and maintain the labor force. But on the other hand, these same norms encourage women across social classes to perform traditionally female low-wage work in the paid labor force as hospital attendants, day-care workers, nursing-home aides, fast-food workers, bank tellers, secretaries, and domestic workers. By encouraging and subsidizing some women to remain at home to nurture the current and future workforce while forcing others into low-wage work, the welfare state uses race, social class, and citizenship differences among women to resolve this conflict. Working-class women of color of varying citizenship statuses bear the brunt of capitalist development. Such women are simultaneously engaged in low-wage work as paid employees doing the reproductive labor for families other than their own.[26]

Third, new reproductive technologies are emerging as central to reorganizing the experiences of all women with motherhood. Working with longstanding patterns of race and social class in the United States, these technological advances fragment the meaning of motherhood. The proliferation of reproductive technologies in the post–World War

II era has allowed the splitting of motherhood into three categories: genetic, gestational, and social motherhood.[27] Genetic mothers are those who contribute the genetic material to another human being. Gestational mothers are those who carry the developing fetus in utero until birth. Social mothers care for children actually born. Traditional views of motherhood put forward by the traditional family ideal present one middle-class White woman as fulfilling all three functions, assisted by domestic servants. But new reproductive technologies have made it possible for women to specialize in one of these mothering categories. With the growing technological ability to make distinctions among genetic motherhood, gestational motherhood, and social motherhood, African Americans, Latinas, and other women of color become candidates for gestational motherhood, supplementing and perhaps even supplanting White working-class women's participation as genetic and gestational mothers.

Fourth, the mother glorification targeted toward middle-class White women coexists with a heterogeneous collection of social policies designed to retain the image of motherhood as vitally important for all women while simultaneously discouraging selected groups of women from becoming mothers because they fail to attain the standards of "real" mothers. For example, 1990s phenomena such as the assault on affirmative-action policies in higher education and the workplace; the passage of the 1996 Personal Responsibility and Work Opportunity and Reconciliation Act, which effectively abolished Aid to Families with Dependent Children by placing it under the supervision of fifty individual states; the emergence of strident anti-immigration rhetoric in public discourse; and the increasing privatization of schools, health care, and selected public services can all be seen as part of an overarching framework designed to maintain differences between fit and unfit mothers. But the rhetoric of mother glorification must be tempered with a long look at how children are actually treated in the United States. Children were disproportionately hurt by social policies of the 1980s and remain the most impoverished age group in the United States. In 1974, 15 percent of American children (under age 18) lived in poverty. By 1986, 21 percent did so—a 40 percent increase in just twelve years. The most recent figures put Black youth poverty at 30 percent, almost twice the rate of general childhood poverty in the United States (16 percent.). Yet despite these startling statistics, infertility continues to be presented as a major public-health issue affecting large numbers of Americans.[28]

A fifth crucial dimension of the new realities concerns the response of the reproductive-rights movement. The struggle for reproductive rights is often seen as spearheaded by White middle-class women, yet Black women, poor women, and women of color all participate in struggles for reproductive rights. For example, the mission statements of the National Black Women's Health Project and the group African American Women Are for Reproductive Freedom spell out the distinctive issues that confront Black women. Similarly, women of color who strive to link struggles for reproductive freedom to human rights point out the need for a broad-based, multiethnic, multicultural initiative that can respond to the challenges detailed in this essay.[29]

Finally, the emergence of new family forms in the United States has the potential either to support or to challenge the traditional family ideal, the edifice of population policies that it sanctions, and fundamental understandings of American national identity as a large imagined national family. For example, growing support for the categories of biracial and multiracial in the U.S. Census speaks to newly emerging family forms that defy boundaries of race. Of particular interest are the White mothers raising biracial or multiracial children through either adoption or biological reproduction. How are we to interpret current efforts to include multiracial categories as part of government data? Are the efforts at reclassification an effort to make such children honorary Whites, with all the benefits that accrue to White middle-class children? Or are the efforts designed to deconstruct a system of racial categorization that routinely distributes privileges based on these classifications? In a similar fashion, the emergence of families organized around gay and lesbian couples with children raises similar challenges to the traditional family ideal and the complex social structures it simultaneously shapes and sanctions. The very existence of these emerging family forms and their increasing legitimacy within state agencies mean that the bedrock of family as defined by the traditional family ideal can no longer serve as the glue linking systems of race, gender, class, nationality, and heterosexist oppression. What comes of these challenges remains to be seen.

II

Ethnicity, Culture, and Black Nationalist Politics

3 Black Nationalism and African American Ethnicity

Afrocentrism as Civil Religion

The changes generated by postcoloniality, global capitalism, and new technologies have sparked a lively debate about the contours and meaning of the new racism in the United States in a greatly changing America.[1] Structurally, Black Americans have lagged behind other groups in enjoying the gains of desegregated housing, schools, and job opportunities.[2] One Atlanta study revealed that neighborhood-level racial resegregation is emerging within major American cities, even those with a politically enfranchised and highly visible Black middle class.[3] Other research points to the growth of a prison-industrial complex as an important new site for the institutionalized racism confronting working-class and poor African Americans and Latinos.[4] Ideologically, a belief in upholding colorblindness masks the continued inequalities of contemporary racism. By proclaiming that equal treatment of *individuals* under the law is sufficient for addressing racism, this ideology redefines *group*-based, antiracist remedies such as affirmative action as being "racist."[5]

How should African Americans respond to the promise and the disappointments of this new racism that operates through the curious combination of a structurally incomplete desegregation cloaked by an ideology of colorblind inclusiveness? In this chapter, I sketch out how some African Americans refashioned the core ideas of Black nationalism in attempts to negotiate the dilemmas of the new racism. Despite considerable variability in how African Americans understand and articulate Black nationalist ideology, I suggest that Black nationalism's main ideas of self-definition, self-determination, and self-reliance resonate with the experiences of large numbers of African Americans and with important cultural norms of American society. In this context, the core ideas of Black nationalism can be used to craft an African American racial/ethnic identity that in turn articulates with historical models of ethnic political mobilization used by other racial/ethnic groups.[6]

My argument constitutes a major departure from standard approaches to Black nationalism. Most scholarship defines Black nationalism as a political ideology, one of many (e.g., socialism or integrationism) that historically have framed African American politics.[7] Such approaches further categorize the philosophical distinctions among Black nationalisms. Cultural nationalism, revolutionary nationalism, religious nationalism, Black feminist nationalism, and the like have all been classified as diverse strands of an overarching Black nationalist philosophy.[8] This approach, while valuable, remains limited, because it ignores how African Americans may use Black nationalist ideology to meet the challenges of contemporary racism. For example, despite social-class differences among African Americans that might catalyze differential voting patterns, African Americans continue to vote along racial lines.[9] Moreover, focusing on ideological strands of Black nationalism also obscures how African Americans may use its core ideas as a system of meaning. Black nationalism can be used to organize social institutions and social relations within African American communities as well as African American group behavior within American society.

Part of Black nationalism's appeal may lie in its usefulness to individual African Americans searching for meaning within their everyday lives; in its utility in mobilizing African Americans as a collectivity for quite diverse activities that are not overtly political; and in its versatility to have diverse meanings for segments of African American civil society distinguished by social class, color, gender, immigrant status, and religion. This malleability constitutes Black nationalism's promise and its danger. Political ideologies and religions both claim this ability to construct group identities that move people to action. Individuals who believe in Christianity, capitalism, Islam, Marxism, and similar systems of thought use the main ideas of these systems of belief to guide everyday decision-making and group mobilization. At the same time, although they share a set of ideas, how individuals interpret these core ideas as well as the actual practices undertaken under their guidance can vary widely.

Honed at the intersection of political ideology and religion, Black nationalism may have a similar utility for African Americans. Historically, Black nationalism's flexibility has allowed African Americans to reshape it in response to the specific political challenges raised by slavery, Jim Crow segregation, industrialization, and urbanization. Given this resiliency and potential functionality for our times, either presenting Black nationalism as an overly homogeneous political ideology to claim or reject it (nationalism versus integrationism) or restricting analysis to the specific content of strands of Black nationalism (cultural nationalism versus religious nationalism) seems shortsighted. Instead, a more intriguing and potentially useful approach lies in exploring the diverse ways in which African Americans deploy Black nationalism as a system of meaning, especially in constructing responses to the new racism.

Racism: The Erasure of African American Ethnicity

Racism and religion were both foundational to the very essence of American national identity as well as the nation-state policies of the United States. The external racism directed against indigenous peoples who occupied the land desired by European settlers and the internal racism directed against enslaved African workers both were integral to the *founding* moments of the United States as a nation-state.[10] During the colonial period in the United States, Whiteness, whether claimed by propertied Whites or White indentured servants, became defined in opposition to and elevated above the non–White status assigned to indigenous peoples and enslaved Africans. This core racial triangle among White settlers, indigenous peoples, and enslaved Africans lay at the heart of the new U.S. nation-state. In forming a settler society that privileged Whiteness, European American settlers saw their search for land and resources as their right as a new people or nation. Because national identity itself was so compromised by such deeply embedded racial processes, it has been virtually impossible to conceive of American national identity in terms other than racial. Moreover, accomplishing this racialized American national identity required reducing the myriad ethnicities that characterized European, American Indian, and African populations into these three core racial categories.[11]

Christian religion mattered greatly during this foundational period and served as a template for the creation of an American civil religion that also articulated with American national identity. On the one hand, a fundamental principle of American national identity—the identity of the American "nation" or "people"—protects religious freedom through the separation of church and state. On the other hand, European colonists were deeply Christian and valued religion, yet this same protection of religious freedom forbade making Christianity the formal state religion of the new nation-state. Crafting an American civil religion that worshipped American national identity, yet did so in a legally secular fashion, addressed this seeming contradiction. By definition, civil religion constitutes the worship of a form of government and the political principles associated with it. The claim that the United States has a civil religion suggests that Americans are not only a religious people in the sense of widespread adherence to religious belief, but that Americans understand American national identity *as* a people in religious terms. In the American context, the substance of civil religion includes the worship of democracy and republican government rooted in principles such as liberty, equality, justice, and law. In short, the American civil religion is patriotism infused with and constructed in tandem with "Christian values." Because the United States explicitly does not have a state religion in which adherence to and protection of a true faith operates as a qualification for holding government authority, the reliance on civil religion emerged as one mechanism for resolving the contradiction between America as a republic and America as a liberal, constitutional state.[12] From its inception, religion and nationalism have been deeply intertwined within American politics in ways that place people of African descent in the strange position of being inside the body politic as workers, yet outside it as either members of the republican community or as full citizens of the liberal, constitutional state.[13]

Arriving with ethnic identities organized around shared language, culture, religion, and customs, new immigrant groups in the early twentieth century established ethnic enclaves that protected their members and established a beachhead in U.S. society. Many groups quickly realized that politicizing these enclosure ethnicities and using them to compete with other ethnic groups yielded tangible political and economic benefits. Deploying a form of competition ethnicity in which groups compete with one another in relation to state power, resources, and development, ethnic groups jockeyed for position within the U.S. racial hierarchy.[14] European immigrant groups were able to use their appearance to become optimally "White," whereas others—Eastern European Jews, for example—settled for becoming "not quite White."[15] The political and economic leverage created via ethnic *group* mobilization generated sufficient opportunities for their children to become "White" *individuals* unencumbered by the limits of enclosure ethnicity.[16] Caribbean immigrants of African descent encountered a different reality. Their challenge lay in trying to be "not Black."

Deploying competitive ethnic identities of Jamaican, Trinidadian, Cuban, and the like served for a time as a shield against falling into the stark racial classification that erased their individuality and made them simply "Black." Rigid racial segregation politicized many, and those who believed that the benefits of first-class citizenship were likely to elude them because they were too "Black" often threw in their lot with African Americans and became "Blacks." Together, in the 1920s, Afro-Caribbeans and African Americans flocked to the Black nationalist Garvey Movement, to date the largest U.S. mass movement of people of African descent.

Whereas the racial category of "White" constructed from European ethnicities remained highly salient within American society, Whiteness ironically became largely un-raced, primarily because it held the power to erase its own operation. Race was certainly real, but because White Americans enjoyed the state protections of being the dominant racial group, they could claim an odd ignorance concerning the privileges that they accrued in their everyday lives because they were White. All White Americans could define themselves as individuals, not as members of a White ethnic group. At the same time, because White Americans were far from homogeneous, some Whites claimed an array of "optional ethnicities" that, depending on historical time and place of arrival in the United States, opened the door to the privileges of first-class citizenship. Structures of racial segregation articulated well with these stark racial categories. For African Americans, ethnicity was denied, and race became paramount. For White Americans, ethnicity operated as a malleable category that could be deployed in defense of the ethnic group or could be shed altogether if the price was right. More important, for White Americans, race disappeared.

Unlike other immigrant groups that typically arrived in the United States with their ethnic cultures intact, African Americans faced the challenge of constructing a new group identity or African American ethnicity that resisted the derogatory meanings attached to the racial category "Black." This new ethnicity had to draw on the syncretic cultural heritage created by diverse African ethnic groups and do so within the distinctly American religious milieu of an overarching American civil religion. In this context, religion culled from Christian theology assumed great importance within African American culture and ethnicity.[17] As C. Eric Lincoln points out: "For African Americans, a people whose total experience has been a sustained condition of multiform stress, religion is never far from the threshold of consciousness, for whether it is embraced with fervor or rejected with disdain, it is the focal element of the black experience."[18] Because the racialized social system itself changed shape over time, African American ethnicity also was continually constructed anew in the context of a persistent core racial triangle, the arrival of new immigrants of African descent, and the importance of religiosity within African American civil society.

Because African Americans have experienced this unique racial/ethnic history in the United States, negotiating the new racism constitutes a special challenge. Historically, African Americans crafted antiracist initiatives in response to deeply entrenched patterns of racial segregation that blocked opportunities in jobs, housing, education, and voting.[19] In the context of legally sanctioned racial apartheid, designing antiracist strategies seemed to be straightforward: Dismantle the legal edifice of racial segregation and racism should wither away. Currently, despite dramatic changes in the legal infrastructure that occurred in the 1950s and 1960s, racial segregation is far from disappearing. As a result, the United States remains characterized by an uneven racial desegregation, especially in housing and schools, with African Americans more heavily segregated in housing, schooling, and marital patterns than any other racial/ethnic group.[20] Moreover, because a sizable portion of the general population believes that American society is more racially integrated than is actually the case, many fail to see new patterns of racial resegregation. Because the victories of the Civil Rights Movement dismantled legal segregation and gave African Americans equal rights, many White Americans feel that to talk of race is tantamount to creating racism. Racially coded language proliferates within this new ideology of colorblindness, with the use of terms such as "street crime," "welfare cheats," "unwed mothers," and "family values" standing in proxy for the racially explicit language of prior eras.[21]

Because the new racism operates in the organizational context of desegregation and with the illusion of equality provided by the logic of colorblindness, it provides new challenges for African Americans. For one, the new racism seems to be replicating the foundational racial triangle, yet it does so by working differently with ethnicity. Changes in immigration legislation dating from the mid-1960s fostered a huge growth of immigration, this time not from European nations but primarily from Latin America, Asia, and, to a lesser extent, the Caribbean and continental Africa. These new immigrants could not fit the biological criteria of Whiteness and thus physically could not be classified as biologically White.

The use of ethnicity by these new immigrant groups provides a fascinating glimpse of how the ethnic identifications claimed by these heterogeneous immigrant groups articulate with the longstanding racial order. Like the Jewish population before them in the 1950s, Asians are also offered the status of becoming "model minorities" as a way to claim the benefits of Whiteness.[22] They remain "not White" but can aspire to be the best of the "not Blacks." The diverse skin colors, hair textures, and physical features of Latino populations, as well as the vastly different histories that distinguish Cuban Americans from Puerto Ricans, Dominican from Mexican immigrants, for example, stimulate interesting challenges for this bureaucratically created "ethnic" group. Moreover, Latino populations typically bring a different sensibility about race and racism that, on the surface, appears to be more tolerant than the stark racial binaries of the United States. However, the absence of a Black–White racial divide in Latin countries does not mean that Afro-Latin populations have not experienced a distinctive form of racism organized around concepts of "whitening." Resembling the situation that confronted Caribbean immigrants during the Garvey era, immigrants of African descent from the Caribbean and from continental Africa encounter similar pressures to flatten their ethnic identities and to become simply "Black." Nigerians, Cameroonians, Somalians, Haitians, and Jamaicans remain "not White," but they also must work to remain "not Black"—that is, to avoid the stigma and stereotyping that Black Americans face. In this case, holding fast to ethnic customs as "foreign Blacks" seemingly provides a shield for the first generation against the assaults of racism where the goal is to be anything but "domestic Black."

Racial/Ethnic Mobilization, Religion, and Black Nationalism

African Americans confront this dynamic racial/ethnic context, where virtually any ethnic identity is deemed to be better than being African American or "domestic Black." For many, claiming African American ethnic identification potentially can serve as a shield against a negative racial classification as well as form a basis for group-based political mobilization. In this political and social environment, the core ideas of Black nationalism may take on importance beyond their logical and empirical merits. Such ideas can guide constructions of an African American ethnicity that can be brokered for political and social power within the context of American pluralism. Moreover, Black nationalist ideas can be reconfigured in ways that draw on the religiosity of African Americans so central within African American culture as well as the climate of American civil religion that frames American society overall.

Despite the fact that the majority of African Americans most likely can define neither Black nationalism nor its major ideological strands, the ideas themselves may circulate in everyday life as a template for African American ethnicity. The ideas need not be associated with formal Black nationalist politics to serve this function for everyday African Americans. C. Eric Lincoln unpacks these interrelationships among ethnicity, religion, and Black nationalism:

> Because black ethnicity and black identity are often expressed through black religion, black religion is often mistaken for black nationalism. They may, and often do, travel together, but the goals and interests of these two aspects of the black experience are not the same.... For the black masses, black religion and black nationalism are often one and the same, *in effect*. Both address the sources of their distress, and these require no labels. Those whose suffering seems most arbitrary are likely to be most impatient with fine distinctions, when in the fervor of black togetherness they finally confront the specter which stalks them all. As a result, black nationalism sometimes assumes the *character* of religion because it promises to the disinherited the swift and certain reversal of the circumstances of their oppression and suffering.[23]

Black nationalism, religion, and African American ethnicity may construct one another in ways that seem remarkably similar to the connections of American patriotism and American civil religion.

Religion, nationalism, and ethnicity certainly are prominent in the Black nationalist projects from the Black Power Movement of the 1960s that somehow survived to the present. The Nation of Islam under the leadership of Louis Farrakhan and Molefi Kete Asante's Afrocentricity constitute two prominent manifestations of contemporary Black nationalism since the mid-1970s.[24] Both forms of Black nationalism work with the paradigm of ethnic mobilization so prominent in American history. Both Black nationalist projects simultaneously draw on the historical religiosity of African Americans yet do so with an eye toward developing ethnic identification among American Americans. At the same time, neither project pushes for political mobilization used by Irish, Italians, Jews, and other European ethnic groups. Dean Robinson contends, "Both make some demands on the state: but, thus far, neither tendency firmly links its political trajectory to the efforts of labor, feminist, or other typically progressive political forces. Both offer, instead, highly idealistic proposals—one explicitly religious, the other quasi-religious—for group empowerment."[25]

Both of these Black nationalist projects came to full fruition during the 1980s and early 1990s, a time when the Christian right made new demands on the U.S. nation-state via the Republican presidencies of Ronald Reagan and George Bush (1980–92), and a time that was characterized by the reworking of religion, ethnicity, so-called family values, and race within American politics.[26] However much its theology deviated from traditional Islamic teachings, by organizing its own mosques and other social organizations, the Nation of Islam (NOI) became recognized as a formal religion. Despite the small number of actual NOI members, much has been written about the intersection of religion and politics of this organization, and I will not summarize this literature here.[27] It seems adequate to point out that ordinary African Americans have either ignored or remain unaware of the often contentious debates among African American intellectuals in the 1990s that castigated the NOI's patriarchal and heterosexist programs. Voting with their feet by attending in record numbers the 1995 Million Man March on Washington organized by NOI and Louis Farakkhan, everyday African Americans apparently found the core ideas of this conservative version of Black nationalism more appealing than arguments advanced by well-known Black public intellectuals who opposed the march.

Afrocentrism raises a different set of issues that pivot on one core question: How does Black nationalism "assume the *character* of religion" to address the "oppression and suffering" caused by the new racism? The emergence of Afrocentrism in the 1980s among African American academics and its dissemination in the 1990s outside the academy into popular culture illustrate how Black nationalist ideology can be recast as a civil religion.[28] Within American higher education, Asante and other African American academics refashioned the main ideas of Black cultural nationalism to guide fledgling Black studies programs.[29] Despite Afrocentrism's expressed function as a social theory within American higher education, its actual use more closely resembled that of a civil religion. As a civil religion, Afrocentrism reinterpreted African American ethnicity by developing African-influenced cultural referents that prescribed the overall values of African diasporic communities, provided social cohesion based on those values, and facilitated the emotional healing of African Americans. In essence,

Afrocentric scholars took the framework of American civil religion, stripped it of the "American" symbols and rituals that were designed to foster patriotic commitment to the U.S. nation-state, and substituted a Black value system designed to achieve similar ends.

One reason that religious expressions of Black nationalism have garnered support is that African Americans have long used religion and faith-based sources of resistance to racism.[30] Unlike the use of religion by immigrant ethnic groups where practicing the traditional religion becomes an important site of a group's success in maintaining its ethnic heritage, for African Americans religion in general, and Christianity in particular, evolved in response to African American suffering under American racism. Initially, African American civil society was virtually synonymous with the Black church. Over time, however—especially with migration from the rural South to urban industrial areas of the South and North—this Black public sphere developed a split between the sacred and the secular as interconnected dimensions of Black community life. The two spheres held a common belief in spirituality. In this sense, the split between the overwhelmingly Christian and largely Baptist formal religious traditions in Black church culture and the secular spirituality that has formed the creative foundation of music, dance, and other aspects of African American creative cultural production constitute two sides of the same coin. When combined, a spirituality that can take sacred or secular form constitutes an important dimension of African American ethnicity.[31]

The sociologist Mary Patillo-McCoy's study of church culture as a strategy of action in one African American community provides ethnographic evidence for the recursive nature of the sacred and the secular within Black civil society and how such a society is infused with an African American religiosity.[32] Existing research indicates that African Americans are, by many measures, highly religious people, as shown by the importance of God and religion in African Americans' lives, the high frequency of church attendance and church membership, and the prevalence of prayer in daily life. Defining church culture as ranging from "the ardent use of formal prayer to the subtle murmurs of encouragement that punctuate public gatherings," Patillo-McCoy contends that "the black church provides a cultural blueprint for community activities and thus influences the script and staging of African American community organizations."[33] As Patillo-McCoy points out, "The power of prayer, Christian imagery, and call-and-response interaction lies . . . in the *cultural* familiarity of these tools among African Americans as media for interacting, conducting a meeting, holding a rally, or getting out the vote. Black church culture constitutes a common language that motivates social action."[34]

This fluidity between sacred and secular provides the historical backdrop for Afrocentric scholars and others to use of the tenets of Black nationalism to craft new ethnic identifications that, because they share some core features with organized religions, link regular churchgoers to African Americans who rarely set foot in a church, mosque, or synagogue. Moreover, Black ethnic identifications that take religious or spiritual forms may be more readily recognizable to far greater numbers of African Americans because they invoke pre-existing religious, spiritual, and cultural traditions. By drawing on this common Black church culture, Afrocentrism attaches the specific content of Black nationalism to the processes of how social action is constructed within African American communities. Afrocentrism aims to provide a template for African American ethnicity grounded in a shared sense of "Blackness" that can be simultaneously theorized (Afrocentricity) and performed (Black church culture).

Black Nationalism as Civil Religion: The Case of Afrocentrism

Examining how Afrocentric scholars have recast the *functions* typically performed by formal religions reveals how Afrocentrism operates as a civil religion. Organized religions have several distinguishing features, some of which Afrocentrism as a civil religion aims to reproduce, and others of which remain less attainable. Here I discuss four overlapping features: (1) shared belief systems that form the core values of the religion; (2) articles of faith that separate the true believers from everyone else and that provide guidance for everyday life; (3) explanations for suffering, death, and other mysteries of life that affect the religion's membership; and (4) organizational structures, especially shared rituals, meetings, and other mechanisms that affirm group membership.

First, organized religions have a shared system of beliefs that constitute the core, enduring values of faith. Without these core ideas, the religion could not exist. Within Afrocentrism, an unconditional love of Black people lies at the heart of this civil religion. Afrocentrism strives to respond to the philosopher Cornel West's suggestion that nihilism constitutes a new, fundamental threat to African Americans. Taking seriously West's claim that "a love ethic must be at the center of a politics of conversion," Afrocentrism strives to affirm the humanity of Black people.[35] Within Afrocentrism as a civil religion, the quest to develop Black consciousness or a love of Blackness stems from efforts to develop unconditional love for one's people or "nation."

Identifying and valuing "negritude" is foundational to Afrocentric efforts to develop this core article of faith. In his 1966 essay "Negritude: A Humanism of the Twentieth Century," Leopold Sedar Senghor offers two definitions of negritude that each serve as pillars for the shared values that constitute Afrocentrism as a civil religion. Senghor suggests that "negritude . . . is rooting oneself in oneself, and self-confirmation; confirmations of one's *being*. Negritude is nothing more or less than what some English-speaking Africans have called the *African personality*."[36] This use of negritude foreshadows Asante's approach to Afrocentricity as being centered in a world of Black beliefs. As Asante observes, "Afrocentricity is the active centering of the African in subject place in our historical landscape. This has always been my search; it has been a quest for sanity."[37] In essence, Afrocentricity enables African Americans to recognize the irrationality of racism and claim "sanity" within it. Elsewhere Asante defines Afrocentricity as "*a perspective which allows Africans to be subjects of historical experiences rather than objects* on the fringes of Europe."[38] Senghor's emphasis on the "African personality" focuses attention on the values and psychological make-up of individual Blacks and encourages efforts to analyze how centered, conscious, African, or Black an individual actually is.

Senghor suggests another meaning of negritude that has influenced another component of the shared system of values that distinguish believers in Afrocentrism as a civil religion from non-members. Here Senghor defines negritude as "*the sum of the cultural values of the world.*"[39] Whereas Asante proposes elements of Black values that form the cultural center of Blackness, Maulana Karenga's creation and dissemination of a Black value system has dwarfed all other efforts. The seven principles of Karenga's Nguzo Saba, or "Black value system," provide organizing principles for Afrocentrism as a civil religion.[40] In describing why he created the Nguzo Saba, Karenga notes that the Nguzo Saba is designed to "organize and enrich our [African American] relations with each other on the personal and community level; . . . establish standards, commitments and priorities that would tend to enhance our human possibilities as persons and a people; . . . and serve as a contribution to a core system of communitarian ethical values for the moral guidance and instruction of the community, especially for children."[41]

These functions routinely are carried out by organized religions and simultaneously articulate with notions of Black solidarity advanced within Black nationalism.

Afrocentrism as civil religion draws from a second feature of organized religions—namely, the importance of articles of faith in guiding the behavior of the true believers. The tenets and beliefs of formal religions are typically preserved in some sort of authoritative scripture—for example, bibles, griots, and other sources of legitimated knowledge. Afrocentrism's tenets seem designed to function as articles of faith. In particular, the significance of evaluating all thought, deeds, and actions in terms of the perceived interests not of God, but of Black people, suggests that centering on Blackness serves as the main vehicle for achieving this state of grace (a respite from White racism). This use of Afrocentricity not only bears striking resemblance to articles of faith that claim that God be considered in every waking action and thought, it dovetails with a pre-existing orientation within African American religious culture whereby spirituality and religiosity infuse African American civil society.[42]

As a civil religion, certain elements of nonacademic Afrocentrism are taken as articles of faith—they are not to be questioned. In this context, just as formal scriptures provide interpretive frameworks for formal religions, Karenga's Nguzo Saba can be deployed as articles of faith that are part a larger authoritative scripture. But if the Nguzo Saba operates as central articles of *faith*, how can it be analyzed or, worse yet, criticized? Who dares argue against creativity, or purpose, or unity? In this faith-based context, what *is* available for interpretation is the question of *how* these articles of faith are being implemented. For example, while the principle of cooperative economics (*Ujamaa*) is endorsed, as was the case during the Black Power era, widely different strategies can constitute cooperative economic effort. These debates within the rubric of the Nguzo Saba are certainly theoretically possible, but they are not common among Afrocentrist thinkers. Rather, just as within formal religions a distinction can be made between articles of faith and religious doctrine, using Afrocentrism as a civil religion can foster an unfortunate slippage between these two uses. Articles of faith are meant to be the principles that pull people together. In contrast, religious doctrines constitute rules to follow that separate the true believers from all others. On the one hand, efforts to hammer out articles of faith in historically specific social contexts—for example, the ways in which African Americans might generate new ways of practicing cooperative economics in the context of the new racism—may breathe fresh life into seemingly failed African American political agendas. On the other hand, as many Black intellectuals quite rightly point out, deploying Afrocentrism as a religious doctrine where some are more authentically Black than others serves to fragment African Americans.[43]

Third, just as organized religions typically provide explanations for suffering, death, and other mysteries of life, Afrocentrism as a civil religion strives to account for the origins and purpose of Black suffering and death under racial oppression. Because organized religions must provide some sort of shared history for their members, narratives explaining the origins of the religion as well as its core principles typically are well known by members of the congregation. For African Americans grappling with the aftermath of the slave experience, this need to establish a point of origin takes on special meaning. The origins of Black suffering are clear: The slave trade constituted the original sin that disrupted what is depicted as harmonious African societies and introduced four hundred years of Black suffering. Afrocentric origin myths identify Africa as the "motherland" or homeland of all people of African descent. Children of the African diaspora have a homeland that they must revere, reclaim, and protect. By seeing their connections with Africa and defining themselves as African people, the lost children of Africa who were enslaved in America can reclaim a Black consciousness and once again become centered in a true African personality.

This attention to explaining Black suffering often accompanies a corresponding emphasis on Black redemption via adhering to articles of Afrocentric faith. Within models that place blame for all Black suffering at the feet of White supremacy, the suffering of African American individuals occurs because they remain mesmerized by White culture. If Whites and the culture they create are in fact "evil," then salvation occurs through rejecting anything labeled "White." Instead, individuals re-centering on Blackness will reverse this lack of consciousness concerning their own importance. "One becomes Afrocentric by exploring the connections, visiting the quiet places, and remaining connected," counsels Asante.[44] By destroying both an authentic African-centered identity and an affirming African-centered culture, institutionalized racism fostered a "psychology of oppression" among African Americans.[45] Within this worldview, Black people suffer when they deviate from their true sense of Blackness and become overly influenced by White-supremacist institutions. As a step toward recovering their identity and subjectivity, Black people needed to undergo a conversion experience from "Negro" to "Black." "Negroes" mesmerized by Whiteness could be distinguished from authentic Black people prepared to participate in liberation struggles by completing a conversion experience. Completing a four-stage transformation— moving through stages of pre-encounter, encounter with Whites, immersion in Black culture, and internalization of a new Black identity— constituted the path toward a new Black identity. Just as members of many organized religions view themselves as the chosen ones because they are true believers, individuals who follow this particular strand of Afrocentrism may see themselves as being more consciously, authentically, and correctly "Black" than others. Moreover, the certainty that accompanies Afrocentrism as a source of faith and the inherent goodness attributed to Black people within this system of thought can be a valuable collective weapon in confronting the daily assaults of White-supremacist institutions and thus can relieve suffering.[46]

A fourth feature of organized religions concerns the need to maintain organizational practices and structures for religious activities. Holding regularly scheduled services in agreed-on places of worship allows communities of faith to re-enact their stories, teachings, and rituals. These repetitive practices are designed to build solidarity among the community of true believers across space and time. In this effort to develop lasting organizational structures for Afrocentrism as a civil religion, being located inside or outside the academy makes all the difference. Just as organized religions have institutional locations where the faith is ritualized, celebrated, and reproduced, Afrocentrism as a civil religion aspired to similar organizational stability. In the 1980s, Black studies programs and departments created institutional bases within seemingly hostile White institutions. From these sites, they aimed to install Afrocentrism as the social theory guiding Black studies scholarship and teaching.[47] Regardless of their intellectual products, the very existence of Black studies initiatives garnered animosity. This very hostility could be used as evidence of the rightness of Black studies and of the martyrdom of its practitioners and disciples. It should come as no surprise that Asante and Karenga chaired two prominent Black studies programs known for Afrocentrism—at Temple University in Philadelphia and at California State University, Long Beach, respectively.

Herein lies the problem: Because Black studies units reside in secular higher education and thus rely on public tax dollars and private fundraising by their institutions to fund their programs, they must be responsive to issues that their host institutions decide are important. The seeming separation of church and state leaves religion with no place in the academy except as a subject of study. As a result, Afrocentrism has great difficulties functioning in this context precisely because it has organized itself as a civil religion, both in content and in practice. This social positioning accounts for academic Afrocentrism's peculiar hybrid identity. On the one hand, positioning Afrocentrism as a civil religion within U.S. colleges and universities exposed it to the epistemological criteria of science that are valued within the academy. The very standards of judgment within the academy eschew faith-based approaches to understanding the world and instead value scientific epistemologies as the currency of acceptability.[48] All knowledge, including Afrocentric scholarship that is infused with the sensibilities of a civil religion, typically garners censure. On the other hand, the antidote to this censure—namely, trying to attract academic credibility for Afrocentrism as a legitimate field of inquiry by establishing itself as a science of Blackness—was equally doomed. Within academe, a visible and virulent backlash against Afrocentrism in the 1990s challenged the flawed knowledge claims of Afrocentrism.[49] Once it became safe to castigate Asante as spokesperson for a narrow version of Afrocentrism, its credibility within the academy, one that had never been high, virtually disappeared.

One important criticism of academic Afrocentrism that fostered its demise as a social theory concerned its exclusionary practices—in particular, its creation of narrow, essentialist definitions of Blackness. Because rituals determine categories of belonging, some versions of academic Afrocentrism degenerated into policing the ever shrinking boundaries of authentic Blackness.[50] Being of African descent makes every African American a potential convert to Afrocentrism, yet being racially categorized as "Black" is not enough. One is both *born* Black and *becomes* Black. Afrocentrism installed rituals to identify the authentically "Black" from their less conscious counterparts. Just as Christians undergo baptism to demonstrate their membership in their faith-based community, Afrocentric true believers were expected to undergo similar conversion rituals.[51] For example, changing one's name from a slave name to an African one; changing one's style of dress to that deemed more closely aligned with traditional African styles; and wearing one's hair in braids, cornrows, dreadlocks, or a some other "natural" style all operated as elements of an individual's conversion experience. All of these indicators were used as ways to signal to the larger community that the individual had undergone the conversion experience from one kind of Blackness to another. The problem with both the narrow definitions of Blackness and the conversion experience needed to accomplish it is that some segments of the African American community could *never* become "Black enough." Within exclusionary versions of Afrocentrism, women, gays, lesbians, and other sexual minorities; biracial and multiracial individuals; and wealthy Black folks were expected to "prove" their right to belong and their rights of entitlement to the unconditional love for Black people. Increasing numbers of people of African descent, especially those in the hip-hop generation, simply refused to do it. Instead, African American youth took Black nationalism in a different direction within Black cultural production.[52] In essence, sexism and homophobia within academic Afrocentrism striving to be a Black civil religion compromised its own claims for a comprehensive love ethic and fostered its demise.[53]

Afrocentrism's organization as a civil religion outside the academy followed a different and more complex path. Currently, a more diffuse Afrocentric sensibility characterizes African American culture, where the meaning of Blackness is increasingly the subject of debate. Interestingly, the holidays, social events, and other practices initially developed by Asante and Karenga within higher education migrated outside the academy and began to fulfill some of the functions of Afrocentrism as a civil religion for churches, community groups, and some urban public school systems. For example, within Black civil society, rites-of-passage programs provide an important example of how the rituals of Afrocentrism as a civil religion have been crafted for nonacademic settings. Such programs aim to give African American youth new identities through a conversion experience of putting them in touch with their true selves and marking their passage to adulthood. Rites-of-passage programs are small-scale, yet the ritual of Kwanzaa has moved beyond the academy and African American communities and is part of American popular culture. Organized around the seven principles of the Nguzo Saba and occurring over a seven-day period between Christmas and New Year's Day, Kwanzaa celebrations range from family gatherings to church-based and other large community events. The success of this holiday is evident in the industry that it has spawned: Commercial greeting cards and other Kwanzaa paraphernalia can be found in local stores. Kwanzaa remains viable in part because it articulates with capitalist marketplace relations. African American consumers have long been targeted with niche advertising for alcohol projects and gym shoes. Adding Afrocentric greeting cards and other paraphernalia associated with African American ethnic rituals constitutes a logical extension of these practices.

Other rituals inspired by Afrocentrism have taken on a more democratic, inclusive aura. For example, the well-attended annual Black family reunions organized by the National Council of Negro Women (NCNW) represent the most visible expression of this organizational "Afrocentric" enterprise. Many extended African American families use these larger events to organize their own family-specific gatherings. Concerned about the erosion of extended family life, the NCNW conceived of the annual reunions as a way to foster family solidarity and thus community and "national" solidarity. These gatherings reflect the family values and faith-based ideology of American national identity and thus dovetail with American civil religion. At the same time, people of African descent constitute the bulk of reunion attendees, but the actual families who attend also include Whites, Latinos, and people from many different racial/ethnic groups. This is not an exclusionary, patriarchal racial identification advanced under some narrow versions of Afrocentrism. Instead, the Black family reunions more closely resemble rituals that are designed to reinforce the core Afrocentric principle of an unconditional love of Black people by recruiting diverse people to that task.

African American Ethnicity and the New Racism

The troubled history of Afrocentrism in the academy does not erase the significance of its approach to ethnic identification. Linking Black nationalist ideas to a pre-existing spirituality has influenced the sacred and secular contours of contemporary African American civil society. Rite-of-passage programs, Kwanzaa celebrations, and Black family reunions constitute tangible actions that African Americans now take to address suffering associated with the new racism. If Cornel West is right about the dangers of nihilism for African Americans, then cultural responses such as those of Afrocentrism that place a love ethic at the heart of Black political mobilization become vitally important.

Beyond the specific case of Afrocentrism, efforts inspired by Black nationalists to construct African American ethnicity raise one crucial question: Can this strategy, or other strategies, of ethnic identification deliver the same economic and political benefits for African Americans grappling with the new racism that ethnic-mobilization strategies of the past did for Irish, Italians, Jews, and other ethnic groups? The increasingly segregated racial landscape obscured by a colorblind ideology eschews group-based politics of all sorts. Under premises of the liberal, constitutional state, groups should not make claims on the American government. That right is reserved for individuals. Thus, the colorblind ideology speaks to equal treatment of *individuals* by the state and before the law as the penultimate expression of the nation-state. Conservative Republicans who attack affirmative action and other group-based remedies for past racial practices believe that any group-based treatment violates the rights of individuals. Social policies that appear to promote group rights, no matter how well intentioned, effectively recognize group-based politics as "special interests" and violates the fundamental tenets of American civil religion that protect individuals from the incursions of the nation-state. Faith-based projects take on added importance within this interpretive context, because they aim to minister not to the group but to individuals.

At the same time, group-based politics remain an important reality within all aspects of American society. Despite expressed commitments to American individualism, the arrival of new immigrant groups of color has revived longstanding understandings of ethnic mobilization as a route to political power within the U.S. nation-state. Racial/ethnic immigrant groups are advised to prove their worthiness for Americanization by not making demands on local, state, or federal governments. Selected Asian groups are depicted as "model minorities" not just because they engage in family businesses and encourage their children to study hard in school. These groups also make limited demands on state services. In contrast, other groups who are deemed to be less worthy are derogated. For example, Mexican American immigrant women are stigmatized as receiving unearned entitlements from the nation-state, primarily because their American-born children consume educational and social services to which they are entitled as American citizens. The message seems clear: Groups are fine, just as long as they make few demands on the state.

This political context of a painfully slow case-by-case remedy of individual claims where the American government has virtually turned its back on reforms to address contemporary racial disparities in health, schooling, education, and employment with targeted group-based remedies leaves African Americans adrift. Traditional civil-rights groups have produced few tangible victories in confronting this non-responsive nation-state. Their efforts quite rightly have been consumed with trying to defend the civil-rights gains that ushered in the period of the new racism. In this situation, the persistence of Black nationalist initiatives cannot be explained away simply as a wrong-headed ideology foisted on falsely conscious African American masses. Despite African Americans' rejection of the politics advanced by both the Nation of Islam and a conservative Afrocentrism, the fact that so many African Americans are familiar with or respect these versions of Black nationalism speaks more to the vacuum in African American politics and intellectual thought than to the strength of the programs offered by either version of Black nationalism. As Robinson observes, "Despite its strange cosmology, the NOI stands as the sole national Black political organization that has a strategy explicitly aimed at improving the lot of the most disadvantaged."[54] As long as this remains the case, Black nationalism is unlikely to disappear anytime soon.

4 When Fighting Words Are Not Enough

The Gendered Content of Afrocentrism

> You cannot escape the pathology of a country in which
> you're born. You can resist it, you can react to it, you can
> do all kinds of things, but you're trapped in it.
>
> —*James Baldwin*

In American higher education, Afrocentrism generates some curious contradictions. On the one hand, many African American intellectuals staunchly support Afrocentrism, contending that its commitment to centering scholarship on people of African descent, its treatment of Black people as subjects rather than objects of history, its valorization of Blackness, and its attempts to speak to and not simply about Black people throughout the Black diaspora provide African Americans with a much needed corrective to existing scholarship on race.[1] Other respected African American academics disagree. Defining Afrocentrism as an ideology or dogma, they claim that it romanticizes the African and rural African American past while ignoring social issues in the urban Black present; suppresses heterogeneity among Black people in search of an elusive racial solidarity; puts forward a problematic definition of Blackness as an essential, innate quality of a general ancestral connection to Africa; and remains male-centered and heterosexist.[2]

Beyond these academic disagreements, Afrocentrism has a broader history and meaning. As one of several Black nationalist projects in the United States in the late twentieth century, Afrocentrism simultaneously represents and shapes Black political aspirations for freedom and justice.[3] Much social theory rarely considers Black audiences except as markers of difference. In contrast, Afrocentrism speaks primarily to Black people by "centering" on their experiences and concerns. In a climate of postmodern criticism where rhetoric of de-centering holds sway, any discourse that seems to center on anything may seem hopelessly flawed. However, Black frustration within the new racism provides one explanation for why African Americans seem more willing to accept Afrocentrism and other Black nationalist philosophies during a period in which academics increasingly view nationalisms of all sorts with disdain. Some see the resurgence of African American interest in Black nationalism in the 1980s and 1990s as a direct result of an increasingly conservative political climate in the United States, the deteriorating economic base in African American communities resulting from changes in global capitalism, and the persistence of an increasingly sophisticated racial segregation.[4]

Because Afrocentrism aims to influence the thinking and behavior of Black people outside academe, it participates in controversies unlike those affecting other discourses. Unlike most other academic discourses, Afrocentrism received substantial media coverage in the 1990s, most of it negative and centering on two themes. One concerned Afrocentrism's inroads into curricular offering of urban public schools. Schools populated predominantly by African American, poor children who had been written off by everyone found themselves the center of attention when they tried to institute Afrocentric curricula. Another area of controversy surrounded the claim by some Afrocentrists that ancient Egypt not only constituted an African civilization, but that it shaped subsequent European classical civilizations. This media controversy, in part, helped to narrow the meaning of Afrocentrism from its initial focus on Black consciousness to so-called authentic Afrocentrists garbed in traditional African attire. Moreover, despite the negative treatment in the popular press of both Afrocentric curricula and claims of African origins of civilization, Afrocentrism as synonymous with Black consciousness remains meaningful to Black youth (see, for example, the autobiography of Sister Souljah), many African American academics, and African Americans of diverse economic classes and genders in ways social theories deemed more respected and prestigious within higher education have yet to accomplish.[5] I have found African American college students receptive to Afrocentric course offerings, symposia, and programs. As part of a larger cohort of Black youth who see the devastation affecting their communities, many see Afrocentrism as the only critical social theory interested in addressing the social problems that they face.[6]

The institutional placement of many Black intellectuals in higher education may also contribute to the persistence of Black nationalism generally and Afrocentrism in particular as one guiding interpretive framework for Black studies scholarship.[7] Despite considerable media attention to selected Black public intellectuals, most African Americans in higher education do not enjoy a comparable elevated status. As Black studies initiatives proliferated at historically White universities in the United States, African American academics gained a crucial institutional niche that allowed them to become Black studies professionals, many within Black studies programs and departments. Moreover, the placement of Black academics in historically White institutions meant that such thinkers routinely encountered the residual effects of scientific racism that viewed Blacks as objects of knowledge in sociology, psychology, history, and other academic disciplines.[8] With limited power to change these institutions, many Black thinkers turned inward toward the task of creating cultural communities that might give themselves and their students solace on what were often hostile White campuses. Afrocentrism flourished in these spaces.[9]

Given Afrocentrism's distinctive political and intellectual ties to Black nationalism, a deep-seated belief in the promise of Afrocentrism by many everyday African Americans cannot be analyzed away as false consciousness. This would only aggravate existing divisions both between Black academics and African Americans outside the academy and among Black intellectuals within higher education. Much more is at stake than questions of the logical consistency or empirical merit of Afrocentrism. Like Black nationalist philosophies in general, the appeal of having Black consciousness or being Afrocentric lies in part in Afrocentrism's ability to mean different things to different African Americans. Rather than trying to define Afrocentrism precisely—or, worse yet, elevating one form of Afrocentrism over another and proclaiming it "correct"—a more intriguing and useful approach lies in identifying the diverse ways in which African Americans employ Afrocentrism as a system of meaning. I suggest that Afrocentrism is alternately used by different segments of African American civil society as a Black nationalist political paradigm, as a civil religion, and as a critical or oppositional social theory.[10]

In this essay, I confine my analysis to Afrocentrism as critical social theory within higher education. As critical social theory, Afrocentrism aims to theorize about social issues confronting Black people with an eye toward fostering economic and social justice. Rather than establishing a taxonomic framework designed to classify Afrocentric scholars (see, e.g., Darlene Clark Hine's useful discussion of Afrocentrism as one of three paradigms operating within Black Studies), I examine selected "orienting strategies" that frame Afrocentrism's practice as critical social theory.[11] As the progeny of a Black cultural nationalism that has been institutionalized within higher education, Afrocentrism strives to challenge the new racism.

A variety of themes lend themselves to analyzing the oppositional nature of Afrocentrism, among them economic class, heterosexism, and religion, yet gender offers a particularly useful lens. Gender operates as a central yet largely unexamined tenet of most nationalist projects, whether the nationalism is forwarded by dominant groups in defense of institutionalized racism, colonialism, or imperialism, or by groups such as African Americans who use nationalist aspirations to challenge hierarchical power relations.[12] The mainstream media portrays Afrocentrism as a monolithic, static doctrine, yet Afrocentric intellectual production remains decidedly heterogeneous and incorporates diverse perspectives on a range of topics, including gender. Despite this heterogeneity among individual scholars, neither Afrocentric intellectual production overall nor Afrocentrism in the academy have shown a sustained interest in gender. Neither the specific experiences of African American women caused by gender oppression nor gender as a major category of analysis framing the experiences of both Black women and men have received sustained attention. Thus, Afrocentrism's treatment of gender might shed light on the challenges confronting critical social theories that try to respond to the new racism.

From Black Cultural Nationalism to Afrocentrism

Evaluating Afrocentrism's effectiveness as critical social theory involves examining the gender politics within the version of Black cultural nationalism that emerged during the Black Power Movement in the 1960s and early 1970s. While Black nationalist movements have a long history in the United States, Black cultural nationalism makes up the political and intellectual predecessor of contemporary Afrocentrism.[13] For African Americans, the 1960s represented a period of rising expectations about Black equality coupled with a growing realization that change would not come easy. The hopes generated by successful decolonization movements in Africa and the dismantling of de jure segregation in the United States stood in stark contrast to the seeming permanence of poverty and powerlessness plaguing Black urban communities. Disenchantment with civil rights, seen as an outmoded solution, led many younger African Americans to Black nationalisms and the search for a heroic national identity or "Blackness" that could serve as the basis for a reenergized political activism. Black cultural nationalism emerged in these social conditions and found its expression in the Black arts movement guided by a Black aesthetic.[14]

In contrast to other Black nationalist projects, Black cultural nationalism concerns itself with both evaluating Western treatment of Black culture as deviant and constructing new analyses of the Black experience.[15] Social-science scholarship on race typically sees Black culture in the United States in one of two ways. On the one hand, African American contributions to mainstream culture have been deracialized and considered simply "American" or "universal." On the other hand, dimensions of African American culture that resist absorption and remain distinctive are either neglected or dismissed as deviant.[16] Consider the differential treatment afforded jazz and Black English in dominant discourse. Despite their shared roots in African-derived philosophical frameworks—their expressiveness, improvisation, and rootedness in dialogue, and the significance of individual sound or "voice"—dominant scholarship identifies jazz as the only classical music produced in the United States and routinely derogates Black language. Ignoring and minimizing the African origins and African American practitioners of jazz, this approach effectively deracializes a major dimension of American culture. In contrast, when assessing Black language, dominant scholarship interprets the same characteristics as pathologies that retard African Americans' social advancement.[17] The Blackness that created jazz remains ignored, while the same Blackness that generates Black English is maligned.

Based on the premise that Black people make up a cultural nation, Black cultural nationalism aims to reconstruct Black consciousness by replacing prevailing discourses on race with analyses that place the interests and needs of African people at the center of any discussion.[18] For African Americans, reclaiming Black culture involves identifying dimensions of an allegedly authentic Black culture that distinguish it from European-derived worldviews. Reconstructing Black history by locating the mythic past and the origins of the nation or the people is designed to build pride and commitment to the nation.[19] These elements allegedly can be used to organize Black consciousness of people of African descent as a so-called chosen people. Identifying the unique and heroic elements of the national culture—in this case, Black culture—ideally enables members of the group to fight for the nation.[20]

Four guiding principles or domain assumptions framed Black cultural nationalism's Black aesthetic.[21] First, in the absence of any substantive African American participation in sociology and other academic disciplines, social-science approaches had long viewed Black culture as primitive, inferior, and deviant. In response to this scientific racism, the Black aesthetic aimed to reconstruct a positive, philosophically distinct Black culture. Central to this reconstructed culture lay the thesis of "soul" interpreted as a condensed expression of the unconscious energy of the Black experience. Soul could not be acquired: You were born with it, or you weren't. Soul or essential Blackness was naturalized, and true believers either believed it existed or discounted it altogether. Thus, the concept of soul aimed to name the essential, authentic, and positive quality of Blackness.[22]

A second guiding principle of the Black aesthetic involved reclaiming Black identity or Black subjectivity via this reconstructed Black culture. For African Americans, institutionalized racism had severed this link between authentic Black identity and an affirming Black culture to create a "psychology of oppression."[23] Internalized oppression substituted this authentic identity expressed via solidarity with the Black community with an identity constructed with premises of scientific racism that deemed Black people intellectually and morally inferior. As a step toward recovering their identity and subjectivity, Black people needed to undergo a conversion experience of Nigrescence from "Negro" to "Black."[24] Completing a four-stage transformation— moving through stages of pre-encounter, encounter with Whites, immersion in Black culture, and internalization of a new Black identity—distinguished "Negroes" mesmerized by Whiteness from authentic Black people prepared to participate in liberation struggles.[25]

A third assumption concerned the significance of maintaining racial solidarity grounded in a distinctive notion of Black community. Race became family; racial family meant community; and Black community symbolized the "imagined community" of nation.[26] Reconstructing Black culture and grounding it in a family model of community organization gave newly "Black" people a home, a family to which they were linked by ties of blood. This stance reinforced the bonds of consanguinity, or blood ties, for the family/race with the sense of political obligation that accompanies blood ties. Family metaphors and their unspoken assumptions about gender permeated Black nationalist discourse of this period. For example, Yosef Ben-Jochannan's influential volume positing African foundations for European civilization and thought was titled, *Black Man of the Nile and His Family*.[27] Family ties of consanguinity demand absolute submission because they are built not on political or social issues but on simple belonging.

Finally, when nurtured by this unified Black community relating as family, this new-found Black identity would stimulate a new politics for African Americans. African Americans in touch with their essential Blackness would be more willing to serve the nation, defined as the Black community/family. This ethic of commitment or service to the Black family/community/nation, one in which Black people would function as "brothers" and "sisters" in fixing the Black family/community/nation, emerged from the conversion experience of immersion in Black culture, reclaiming Black identity via racial solidarity.[28]

In the 1980s, Molefi Asante, Maulana Ron Karenga, and other African American intellectuals basically imported these four principles into Black studies programs and departments and recast them as premises of Afrocentrism in the academy. Yet while each core theme traveled into the academy, each received a distinctive treatment, reflecting the new racism of the 1980s and 1990s. By 2000, the bulk of contemporary Afrocentric intellectual production, particularly that housed in Black studies programs, emphasized the first core theme of the Black aesthetic. Such scholarship explored the distinguishing features of Black culture through identifying the distinctive elements of an Afrocentric worldview.[29] Even though the term "soul" disappeared and was replaced by the search for the "essence" of Blackness, Afrocentrism retained this focus on opposing social-science constructions of Black culture as deviant. Recasting Black culture through an essentially Black and often celebratory corrective lens, African history, philosophies, religions, and social systems all generated new interest.[30] The assumption guiding much of this research was that Black culture had an essential core and that uncovering the philosophical foundations of a distinctive African-centered, Black, or Afrocentric worldview expressed differently throughout the Black diaspora would provide a new Afrocentric context for examining Black community organization.[31]

Building on the Black arts movement's search for soul, Afrocentric scholarship posited several distinguishing features of essential Blackness. These features were: (1) a distinctive relationship of the Black individual to the Black community that fosters a connected definition of self; (2) a concern for harmony as a fundamental principle of community organization where individuals find their worth in relationship to a community, to nature, and in to some supreme idea or being;

(3) the relationship between the spiritual and material aspects of being where material life is not privileged over spirituality; and, (4) a cyclical versus linear conception of time, change, and human agency where individuals see their connectedness to all life and where the appearance of phenomena always change while the underlying essence remains basically unchanged.[32]

Efforts to verify how these key elements of the African philosophical tradition shape African-influenced cultures throughout the Diaspora also stimulated scholarship on so-called classical African civilizations.[33] Investigations of the roots of Black culture parallel efforts to reclaim Black history by empirically verifying how the elements of an African philosophical tradition have shaped both Black history and, in some versions, Western civilization itself.[34] This component has led to increased interest in African civilizations and cultures, especially the study of ancient Egypt. Interest in ancient Egypt, or Kemet, perceived as the original "Black" civilization serving as the philosophical foundation for all subsequent societies formed by people of African descent, increased.[35]

Identifying elements of a distinctive Afrocentric worldview created the conceptual space for scholars to begin the painstaking task of reinterpreting a range of social institutions in Black civil society. Black family studies represent one area in which Afrocentric interpretations have challenged social-science assumptions of Black family deviance, especially in female-headed households. Studies of Black religious expression and spirituality comprise another important area of scholarship on Black culture. Black cultural production, especially music, dance, the visual arts, and literature, made up yet another area of important reinterpretation. Finally, Black language has benefited greatly from establishing a new normative center that is derived from African societies.[36]

Despite these contributions of thirty years of Afrocentric scholarship aimed at addressing more than 150 years of scientific racism, the definition of culture currently shaping much Afrocentric intellectual production runs the risk of limiting its effectiveness. Black cultural nationalism in the 1950s and 1960s was inspired by the use of culture in *actual* and not *imagined* national liberation struggles. As a result, the definitions of culture put forward by thinkers such as Amilcar Cabral and Frantz Fanon differ markedly from those of today. These and other Black nationalist thinkers saw culture as dynamic and changing, as a complex network of social practices that determine positions of domination, equality, and subordination. The close links that ideas and actions had in political struggle fostered a particular view of praxis grounded in a constantly tested Black culture.[37]

In contrast, by 2000, Afrocentric constructions of Black culture had replaced this dynamic self-reflexivity with an a priori set of cultural norms culled from the belief systems of selected African societies. These norms were often used as yardsticks for assessing normative qualities of Black culture.[38] Afrocentric preoccupations with putting forward "positive" views of Black culture stem from these efforts to extract it from the uniformly "negative" constructions that have long permeated Western scholarship and popular culture. However, as Michele Wallace observes, "Focus on good and bad images may be more fundamentally connected to the western metaphysical dualism that is the philosophical underpinning of racist and sexist domination than with radical efforts to reconceptualize black cultural identities."[39] Ironically, this type of thinking reifies the notion of a fundamentally good, essential Blackness increasingly submerged by an encroaching and inherently bad Whiteness. From this perspective, essential Blackness has much to offer an intellectually and spiritually bankrupt White world that has little of value.[40]

Reconstituting Black identity, the second core theme of the Black aesthetic, may remain a less focused goal, yet unstated assumptions about identity permeate Afrocentric intellectual production. Work in Black psychology demonstrates efforts to use the core elements of Black culture to assist African Americans in dealing with racial oppression. As the prominent Afrocentrist Na'im Akbar observes, "We now know that psychology is not only what the European behavioral scientists have taught. We have a new grasp on the concept that Africans view the world differently."[41] Substantial scholarship aims to redefine a new basis for viewing African American identity and personality.[42]

As was the situation with Black culture, reconstructing Black identity faced its own set of challenges. In some cases, constructing a normative Black identity easily slipped into attempts to describe the ideal, normative, and "authentic" Black person. The search for the "authentic" Black person as shown in the glorification of "pure" African biological heritage; the displacement of an essential Blackness from sight to sound by viewing orality, rhythm, and "soul" as the source of Blackness; the listing of components of the "normative" Black personality that can be used to measure African American mental health; the belief that a Black essence or "soul" exists that is distinctive to Black people and that only Blacks can access—all became stigmatized as examples of Black essentialism.[43] In essence, this Afrocentric approach to identity construes Black culture as a package of insulated traits possessed in varying degrees by Black individuals and then assesses Black mental health using the normative yardstick of Black cultural traits.

Although developed in opposition to domain assumptions of positivist science, Afrocentric definitions of culture and identity inadvertently rely on the same assumptions. For example, one assumption of positivist science is that the tools of science can accurately represent or depict reality. Within scientific contexts of justification, empiricism and rationality become tools to uncover the "truth" of social phenomena. Afrocentric views of culture and identity share this belief in a truth that is waiting to be discovered by the science of Afrocentrism. This theme of the embeddedness of Afrocentrism in scientific assumptions concerning culture and identity has had a deep impact on Black cultural criticism. African American writers whose work seems to challenge dimensions of essential Blackness depicted as "truth" often encounter censure. For example, criticisms of Alice Walker's novels *The Color Purple* and *Possessing the Secret of Joy* often challenged Walker's accuracy in portraying the Black experience. Even though Walker never claimed that she was trying to represent or depict the Black experience, holding her work to this standard allowed for its dismissal.

In contrast to the treatment of culture and identity, the themes of racial solidarity and the ethic of service are treated less as areas of scholarly investigation than as unquestioned rules that regulate relationships among professionals in some Black studies programs. Much less attention has been paid to examining the actual and potential mechanisms by which African Americans create racial solidarity or engage in community service in Black civil society. Instead, Black-on-Black surveillance seems designed to ensure that racial solidarity and an ethic of service as articles of faith are observed. On some college campuses, maintaining racial solidarity at all costs often degenerates into policing the borders of who is authentically Black. At times, this posture has proved to be extremely costly. For example, during the confirmation hearings of Supreme Court Justice Clarence Thomas, conservative Republicans manipulated this automatic invocation of racial solidarity to their own advantage. Many African Americans made the misguided assumption that, once on the bench, Thomas would demonstrate his racial loyalty by expressing an ethic of service to the Black community. They were wrong.

The lack of attention within Afrocentrism to current political and economic issues may stem in part from academic norms. Such standards support apolitical scholarship on culture, especially when displaced to a distant and safe past while eschewing more contentious contemporary African American political realities. Asante has been writing Afrocentric analyses for years. When his work was deemed to be politically ineffective, he was left alone. But Asante's work became the center of controversy when it began to be used in shaping school programs in Milwaukee, Detroit, and Portland, Oregon. Only then was it publicly censured. Afrocentric analyses that suggest that psychological freedom must precede concrete political action also uphold academic assumptions. Treatments of Black identity, when confined to analyses of poor Black self-esteem and the need for more role models, represent another safe topic. Unfree minds limit Black participation in both racial solidarity and an ethic of service. The solution: Fix the mind. These approaches both sever analyses of culture and identity internal to African American civil society from political challenges such as racial segregation and surveillance that originate outside Black communities. In other words, not only are culture and politics severed—a shrinking of the notion of praxis—but the meaning of each becomes changed as a result of this separation. Thus, restricting Black intellectual activity to the terrain of culture and psychology may signal yet another strategy of co-optation that characterizes the new racism.[44] As Barbara Ransby and Tracye Matthews point out, "The Afrocentric prescription for progress is predicated upon the notion that the main problems confronting the African American community and diaspora at this historical juncture are internal to the Black community itself. The problems are defined as cultural, behavioral and psychological, not as political, economic or structural. In other words—our problem is us."[45]

Comparing the power relations confronting Black cultural nationalism in the 1960s to those facing Afrocentrism in the 1990s sheds light on the contrasting views of culture deployed by both. The Black arts movement of the 1960s clearly reflects a stance of "strategic essentialism" where an essentialist Black culture played a pivotal role in Black nationalist struggles.[46] However, intellectuals from that era recognized that national culture could become problematic for liberation struggles if the moment of strategic essentialism hardens into dogma. Cabral, Fanon, and others never meant Black essentialism to be the organizing principles of Black social organization. Instead, they saw culture as one essential tool for political liberation.[47]

The question for African Americans concerns whether we are still in such a historical moment. Will producing a national culture of Blackness yield similar political results as those characterizing earlier historical periods? More important, who benefits from Black essentialist positions that appear unable to generate theoretically compelling arguments for political practice? In a paper appropriately titled "Afro-Kitsch," the film critic Manthia Diawara scathingly alludes to the political limitations of some versions of Afrocentrism:

> Until Afrocentricity learns the language of black people in Detroit, Lingala in Zaire, and Bambara in Mali, and grounds itself in the material conditions of the people in question, it is nothing but a kitsch of blackness. It is nothing but an imitation of a discourse of liberation. Afrocentric academics fix blackness by reducing it to Egypt and *kente* cloth. Hence, like Judaism, Christianity, and Islam, Afrocentric social theory has become a religion, a camp movement, where one can find refuge from the material realities of being black in Washington, D.C., London, or Nairobi.[48]

As currently constructed, some dimensions of Afrocentrism seem designed to sooth their advocates who are comfortably ensconced in teaching and research positions in higher education. Their value as critical social theory seems much more questionable.

Gender and the Black Aesthetic

Afrocentric domain assumptions of culture, identity, solidarity, and service have markedly different implications for African American men and women. These differences stem in large part from Afrocentrism's reliance on Black aesthetic notions of community, which in turn relies on mainstream views of family.[49] Like nationalist movements globally, women and gender have prescribed functions.[50] Using the experiences of selected White middle-class families as normative, 1960s gender ideology posited that so-called normal families divided the public sphere of the political economy reserved for men from the private sphere of family relegated to women. These nuclear families where benevolent male authority ruled, with women assuming their proper, natural roles as wives and mothers, reproduced appropriate gender roles for men and women.[51] Within this interpretive framework, strong African American women in Black families and Black civil society were labeled deviant.[52] Moreover, the seemingly flawed gender roles in African American families fostered a slew of problems, among them Black poverty, criminality, poor school performance, and adolescent child-bearing. In other words, by not reflecting dominant gender ideology, Black families reproduced a Black cultural deviance that in turn fostered Black economic-class disadvantage.[53]

Despite the writings of Black feminists disputing these views, in the absence of a Black feminist political movement, these views were incorporated into Black cultural nationalist agendas.[54] Autobiographies of Black women activists from this period describe the sexism in Black cultural nationalist organizations. For example, Elaine Brown, a former leader of the Black Panther Party, describes the sexism in her own political organization. Brown identifies similar practices in US, a Black cultural nationalist movement led by Karenga, the creator of Kwanzaa and a figure closely associated with institutionalizing Black studies programs in higher education.[55] Echoing Brown, Angela Davis also reports elements of sexism in Karenga's Black cultural nationalist organization. Brown, Davis, and other Black women activists assumed a particular place in Black cultural nationalist efforts to reconstruct authentic Black culture, reconstitute Black identity, foster racial solidarity, and institute an ethic of service to the Black community.[56] While Black cultural nationalism staunchly opposed racial oppression, it uncritically incorporated dominant ideologies about White and Black gender roles into its domain assumptions. Consider the following passage, quoted at length, from Imamu Amiri Baraka, at the time a prominent Black cultural nationalist in the United States. In his 1970 article "Black Woman," Baraka offers a particularly concise example of the gender ideology that permeated Black cultural nationalism:

> We do not believe in "equality" of men and women.... We could never be equals...nature has not provided thus.... But this means that we will complement each other, that you, who I call my house, because there is no house without a man and his wife, are the single element in the universe that perfectly completes my essence. You are essential, to the development of any life in the house, because you are that house's completion. When we say complement, completes, we mean that we have certain functions which are more natural to us, and you have certain graces that are yours alone. We say that a Black woman must first be able to inspire her man, then she must be able to teach our children, and contribute to the social development of the nation. How do you inspire Black Man? By being the conscious rising essence of Blackness.... By race, by identity, and by action. You inspire Black Man by being Black Woman. By being the nation, as the house, the

smallest example of how the nation should be. So you are my "house," I live
in you, and together we have a house, and that must be the microcosm, by
example, of the entire Black nation. Our nation is our selves.[57]

Participants in Black nationalist projects certainly differed in their
adherence to these beliefs, yet in his bold assertion of typically more
diffuse assumptions, Baraka's rendition remains unusual and therefore
useful. The passage's significance lies in its particularly concise statement of the gender ideology permeating 1960s Black cultural nationalism. Moreover, it illuminates how key ideas about gender framed
subsequent assumptions of Afrocentrism. Four areas are of special
significance. They are (1) the importance attached to controlling Black
women's reproduction and sexuality; (2) the significance of Black
mothers in passing on Black culture; (3) the notion of complementary
gender roles as points of departure in constructing Black masculinity
and Black femininity; and (4) the symbolic association of Black women
with the nation.

First, since women are the only group who can biologically reproduce the population of the Black family, Black community, or Black
nation, regulating Black women's reproduction becomes central to
nationalist aspirations. Controlling biological reproduction to produce
more of one's own "people" or, depending on political and economic
policy, more or fewer of an outsider group's "people" typifies nationalist philosophies generally, and Black nationalist philosophies in particular.[58] Responding in large part to eugenicist scientific and public
policies long leveled against Black people and others deemed socially
undesirable, Black nationalist projects claim that without sufficient
population there can be no Black individuals whose identities are in
question.[59] Without population, the Black nation ceases to exist.
Within this intellectual and political context, Black nationalist projects
of the 1960s often opposed contraceptive and reproductive services for
African American women. Viewing such services as "genocide," they
argued that because family-planning services were largely run by
Whites, such services represented a continuation of longstanding eugenics policies targeted toward Blacks. In a climate of medical experi-
mentation on Blacks typified by the Tuskegee syphilis experiment,
which was then in progress, claims of government-initiated efforts to
eliminate the Black population appeared highly plausible.[60] However,
while the Black nationalist phrase "Have a baby for the nation" made
good political rhetoric, it failed to address the issue of who would
care for the population actually born. Despite their analyses, Black

nationalist groups often found themselves at odds with the African American women left to raise the future warriors of the nation with few resources. These women often viewed the denial of reproductive services quite differently.

Controlling Black women's biological reproduction raises an accompanying issue of who would control Black women's sexuality. Assumptions about Black women's sexuality central to relations of ruling also influence Black nationalist projects.[61] For example, Baraka's passage mirrors dominant gender ideology dividing women into two categories: that of the virginal, married, good girls, contrasted to the sexually promiscuous, immoral, unmarried bad girls. Within this binary logic, good girls are sexually active only within the context of marriage and family. In contrast, bad girls represent the sexualized woman, one lacking the protection of marriage and whose sexuality renders her deviant. Within this context, African American women who make up the "conscious rising essence of Blackness" are to be protected, revered, and seen as "good" women, while those who fall outside of this union with Black men garner less favor. This model legitimates Black women's sexuality only in relation to Black men, yet it offers no parallel legitimation of Black men's sexuality in relation to attachment to Black women. Moreover, statements such as "a Black woman must first be able to inspire her man" suggest that all Black women should be heterosexual and that the primary utility of Black women's sexuality lies in inspiring her Black man in the privacy of their home. Her own pleasure is rarely mentioned.[62]

Controlling Black women's sexuality simultaneously addresses another issue of great concern within Black nationalist projects. By reversing the color hierarchy of White-supremacist beliefs that derogate darkness, Black becomes beautiful. If "the blacker the berry the sweeter the juice" typifies standards of Black beauty and moral authority, Black women remain far superior to White women and other women of color in their ability to produce the "authentic" Black bodies that this ideology requires. Moreover, keeping the race biologically Black and pure directs attention to policing Black women's sexuality. Black women who sleep with the enemy place the Black race/family/community at risk, for this choice perpetuates the bastardization of the Black race. As mothers of the race, Black women need to be heterosexual and should be good girls, and good girls do not sleep around. Within a sexual double standard, Black women become mothers of the nation, while Black men serve as warriors in the revolution. As warriors, they maintain the right to sleep with, own, and, in some cases, rape the women of the alien nation—in this case, White women—while receiving praise for these actions.[63] This ideological framework constrains Black women and Black men differently, with patterns of choices made by actual African American women and men reflecting their struggles with this unstated yet powerful gender subtext of reproduction, sexuality, and Black cultural nationalism.

The significance of African American women as mothers in passing on Black culture also constitutes a significant feature of Black nationalist projects. Within nationalist philosophies, the people of a nation exist not just as a measurable, quantifiable population; they also represent a group that actually occupies or is dispersed from a homeland and possesses a national culture symbolic of the nation.[64] Since nationalism remains closely associated with notions of self-determination over territory and homeland, Black women, by virtue of their association with land, family, and homes, become keepers of the family, home, community, and nation. For example, Baraka notes that the collective self-determination of a people is expressed through building a nation composed of "houses." These houses form a microcosm for the nation as a whole. Thus, the idealized traditional family becomes the approved, natural site where Black culture and racial identity are reproduced. Viewing families as the building blocks of nations, in conjunction with identifying women's actions as more central to the family's well-being and functioning within the house/community than men's, elevates Black women's responsibilities as mothers in certain ways. Since women typically carry the burden of child-care responsibilities within African American households, conceptualizing family as intricately linked with both community and nation effectively joins women's activities in socializing the young in individual households to that of transmitting the symbols, meanings, and culture of the Black nation itself. Viewing African American women as moral mothers or keepers of the nation, Baraka argues, Black women must be able to "teach our children and thus contribute to the social development of the nation." Maintaining the elements of culture such as learning language, ways of living, and cultural values of a "people" is essential to the continuation of the national group. Through their activities as mothers, Black women reproduce "authentic" Black culture—in this case, the allegedly positive qualities that would ensure the loyalty of members of the national group. Thus, Black women's highest accomplishments become inspiring Black men and keeping "house," the building blocks of the nation.

With so much vested in glorifying the mother, Black women who fail to fulfill these functions can only face censure. A distinction can be made between those women who uphold the values of the nation but do not adhere to them and those women who, by refusing protection, challenge the premises of the system. Within this framework, Black gays, Black lesbians, and Black women who embrace feminism all become suspect, because each group in its own way challenges the centrality of motherhood for Black families, communities, and ultimately the Black nation. The homophobia in Black cultural nationalism seems linked to this belief that maintaining a conservative gender ideology is essential for Black families, communities, and the Black nation as family. As Henry Louis Gates points out, while the ideology of Black nationalism does not have any unique claim on homophobia, "it is an almost obsessive motif that runs through the major authors of the black aesthetic and the Black Power movements. In short, national identity became sexualized in the sixties in such a way as to engender a curious subterranean connection between homophobia and nationalism."[65] Overall, those Black women who fail to have children or who reject the gender politics of the heterosexist nuclear family, face being labeled traitors to the race, too "White," or lesbians.

As Baraka points out, while extremely important, Black women's actions as mothers remain secondary to the objective of "inspiring her man." Thus, Black women's partnership with Black men toward a common goal of nation-building, or service to the nation in gender-appropriate endeavors, makes up a third key idea about gender. The thesis of complementarity of men and women, working in partnership in building a strong Black family and community, functions as a deep root in Black cultural nationalism. In this discourse, complementary symbolizes equality, one where the revered Black mother role complements the benevolent yet warrior-like father. While equality and complementarity are related, they are not the same. Baraka flatly states that African American men and women can never be equal. In saying this he endorses natural, separate identities for men and women that parallel the notion of natural, complementarity identities for Blacks and Whites. This notion of gender complementarity dovetails with an ethic of service in which Black women and men demonstrate racial solidarity by submerging their individual needs, goals, and concerns to those of the Black community as a collectivity. Theoretically, all make sacrifices so that racial solidarity can be maintained. But in actual everyday life, African American women typically sacrifice more.[66]

Not only are Black women supposed to reproduce the population of the new nation and pass on national culture, within the confines of gender complementarity, they also are expected to serve as symbols of the national family or national culture to be protected and preserved. Symbols of American nationalism, such as "mom," "God," the "flag," and "apple pie," are deeply gendered images. They revolve around a nexus of traditional nuclear-family values with a nurturing mother at the center under the watchful eye and protection of a supportive husband/father good citizen, and watched over by a powerful male God. While Black cultural nationalism alters the symbols of the nation—the creation of a Black liberation flag, the Black value system, Black holidays such as Kwanzaa—it simultaneously imports the notion of women as symbolic of the nation. Tactics such as referring to Africa as "Mother Africa" and identifying it as the mythical homeland of Black people scattered throughout the Black diaspora operate as gender-specific images. Within Black cultural nationalism, as "conscious, rising essence," only certain Black women symbolize the nation itself, "by race, by identity, by action." In this sense, Black women become defined as "keepers of the race" both literally and symbolically.

Black community, race, and nation understood through the rubric of family thus become constructed in relation to certain notions of gender that, although not as explicit as Baraka's rendition, depend on African American women and men adhering to a particular gender ideology. A Black woman must be able to "teach our children, and contribute to the social development of the nation." Black women's contributions remain biological (as mother, she physically produces the children for the nation and provides sexual services for male warriors) and symbolic or cultural (as mother, she socializes Black children for the nation through exemplary role modeling of authentic Black femininity). In contrast, Black men claim masculinity by protecting their households, their communities, and their nation, as symbolized by their Black women.

The dangers here for African American women become clear. If protecting Black women becomes conflated with the construction of Black manhood, any woman who is seen as unworthy of this type of protection becomes a threat to the entire community and is thus open to group censure. It is one thing to refuse to have a baby for the nation and yet support the importance of that activity. It is quite another to reject the role itself—namely, the heterosexual nuclear family under Black male leadership. The actions of the individual woman are far less threatening than what her rebellion symbolizes to the entire community.

Gender and Afrocentrism

The guiding principles of Afrocentrism embraced Black cultural nationalism's emphases on reconstructing Black culture, reconstituting Black identity, using racial solidarity to build Black community, and fostering an ethic of service to Black community development. More important, Black cultural nationalism's unexamined yet powerful gender ideology concerning reproduction, motherhood, gender complementarity and Black women's symbolic association with nationalist aspirations also found its way into Afrocentric scholarship.

Most commonly, discussions of Black culture operating within Afrocentric domain assumptions merely exclude gender altogether and discuss Black "people." In some versions, the phrase "the Black Man" stands as proxy for "Black people." However, in far too many cases, the phrase "the Black Man" really refers to men, suggesting that the experiences of Black men adequately represent those of African Americans overall. This approach both renders the distinctive experiences of African American women invisible and reinforces the notion that, if Black women are not explicitly discussed, then the discourse itself lacks a gendered analysis. Thus, while it may appear that Black women as individuals and a gendered analysis in general remain absent from efforts to reconstruct Black culture and Black identity, African American women's absence and invisibility works to structure the very terms of the argument advanced.

Another approach consists of including the work of a few clearly exceptional Black women, only if they do not challenge pre-existing Afrocentric assumptions. For example, incorporating selected Black women if they meet a standard of greatness derived from male experience allows Harriet Tubman to be routinely portrayed as the "Moses of Her People." This treatment reinforces notions of greatness derived from male standards of military leadership and warfare. Women whose accomplishments seem to advance dual goals of furthering the development of a positive Black culture and fostering positive Black identities without challenging prescribed gender roles within Black communities also garner the status afforded Black women worthies. In some cases, only part of the African American woman worthy can be claimed: Her nationalist part is embraced, while any feminist, socialist, anti-heterosexist ideas that challenge Afrocentric domain assumptions are conveniently omitted. For example, if she is mentioned at all, Mary McLeod Bethune's contributions to Black civil society by founding a college and caring for the community's children remain more prominent than her contributions as a skilled negotiator within Franklin Delano Roosevelt's "kitchen cabinet." Her community-development activities reinforce norms of Black motherhood within Black civil society, while her participation in the public sphere challenges views that such activities are best left to African American men. Even the most radical Black women worthies may have trouble recognizing themselves within the Afrocentric canon. Despite her socialist-feminist, antiracist political analysis, reconfiguring Angela Davis's image as the essence of a 1960s-style "natural" or "authentic" Black woman— signified by presenting Davis as wearing a large "natural" hairstyle— effectively recasts her complex political activism in terms of a more simplistic cultural nationalist framework. As Davis herself notes, "It is both humiliating and humbling to discover that a single generation after the events that constructed me as a public personality, I am remembered as a hairdo. It is humiliating because it reduces a politics of liberation to a politics of fashion."[67]

In response to the obvious exclusion of Black women in analyses of Black culture, some Afrocentric scholarship tries to present African American women's experiences as equal and complementary to those of African American men. Responding to earlier patterns of the exclusion and marginalization of African American women, Black women scholars in particular aim to correct the Afrocentric record by highlighting Black women's activities in shaping Black culture and history. While edited volumes such as *Women in Africa and the African Diaspora* foster Black women's visibility within Afrocentrism and work within the assumptions of complementarity, because they highlight Black women's activities in Black civil society, they disrupt gender ideology that relegates Black women exclusively to home and family.[68] In this volume exploring Black women's resistance in African, Caribbean, and African American societies, several authors suggest that Black women's activities have not been confined to the so-called private or domestic sphere. Works such as these create conceptual space to investigate how African American men and women both have been central to the creation and continuation of Black culture in the areas of religion, music, language, and families. This focus on Black women's complementary contributions to Black culture challenges views of Black culture as male-created and male-defined. For example, by demonstrating that Black women have been central in the creation and continuation of Black culture, Bernice Johnson Reagon's work on Black women as cultural workers deepens Afrocentric analyses of Black culture. Similarly, Niara Sudarkasa's analysis of African women's gender activities provide a much needed perspective for understanding African American women.[69]

The outpouring of works by contemporary Black women writers in the United States can be seen as an initial corrective to the male bias in African American literature. By focusing on different yet equally important themes permeating Black civil society, such writers illustrate complementarity and demonstrate solidarity with Black men.[70] For example, the anthropologist and novelist Zora Neale Hurston writes of Black life and culture; contact with Whites does not figure into her greatest work, *Their Eyes Were Watching God*. In contrast, Richard Wright, her contemporary, writes about interracial interaction, primarily among men. Hurston's work is affirmation; Wright's is protest. Both offer valid approaches to African American experience, for Black affirmation and protest against White domination can be seen as complementary parts of the same process. Yet one has traditionally been elevated above the other as superior. Reclaiming the ideas of Hurston and other Black women writers redresses these longstanding imbalances.[71]

At the same time, African American women writers' treatment of reproduction, sexuality, and motherhood definitely breaks with Black cultural nationalism's idealized gender ideology of men as warriors and women as nurturers. The works of Black women writers are revealing on this point, primarily because, unlike social scientists or historians, fiction writers encounter few requirements to depict reality and instead can explore its contested nature. For example, Alice Walker's fiction has long been criticized because, while it invokes traditional Black culture, it simultaneously refuses to valorize that culture's construction of gender. Like Walker, African American women writers increasingly eschew uniformly positive treatment of Black culture and instead situate themselves within the space created by Black nationalist discourse to rework some of the very themes of that discourse.[72]

Despite its appeal in reinforcing longstanding norms of racial solidarity, the hypothesis of gender complementary can be applied only to selected topics. Far more attention has been paid to positing areas of Black women's equality with Black men in an imagined ancient African past than on gender complementarity within either contemporary Black civil society in the United States or in contemporary African societies themselves. For example, in her popular volume *The Isis*

Papers: The Keys to the Colors, Frances Cress Welsing claims that the Black classical civilization of Kemet fostered a gender complementarity in which women and men were essentially equal. Her argument suggests that prior to European-installed institutionalized racism, Africans in Kemet lived an idyllic life.[73] Ransby and Matthews disagree, claiming that "the great African past which we are told we need to recreate is also a patriarchal past in which men and women knew their respective place. These unequal gender roles are then redefined euphemistically as 'complementary' rather than relationships of subordination and domination."[74] Historical settings of African antiquity appear to be more amenable to this type of reinterpretation than contemporary African American civil society, in part because historical analyses of this nature cannot be easily disproved, and in part because applying similar arguments to contemporary conditions would generate a storm of protest. Reactions such as those of the historian E. Frances White, who notes that "the ideology of complementarity and collective family continues to work against the liberation of black women," would surely arise.[75] Given these caveats, locating complementarity in the distant past represents a wise decision.

In part in response to sustained Black feminist criticisms from Toni Cade Bambara through E. Frances White, more recent Afrocentric scholarship acknowledges the significance of gender but relegates it as secondary to the more pressing cause of fighting racism. Working within the assumptions of gender complementarity, scholars such as Asante, Linda Jane Myers, and Haki Madhubuti acknowledge differences in men's and women's experiences while minimizing the effects of gender oppression in the lives of both Black women and men.[76] Paying lip service to Black women enables gender as a major category of analysis to be ignored. For example, in *Kemet, Afrocentricity and Knowledge*, widely acknowledged as a central text in contemporary Afrocentrism, Asante advises his readers to incorporate gender as a principal cosmological issue in Afrocentric inquiry. Afrocentric researchers must be cognizant of "sexist language, terminology, and perspectives," counsels Asante, and should investigate the "historic impact and achievement of women within the African community."[77] Asante advises his readers to "examine the roles women have played in liberating Africans and others from oppression, resisting the imposition of sexist repression and subjugation, and exercising economic and political authority."[78] Asante's advice is especially odd, given that he makes little mention of gender in his own volume, despite his advice that it be taken seriously. Eschewing intersectional analyses of race, class, gender, and sexuality, this approach assumes that only Black women are affected by gender and sexuality; that Black women's political activism can be analyzed solely within the Black nationalist "race-as-family" framework; that sexism is something that exists outside the domestic sphere of the Black racial family; and that Black lesbian, gay, bisexual, and transgendered people are not authentically Black. As a result, gender has little explanatory power.

Including Black women worthies, incorporating material on Black women, and investigating Black women's experiences within assumptions of gender complementarity all expand the knowledge base about Black women. Given the sorry history of social-science scholarship on African Americans in general, and on Black women in particular, Afrocentric efforts, however flawed, can serve a purpose. Unfortunately, these correctives typically fail to challenge the gendered domain assumptions of Afrocentrism concerning culture, identity, solidarity, and service. They simultaneously reinforce notions of Black women as people who strangely escaped the full brunt of racism and for whom sexism is a minor problem. Within these constraints and in the absence of any sustained interest in intersectional analyses of race, class, gender, and sexuality, certain dimensions of Black women's experiences in the United States cannot be adequately addressed. Reconceptualizations of rape, violence, and the overarching structure of sexual politics; of Black women's political activism and resistance outside traditional family models; of the relationships between work and family for both Black women and Black men; of reproductive-rights issues such as sexuality, access to family planning services, and Black women's rights of choice; of homophobia and its impact on Black identity, families, and communities; and of how race, class, and gender interlock in framing Black women's poverty are all topics explored in Black feminist thought that are routinely neglected by those working exclusively within Afrocentric domain assumptions.[79]

Despite its contributions, Afrocentrism as critical social theory remains unable to address the inherently problematic stance toward gender that plagued the Black arts movement. The Black arts movement did contain the seeds for a quite different gender ideology. For example, the first groundbreaking book of contemporary Black feminist theory, Toni Cade Bambara's edited volume *The Black Woman* published in 1970, contains several essays by Black women whose feminist ideology developed in large part within the context of Black nationalist struggle.[80] Despite this resource, Afrocentric scholarship conveniently ignores these Black feminist analyses, choosing instead to incorporate a gender analysis resembling that of dominant social science and a gender politics that at times is indistinguishable from the "family-values" posture of conservative Republican politicians. It did not need to be this way, because the Black arts movement served as a catalyst not only for Afrocentrism but also for a Black feminist movement in the 1970s and 1980s.[81] Afrocentrism's failure to examine its own gendered ideology represents a profound missed opportunity.[82] Unfortunately, as a discourse following both Black cultural nationalism of the 1960s and 1970s and Black feminist analyses of the 1970s and 1980s, contemporary Afrocentrism seems to have taken only one to heart.

How Oppositional Is Afrocentrism?

In the context of the new racism, the very existence of Afrocentrism as an avowedly antiracist project speaks to its oppositional intent. As its treatment of gender illustrates, because Afrocentrism's guiding principles have been formed largely within the domain assumptions of a science it opposes, it remains limited as critical social theory. Unfortunately, for African Americans in search of antiracist critical social theory grounded in lived Black experience, Black nationalist projects such as Afrocentrism often appear to be the only game in town. Afrocentrism seems increasingly effective in attracting those segments of Black civil society who, for a variety of reasons, see little hope that racial integration can solve economic and social injustices. Given the racial polarization in the United States, Afrocentrism's reliance on Black essentialism may not be as misplaced as a *political* strategy, as some Black public intellectuals believe. Afrocentric discourse that treats Blackness as a free-floating, ahistorical Black essence expressed differently at different historical moments provides continuity with the past and gives members of communities so constructed an identity and purpose that provides guidance for the future.

In a context where Black nationalist ideas may be used for Black Americans' ethnic mobilization, criticisms that Afrocentrism remains riddled with troublesome essentialist thinking that harms both women and men, especially when advanced by Black intellectuals with minimal current contact with racial segregation may fall on deaf ears. Afrocentrism may be limited as critical social theory, yet its strong pro–Black posture, combined with its masculinist thrust, may also contribute to its popularity among many African Americans. The Nation of Islam, a competing Black nationalist project, has long recognized the effectiveness of us–them binary thinking as a strategy for mobilizing African Americans. Few of the estimated 800,000 Black men and their female supporters who attended the 1995 Million Man March in Washington, D.C., expressed concern about Black essentialism and its purported suppression of differences among Black people. They were there as a show of unity. If all Black academics in the United States tried to organize a rally of that magnitude, how many African Americans would attend? Moreover, in a climate where hate speech escalates and racial violence targeted toward African Americans gains strength from the resurgence of scientific racism resurrected by the far right, essentialist thinking continues to enjoy widespread success in mobilizing large numbers of Whites in defense of White privilege. In a situation like this—a situation in which, for example, thirty-two Southern Black churches in the United States experienced arson fires in an eighteen-month period preceding the 1996 presidential campaign—Black nationalism may be the best strategic defense against White essentialism. While intellectuals in academe deconstruct everything, including their own leftist politics, little remains on which to construct a new politics capable of responding to unemployment, police brutality, teen violence, adolescent childbearing, AIDS, and other social issues of pressing concern to African Americans.

Black people in the United States need critical social theory that provides leadership and hope in the face of these troublesome conditions. In this sense, Afrocentrism's distinctive and fundamental contribution may be one that, as yet, other theories cannot match. Cornel West suggests that nihilism, or the feeling that life has no meaning, constitutes a new, fundamental threat to African American existence. West contends, "Nihilism is not overcome by arguments or analysis; it is tamed by love and care. Any disease of the soul must be conquered by a turning of one's soul. This turning is done by one's own affirmation of one's worth—an affirmation fueled by the concern of others. This is why a love ethic must be at the center of a politics of conversion."[83] West may have touched on why, despite its problematic treatment of gender, economic class, and sexuality, Afrocentrism remains important to both Black men and women. In a climate of institutionalized racism that valorizes Whiteness, Afrocentrism offers an affirmation of Blackness, a love ethic directed toward Black people. In this sense, it reaches out to everyday African American women and men in ways lost to even the best academic antiracist, feminist, Marxist, or postmodern social theories. While sociology provides knowledge and postmodernism stresses tools of critique, Afrocentrism offers hope.

Despite this essential contribution, current manifestations of Afrocentrism have been ineffective in both changing higher education and guiding Black political activism. Exclusivity in the name of nation-building eventually fails. Fear of dissent undermines the creativity that must lie at the heart of truthful, sustained, and meaningful struggle. A Black nationalist politics that remains analytically self-critical of its own ideas, practices, and practitioners could seriously engage questions of race, gender, economic class, nation and sexuality. By situating itself in dynamic, versus essentialist, definitions of Black culture, such a re-vitalized Black nationalism might manage to craft an elusive Black solidarity that is simultaneously sensitive to differences among Black people and prepared to engage in principled coalitions with Latinos, women, and other social movements for social justice. Until that day, domination is domination, no matter who is doing it. Any critical social theory that counsels African American women or any other group to be silent and step back in the name of an ill-defined unity hurts Black women, cheats African American communities of the best talent and leadership, and ultimately impoverishes us all.

III

Feminism, Nationalism, and African American Women

5 Why Collective Identity Politics Matter

*Feminism, Nationalism, and
Black Women's Community Work*

I used to think that if I could go North and tell people
about the plight of the black folk in the state of Mississippi, everything would be all right. But traveling
around, I found one thing for sure: it's up-South and
down-South, and it's no different.... We have a problem, folks.... I'm not hung up on this liberating myself
from the black man, I'm not going to try that thing. I got
a black husband, six feet three, two hundred and forty
pounds, with a 14 shoe, that I don't want to be liberated
from. But we are here to work side by side with this black
man in trying to bring liberation to all people.

—*Fannie Lou Hamer*

Occupying the same geographical terrain are both the
ghetto, where we are penned up in a concentration-camp
horror, and the community, wherein we enact daily rituals of group validation in a liberated zone—a global
condition throughout the African diaspora.

—*Toni Cade Bambara*

Generally, male crimes against women with whom they
are, or have been, intimate, are grouped together under
the term "domestic violence." Notice how the phrase
sounds somehow less horrible because of that word
"domestic" in it? Just the word "domestic" calls up images of lovely little homes, presided over by a strong,
generous dad and a smiling, well-organized mom. Things
that happen in such an environment might be a little
unpleasant from time to time, but that's about as bad as
it gets. The word violence tacked on the end seems almost benign.

—*Pearl Cleage*

ecause Fannie Lou Hamer, Toni Cade Bambara, and Pearl
Cleage worked tirelessly to address the needs of the Black
community, few would question their commitment to African
American freedom struggles.[1] Hamer's biography—that of a
prominent African American Southern Civil Rights activist in the
1960s—reveals a remarkable history of championing empowerment for
the dispossessed.[2] In 1970, Bambara served as the editor of *The Black
Woman*, a groundbreaking volume in Black women's studies. As a
self-proclaimed writer, "engaged artist," media activist, and "cultural
worker," Bambara spent her life working on behalf of the poor and
working-class neighborhoods of Philadelphia that bore the brunt of the
costs attached to globalization.[3] Cleage, an Atlanta playwright and
performance artist, cut her teeth on Black activist politics during the
Black Power Movement. Cleage is the daughter of the Reverend Albert
Cleage, a major figure in fusing Black nationalist politics with Christianity in Detroit. Her essays and fiction remain staunchly pro–Black.[4]

Are these African American women "feminists"? Does it really
matter what they call themselves? Seemingly endless debates about
classifying people into identity categories of who is "Black" and who is
not, who is "feminist" and who is not, and whether a "transsexual"
individual can join the women's tennis team sap energy from more
pressing concerns. These *personal* identity politics are certainly important to the individuals involved, but such disputes also obscure a
more fundamental *collective* identity politics that is essential to successful social movements.[5] One working definition of collective identity is "an individual's cognitive, moral, and emotional connection with
a broader community, category, practice, or institution. It is a perception of a shared status or relation, which may be imagined rather
than experienced directly, and it is distinct from personal identities,
although it may form part of personal identity."[6] Taking a closer look
at the kinds of collective identity politics that have influenced African
American women might shed light on the type of Black politics needed
to address adequately the issues confronting the hip-hop generation.[7]

Hamer, Bambara, and Cleage participate in a kind of community
work that grows from a collective Black identity that emphasizes the
needs of African American communities. Primarily because of this
participation and because all three perceive antiracist agendas in terms
that are broader than American race-relations frameworks, all three
women place varying degrees of emphasis on gender. Instead, their
perceptions of how gender oppression affects African American women

become filtered through the framework of "trying to bring liberation to all people" through the strategy of Black community development. For example, in her 1971 speech given at a NAACP Legal Defense Fund gathering, Fannie Lou Hamer refuses to separate African American women's issues from those of African American men. Instead, she perceives the dual themes of racism and social class exploitation in the "down-South" and the "up-South" as more significant in her personal life. For Mrs. Hamer, her personal experiences as a woman seem less important than analyzing the social issues facing African American women and men as a class or group. For Bambara, the Black community to which Mrs. Hamer is so committed contains the contradictions of violence and love—a juxtaposition of "ghetto" as a place of "concentration-camp horror," and "community" as a "liberated zone" where African American men and women can gain respite from racism and organize against it. Bambara sees the contradictions of Black communities where Black men can commit "crimes against women" and receive the type of love and loyalty from Black women engendered in Mrs. Hamer's statement, "I got a black husband, six feet three, two hundred and forty pounds, with a 14 shoe, that I don't want to be liberated from."

Cleage also wishes to "work side by side" with Black men to foster the liberation of all people. In her case, African American men's violence against African American women is an obstacle to fostering a Black community that acts as a "liberated zone" in confronting racism. More important, violence coupled with love harms African American women and should not be tolerated. The corpus of her work clearly identifies how violence in American society associated with intersecting oppressions of race, class, gender, sexuality, and nationalism frame Black community life, but her challenge to rethink the term "domestic" throws down the gauntlet for Black women and men to rethink the terms of "community." Just as violence against women can occur in "domestic" family spaces with little retribution, so can collective violence against Black women at the hands of Black men tear at the very fabric of Black neighborhoods and the organizations of Black civil society.

The history of residential racial segregation that has plagued African Americans more than any other racial/ethnic group meant that Black women such as Hamer, Bambara, and Cleage engaged in an array of activities known as *community work*. As a form of reproductive labor, community work was designed to (1) ensure the physical survival of

African American children; (2) build Black identities that would protect African Americans from the attacks of White supremacy; (3)
uphold viable African American families, organizations, and other institutions of Black civil society; and (4) transform schools, job settings,
government agencies, and other important social institutions to ensure fair and equal Black participation.[8] Prior to the 1960s and 1970s,
African American women's community work lay at the heart of African
American politics. Empowering African Americans meant "trying to
bring liberation to all people." Working to change institutional practices such as segregated schools, biased election procedures, racial
steering in housing, and discriminatory employment policies was seen
as the path to personal dignity and individual freedom for African
American men and women, and constituted one important dimension
of Black women's politics. At the same time, Black women also worked
to develop African American communities by working collaboratively
with Black men, by pointing out the internal contradictions of violence and love within Black civil society, and by speaking out against
violence against Black women and other similar social problems.
Black women's community work aimed to foster group survival. Thus,
Black women's political activism was expressed by working both for
institutional transformation and for group survival within a larger
framework of collective struggles for social justice.[9]

Since the 1960s and 1970s, the changing contours of African American communities and of social movement politics have raised new
challenges for the type of collective identity politics upheld by Hamer,
Bambara, and Cleage. This chapter takes a closer look at the relationship between collective identity politics of Black women's community work, how it has changed in the period from Black power to hip
hop, and how it might be revitalized by synthesizing ideas gleaned from
both feminism and nationalism. Just as the actual contours of African
American communities have undergone substantial change, so have the
contours of Black women's community work.

The Changing Contours of
Black Women's Community Work

Within the rights-based, individualistic assumptions of Western feminism, Mrs. Hamer's statement, "I'm not hung up on this liberating
myself from the black man, I'm not going to try that thing," seemingly
lacks feminist consciousness and demonstrates political naiveté.[10] Yet

Mrs. Hamer was far from naive, and her politics might be better understood within the context of Black women's community work. As mothers, wives, and churchwomen, African American women such as Mrs. Hamer have long assumed responsibility for maintaining Black community institutions that shield Black children from and prepare them for the poor treatment afforded Black people in America. Black women participated in community development activities on behalf of future generations, just as prior generations had labored for them. Historically, many women approached their families, churches, and communities as important and valued members of Black civil society. As illustrated by the case of African American churchwomen, when challenged by their churches, many women respond, "If it wasn't for the women, you wouldn't have a church."[11]

Whether in the South or the North, growing up under racial segregation meant that African American women such as Hamer, Bambara, and Cleage came to political struggle *both* as unique individuals *and* as members of a historically constituted, oppressed racial group. Prior to the racial desegregation that gathered momentum after the passage of civil-rights legislation in the 1960s, it was virtually impossible for African American individuals to grow up without knowing that they were Black and what that meant in America. Historical legacies of *group*-based oppression such as slavery, colonialism, and racial segregation stimulated *group*-based collective identity politics crucial to struggles against racism. For example, in her study of African American political life in the transition from slavery to freedom, the historian Elsa Barkley Brown examines the distinctive dynamics of this orientation toward racial-group membership in Richmond, Virginia:

> An understanding of collective autonomy was the basis on which African Americans reconstructed families, developed communal institutions, constructed schools and engaged in formal politics after emancipation. The participation of women and children in the external and internal political arenas was part of a larger political worldview of ex-slaves and free men and women, a worldview fundamentally shaped by an understanding that freedom, in reality, would accrue to each of them individually only when it was acquired by all of them collectively.[12]

During the Jim Crow era, social policies of legal racial segregation left African Americans far more segregated within American society than any other group. This racial segregation in turn shaped Black women's political activism.

Under segregation, Black solidarity was a vital element of African American politics. In social conditions where racial violence targeted toward Black women and men was routinely interwoven into all aspects of American society, Black solidarity was not a luxury. It was essential.[13] Sticking together and remaining unified often meant the difference between survival and death. In this context, fostering Black unity emerged as both a fundamental goal of Black political activism and a strategy for achieving other Black objectives. This ethos of Black solidarity also served to protect Black individuals from continual assaults by White supremacist images and ideologies on their identities as Black people. In a climate that routinely portrayed African American women as sexually available servants; Black men as violent, criminal rapists; and African American children as miniature versions of their parents, Black American community institutions worked to shield their members from these negative representations. Families, churches, and other institutions provided buffers against routine negative stereotyping within news media, school curricula, movies, books, television, advertisements, and public transcripts of government and industry.[14] As a way of preserving their individual human dignity, Black children of both genders were encouraged not to take racism "personally." At the same time, a syncretic cultural value system from the African diaspora fostered a collective "I," a sense of Black solidarity needed to both preserve traditions and offer a united front in response to White-supremacist treatment.[15]

This deep-seated belief in the importance of Black solidarity also fostered a parallel emphasis on structural versus individual remedies for African American disenfranchisement and poverty. The goal of Black American politics may have been gaining the rights of first-class citizenship, in particular the protections and privileges afforded individual White citizens, but Black solidarity and collective action seemed to be the best way to achieve that objective. Under conditions of racial apartheid, Black solidarity represented a reasonable and effective response to the institutionalized racism operating within housing, education, employment, health, and public access. Such racism was targeted not toward African American *individuals* but toward people of African descent as a *group*. Without changes in rules, laws, practices, and customs that routinely discriminated against African Americans as a group, little space for Black individualism existed outside African American communities. An entirely different story often existed within Black communities, especially Black urban neighborhoods. There, Black individuality and style flourished.

Under racial segregation, African American women's community work consisted of activities to combat racism and empower their communities to survive, grow, and advance in a hostile society. Some organizations, such as fraternities and sororities, the Black independent schools movement, and Black churches, focused inward and targeted Black community-development efforts in education, cultural activities, and community-based social services. Other organizations, such as the NAACP and the Urban League, assumed an external focus by challenging institutional policies that discriminated against African Americans. African American women also founded Black female-run organizations—for example, the National Council of Negro Women—that allowed them to exert a distinctive form of leadership as "race women."[16] Historically, African Americans infused the term "race" with deeper meaning signifying cultural identity and heritage, not biological inferiority. The historian Evelyn Brooks Higginbotham refers to this as "the power of race to mean nation—specifically, race as the sign of perceived kinship ties between blacks in Africa and throughout the diaspora."[17] In this context, working for the "race" via community work had nationalistic implications that transcended individual concerns.

Black women's community work was a constant reminder of the centrality of social justice for the Black freedom struggle. Social justice traditions emerged not solely from abstract theology but from concrete political action. The historian Darlene Clark Hine describes how this tradition operated for Sojourner Truth and Harriet Tubman: "For both Truth and Tubman, freedom, and the unrelenting quest for freedom, was the mainstay of their identities. Their passionate embrace of freedom was born not of some abstract commitment to the Constitution or the noble sentiments embodied in the Declaration of Independence, but out of the reality of their enslavement and oppression. They knew firsthand what it meant to be owned by another, to be considered little more than a cow or a mule. . . . Slavery, and resistance to it, were the defining moment of the birth of black women's oppositional consciousness."[18]

When it came to racial equality, this belief in social justice also worked closely with the theology of Black Christian churches.[19] When joined to an organizational base provided by Black churches, African American women were able to find both institutional support for and tap an ethical tradition grounded in a broad view of social justice.[20] African American women's importance within Black churches as fundamental organizations of Black civil society provided an important arena for Black women's political activism as well as their consciousness concerning the political. This moral, ethical tradition, especially as expressed via institutional carriers of Black Christian churches, provided another context in which African American women were encouraged to relinquish their so-called special interests as women for the greater good of the overarching community. Within this interpretive framework, fighting on behalf of freedom and social justice for the entire Black community and for a more inclusive society based on social justice was in effect fighting for one's own personal freedom. The two could not be easily separated.

Grounded in these social-justice traditions, Black women community workers routinely advanced more complex political agendas *within* the contours of Black solidarity than is commonly realized. But as scholarship on African American women as political activists indicates, Black women's feminist/womanist activities occurred within all types of organizations.[21] For example, to this day the Universal Negro Improvement Association (UNIA), led by Marcus Garvey in the 1920s, remains one of the largest Black organizations ever developed in the United States. Amy Jacques Garvey, wife of Marcus Garvey, not only participated in shaping the organization through her influential newspaper column, but she actually ran the organization in Marcus Garvey's absence. Especially striking in Amy Garvey's ideological analyses is the fundamental connection she makes between nationalist and women's liberation movements. Despite Garvey's claim that her primary dedication was to Black liberation, she believed that Black women represented the backbone of Black nationalist struggle.[22] Subsequent Black women's activism has reflected this template of working for women's issues as part of a broader social-justice project within the context of Black community struggles—for example, the leadership strategies of Black women in the 1950s Civil Rights Movement.[23] Moreover, African American women were not merely participants in Black political struggle. They often performed important albeit unrecognized leadership functions.[24] In all, as was the case of Amy Jacques Garvey, African American women approached women's issues through a pre-existing network of organizations already positioned to work for social change in the area of race. As a result, expressions of Black feminism emerged within these organizational structures and reflected these concerns.

Within Black churches and other organizations of Black civil society, African American women expressed a more comprehensive commitment to social justice than that initially advanced within Western feminism.[25] In contrast to the model of organizing first around personal advocacy for one's own interests, a model that assumes the rights of first-class citizenship, Black women often first became involved in community work on behalf of others. A personal incident with racism may have catalyzed their involvement—for example, being treated badly by their child's teacher—yet concern for a specific loved one in their lives, most often their children, sustained long-term commitment.[26] African American women have seen their fathers and sons lynched, lost their children to guns and drugs, cared for their adolescent daughters' children, and visited their brothers in jail. The personal suffering of their loved ones continues to function as a powerful catalyst for action. One outcome of this mode of entry is that African American women typically developed a sensibility for women's issues by broadening pre-existing analyses concerning racism and social-class exploitation to include the additional oppression of gender. Working for social justice for a particular loved one often stimulated a heightened consciousness about the effects of oppression on African American people as a group.

Then and now, Black women's motherwork often emerges as a powerful catalyst for their activism that simultaneously politicizes them and serves as the primary location for their activism. Motherwork consists of a cluster of activities that encompass women's unpaid and paid reproductive labor within families, communities, kin networks, and informal and formal local economies. By going quietly about the business of refusing to accept what is expected of them and their children, Black women engage in community work that remains un-recognized. For example, after an evening talk that I gave at a college in Detroit, Michigan, with a high enrollment of female adult learners, one African American woman approached me to ask whether I planned to write some of the ideas in *Black Feminist Thought* in a format suitable for teenage girls. As we talked, she shared a bit of her life. Even though she worked in a full-time job, this mother had decided to return to school after her marriage dissolved. Her husband had left her with eight children. As she described it, her children wanted to know what she was learning in school, and when they asked, "What you reading, Mamma?" she stopped and read to them from her college assignments. When her two teenage daughters saw her reading *Black Feminist Thought*, they asked about it. She translated the ideas for them but wanted something similar that she could place directly into their hands. The actions taken by this mother are certainly exceptional, but the way she conceptual-ized her motherwork is not.

Like the African American mother in Detroit, some women choose to become "mothers of the community." Others find it thrust upon them. Seeing the racial and gender politics that confine their mother-work can catalyze Black women to take actions that they otherwise might not have considered. For example, when Mamie Till Bradley's fourteen-year-old son Emett Till was brutally murdered in Mississippi in the summer of 1955, Bradley found herself in the center of a national controversy. This thirty-three-year-old Chicago resident "wanted the whole world to see" what had happened to her son. Bradley certainly understood the various dimensions of motherwork. Her decision to send her son South most likely was stimulated by family circumstances and the challenges of raising an adolescent boy in urban Chicago. At the same time, her actions to help the "whole world to see" what had happened to her son clearly politicized her.[27] Sadly, in this case, her son could not directly benefit from his mother's actions on his behalf. Her politicized motherwork in this case occurred on behalf of the many other young African American men who faced challenges similar to that of her son.

Despite the fact that without Black solidarity there could be no effective freedom struggle, Black solidarity was neither inherently desirable nor effective. Armed with a social-justice tradition that linked politics, ethics, and equality, for some women political work within Black organizations sensitized them to gender issues. For example, many African American women who worked in the Student Nonviolent Coordinating Committee (SNCC) during the Civil Rights Movement experienced a growth in feminist consciousness as a result of the organization's gender politics.[28] Other African American women used a male-run church to advocate women's issues, whereas others came to question the interpretations of Christian scripture preached by their ministers on the rightful place of women.[29] Thus, Black women often encountered women's issues not in the context of feminist groups organized to raise their consciousness, but via daily interactions within organizations that formed the public sphere of African American communities.

Black Women's Community Work and the New Racism

In the decades since the 1970s, the need for Black women's community work has not lessened. In fact, if the status of African American children and youth is any indication, many African American communities are in crisis. Problems in housing, schools, poverty, jobs, and health still plague sizable segments of the African American population.[30] For many, the influx of drugs into Black urban neighborhoods in the 1980s turned once thriving Black working-class neighborhoods into the "concentration-camp horror" chillingly described by Bambara. Drugs, crime, and joblessness have eroded the very fabric of Black urban neighborhoods in Philadelphia, Baltimore, Detroit, Cleveland, Washington, D.C., and other cities with large African American populations.

The failures of local and national politics have been especially hard on Black youth in the hip-hop generation, a group that should have benefited from the struggles of the Civil Rights and Black Power movements, and a group of special concern for African American women. The punitive policies targeted at poor and working-class Black youth who are locked up in large urban ghettos with poor schools and no jobs, and who are targets of a growing prison-industrial complex, has been a special concern for their mothers, grandmothers, and community "other mothers." Despite a powerful mass media that simultaneously saturates the airwaves with images of successful Black individuals (the 1980s *Cosby Show*) and profiteers from Black poverty and anger by turning the music, fashion, and lifestyles of U.S. Black urban youth into commodities, Black women have recognized how difficult things have become for the majority of Black youth.[31] Many African American women also realize how basic changes in Black civil society that have accompanied middle-class Black migration from inner cities and the intensification of Black poverty within those same cities has eroded the Black institutional base for antiracist political struggle.[32]

In this context, important shifts in Black women's work and family experiences continue to erode the organizational bases for Black women's activism within African American neighborhoods. Several important factors now affect African American communities, which in turn influence the contemporary contours of Black women's community work. First, the geographic dispersal of some African Americans into desegregated neighborhoods has masked continued high levels of residential racial segregation overall, leaving many with the impression that many more Black people live integrated lives than actually do.[33] Second, African Americans have become far more heterogeneous regarding social class, as shown by a new and expanded Black middle class and a seemingly permanent poverty population. The increased visibility of both groups not only challenges longstanding notions that racism is the fundamental cause of Black disadvantage; it also renders increasingly invisible the much larger group of working-class Black Americans who are struggling to get by.[34] A third trend reflects this convergence of geographic change and social-class heterogeneity. Although there is recent evidence that this situation is lessening, African Americans living in poverty remain more concentrated in poor, racially segregated, inner-city neighborhoods than other groups.[35] With this concentration factor came a startling change in Black working-class community organization: The drug industry and crime, eroding family structures, poor employment prospects, gangs, and other social problems associated with blocked opportunity structures emerged with a vengeance in many African American inner-city neighborhoods.[36] Finally, family structures and gender relations among African Americans showed a significant shift under the new racism. Black women found themselves as single mothers, shouldering more financial responsibilities and unpaid family labor than ever before. In the general speed-up of American society, in which large numbers of women from all racial groups now work to make ends meet, Black women's workload increased.[37]

These changes greatly altered the types of neighborhoods in which African American women live and their ability to perform work on behalf of Black communities. In essence, as Black families, churches, grassroots organizations, and civil-rights organizations floundered in responding to a new racism that has left large concentrations of poor Black people in many large cities, Black women faced increased pressure to take up the slack with seemingly fewer resources to do so.[38] Overall, with the disappearance of self-contained African American neighborhoods that supported a variety of Black community organizations, the need to work longer hours and to take more time getting to jobs, the growing double day of being single parents, the dangers associated with living in impoverished communities, and the overall speed-up of the pace of everyday life all affect Black women's activism. Fewer Black women engage in community work in the way it traditionally was organized within class-homogeneous, racially segregated African American neighborhoods.

Given social changes of this magnitude, what types of Black women's community work can be carried out under these new political, geographic, ideological, and social conditions? Moreover, what are the implications of these changes for African American women who see gender as an important component of Black community development? African American women have shown a range of responses both to the norms of Black solidarity associated with racial segregation and to the legacy of Black women's community work that has accompanied them.

In many cases, the foundation provided by Black women's community work enabled African American women to continue traditional forms of Black women's political activism through their churches, as well as to attend college and move into broader arenas. For example, some Black women organized projects within African American communities that were specifically targeted toward African American women's special concerns—for example, the case of the National Black Women's Health Project.[39] Grounded in the religious ethos of Black civil society, other women used Black churches and religious organizations to raise issues of gender in Black communities. For example, Black women theologians and Black feminist thinkers have been at the forefront of bringing womanist ethics and practices into African American churches and have launched significant challenges to Black Christian teachings on gender and sexuality.[40] Others worked within Black grassroots organizations. For example, women helped organize the 1995 Million Man March, an event criticized by some as upholding Black patriarchy but seen by others as supporting the need to examine Black masculinity.[41] Still other African American women advocate the specific economic and political issues that affect segments of the Black American population but do so within multiracial, multiethnic alliances. Take for example, efforts to organize workfare workers as part of the union movement.[42] In this same tradition of "working for the liberation of all people," other Black women have formed class-specific alliances with women from other groups—for example, Black women's efforts to attain social-welfare benefits.[43] In essence, African American women may advance a kind of "everyday feminism" that is rarely labeled as such but that contains an important gendered agenda.[44] To engage the traditions of Black women's community work, specific actions need not occur primarily within the contours of actual African American neighborhoods or within Black nationalist–influenced organizations. At the same time, these very same communities remain places where the major tenets of Black women's activism remain most needed.

Feminism, Nationalism, and Black Women's Community Work

In *Further to Fly: Black Women and the Politics of Empowerment*, Sheila Radford-Hill contends that African American women's traditional politics of empowerment, the kind identified here as community work, have actually deteriorated since the emergence of modern Black feminism.

She claims that, "compared to our historical traditions, black women's empowerment—which I defined as black women's agency expressed through social and political action—had actually declined."[45] Seeing the myriad social problems that African American communities continue to face and recognizing the need for an incisive analysis of how gender oppression affects African American communities, Radford-Hill places little faith in feminism's ability to empower Black women. In this context, she suggests, "The challenge of black feminism is to connect black theories of gender oppression with a renewed grassroots activism that resurrects black cultural power to rebuild black communities."[46]

This is a serious challenge. If Radford-Hill is correct, not only has modern Black feminism *not* empowered African American women and girls, but the accolades given to Black feminism within American colleges and universities occurred during a period in which African American women as a collectivity were *losing* traditional sources of power. Several authors point to the gender problems that plague American communities. For example, basically supporting Radford-Hill's thesis, in *Gender Talk: The Struggle for Women's Equality in African American Communities*, Johnnetta Cole and Beverly Guy-Sheftall suggest that women's issues are still not granted the same importance as those of Black men within Black civil society. Similarly, in *Black Sexual Politics: African Americans, Gender, and the New Racism*, I explore how gendered structures of power continue to impede Black community development.[47] If Black feminism in fact has an impact on African Americans, what accounts for the sustained support for Black rap artists whose work is riddled with misogyny, the cavalier use of terms such as "bitches" and "hos" to refer to Black women in everyday speech, or the popularity of the term "wife beaters" to describe the sleeveless white T-shirts worn by young Black working-class men?

Answering these questions requires returning to the theme of collective identity politics to ask not whether collective identity politics should guide Black feminism but, rather, what kinds of collective identity politics are tenable and effective for contemporary Black feminism. In the 1990s, the notion of collective identity politics and the social movements that they can engender fell out of favor within academic arenas, a reflection both of postmodernist and poststructuralist analyses that so captured the attention of Western academics as well as the inability or unwillingness of academics and intellectuals to take on the increasingly conservative social policies that harmed African American youth. Black feminism became caught up in these politics and, as a result, found itself engaged in heated debates that concerned academics but not those of greatest concern to African American women. Given this situation, I suggest that we need to revitalize Black women's community work with an eye toward empowering Black women. Doing this requires recontextualizing Black women's community work generally and Black feminism in particular within a new framework of Black feminist nationalism/Black nationalist feminism.

Because dominant views of power and resistance typically ignore the significance of all women's work, community or otherwise, as a site for political analysis, Black women's behavior as political actors and agents, whether within or outside African American communities, is routinely ignored. Universalistic theories of power that use as the unit of analysis a raceless, genderless, and classless Western citizen erase the racism, sexism, class exploitation, heterosexism, and nationalism that make these theories of power possible. In contrast, both feminism and Black nationalism do view Black women as political actors as well as recognize the significance of Black women's labor. Yet despite the importance of community work for women of African descent, both in the United States and globally, neither Western feminism nor Black nationalism fully acknowledges the complexities that surround this type of women's reproductive labor. Because Western feminist and Black nationalist ideologies work within gender- and race-specific paradigms, respectively, both have partial perspectives on Black women's community work.

Western feminism criticizes the exploitation inherent in Black women's work and family experiences yet misreads the possible significance of community work for Black women's political activism. In particular, Western feminism provides an important critique of the Western nuclear family that uncovers how community work can be exploited within patriarchal assumptions concerning reproductive labor. Yet at the same time, its reliance on an individual-rights framework that counsels personal advocacy as the highest form of politics simultaneously fosters a misunderstanding and misreading of Black women's community work as part of a politics grounded in collective racial/ethnic identity. Black nationalism provides a similarly narrow understanding of community work, but for different reasons. Black nationalism's recognition of group solidarity as the basic unit of political action fosters a recognition of Black women's community work, especially Black women's contributions to the well-being of racial/ethnic groups. At the same time, Black nationalism's uncritical

acceptance of dominant family rhetoric supports a troublesome patriarchy and fosters an appropriation of Black women's labor that often
harms Black women. Overall, Western feminism provides a much
needed critique of the exploitative dimensions of Black women's
community work yet fails to recognize its empowering dimensions,
whereas Black nationalism acknowledges the power inherent in Black
women's community work yet simultaneously aims to place that power
under male stewardship and often male exploitation.

Western Feminist Interpretations of Black Women's Community Work

Western feminism has made important contributions in identifying the
gender oppression of women within the United States, Canada, Great
Britain, France, and other similarly advanced industrialized Western
societies.[48] Within Western feminism, claiming a new identity as
a woman allied in sisterhood with other women means engaging in
personal advocacy on one's own behalf to overturn the exploitative
dimensions of women's reproductive labor. Western feminists argue
that, despite a history of liberalism that promises equal protection for
individual citizens, gender oppression has given more rights to men,
primarily by relegating women to the devalued and seemingly private
sphere of the family. In family settings, women contribute unpaid labor
that benefits men and boys more than it does women themselves and
girls. In response to this liberal, Western form of patriarchy, women's
politics consists of challenging the seeming public–private binary that
distinguishes two spheres of society by capturing good jobs, voting,
running businesses, and enjoying the individual rights long held by
men. Once women gain their rights within the public sphere, they can
be assured of getting an education, pursuing careers commensurate
with their talent, choosing love partners without family intervention,
embracing religious practices without gaining consent of their families,
and moving about in public without restriction. Within the parameters
of Western feminism, the individual constitutes the primary unit of
political action and personal advocacy on one's own behalf constitutes
the highest form of politics.

Western feminist analyses of work and family have raised important issues concerning women's oppression within advanced industrial
societies and modern democracies of Western Europe and North
America. Western feminism quite rightly points out that the mother-
glorification that originated within the idealized, middle-class nuclear

family lies at the base of many social practices that subordinate all women in such societies. For example, keeping women out of the labor market altogether minimizes competition with men for good jobs, and paying women less than men for the same work disadvantages women who lack access to male income. Western feminists also point out that the attributes associated with motherhood, namely, an allegedly natural capacity for nurturing, emotionality, and willingness to take care of others, have been used to shunt women to lower paying jobs such as nursing, teaching and secretarial work in an expanding service sector.

Western feminism's critique of the nuclear family has made important contributions in challenging the seeming naturalness of family (as well as the related concept of community) as a foundational concept within the political systems of diverse societies.[49] Families constitute sites for the intergenerational transfer of wealth and poverty in ways that normalize social hierarchies of class, race, ethnicity and religion. The dynamics *within* families also serve to naturalize hierarchies of gender, age, and sexuality. In other words, it becomes natural for some groups to submit to the authority of others within family structures. In this sense, family members recognize their natural, hierarchical difference and tolerate one another across these differences.[50] In the United States, for example, women learn their subordinate roles within family structures in which male domination is naturalized and thereby normalized by the American family ideal. Overall, Western feminism's criticism of the family has also been crucial in spurring analyses of the idealized nuclear family as a template for inequalities of race, ethnicity, class, nation, and gender.[51]

Western feminism's critique of the family, and the feminism its critique seemingly supports, remain a sore point for African American women. For example, Cheryl Gilkes points out that, "where white feminists identified the family as a primary site of oppression, black women, in spite of the troubles that intrude on their family lives, do not."[52] Many Black women perceive Western feminism as being basically antifamily, an interpretation fueled by the Western media, and this perception constitutes one important reason that they reject it. Moreover, the perception that Western feminism is inherently anti-motherhood is especially problematic in that it misreads the significance of motherwork within Black women's community politics. Within an overarching global, transnational, political economy, all women encounter the norms and social practices associated with the forms that motherwork takes in their respective societies. Yet African

American women's history within intersecting systems of oppression of race, class, nation, gender, and sexuality in the United States has catalyzed recurring themes concerning family and motherhood.[53]

This resistance to Western feminist frameworks neither means that African American women are happy and satisfied with family dynamics nor that they lack a critique of the family or Black community politics. Rather, problems within families are not seen as *inherent* in families themselves primarily because African-influenced understandings of family and kin are not organized around the patriarchal structures of the Western nuclear family and because, in the wake of the attacks on Black families ushered in by the 1965 Moynihan report, *The Negro Family: The Case for National Action*, African Americans are suspicious of any perceived attacks on Black families.[54] Overall, the centrality of critiques of the family to Western feminism, coupled with a perceived insensitivity to Black women's family issues, leaves the impression that Western feminism is unable to understand Black women's community work, let alone see women's work in building communities as anything but a site of their oppression.

Western feminism's grounding in a liberalism that can foster an individualistic personal politics also does not sit well with the group-based traditions of people of African descent.[55] Western European feminism has been especially critical of nationalism as an ideology, with some strands castigating nationalism as inherently oppressive to women. Cast in broad brushstrokes, Western feminism positions itself in the camp of Western civic nationalism, with its assumptions of individual rights and the rational man. This framework has been juxtaposed to that of ethnic nationalism, where nationalism connotes a backward, less enlightened tribalism—family, tribe, and ethnic group writ large onto the larger template of nation.[56] Feminist critiques of the patriarchal family and of nations constructed from the building blocks of allegedly patriarchal nationalism constitute one important site of Western feminist theorizing about women's oppression. Thus, family, ethnicity, race, and nation were intertwined, and this nexus serves as an interdependent site of women's oppression. Given the history of National Socialism in Germany, of Italian fascism, the longstanding ethnic conflict in Northern Ireland that is ostensibly between Catholics and Protestants, and the more recent violence associated with "ethnic cleansing" in Bosnia and Eastern Europe in the 1990s, this antipathy on the part of Western European feminists to nationalisms of all sort seems justified.[57] The commitment to a liberal agenda that would grant women individual rights within this history of ethnic conflict or "nations within nations" represents one important pillar of women's empowerment.

Despite these good intentions, the reliance on an individual-rights framework of civic nationalism that views personal advocacy as the most significant form of women's political activism can foster a misreading of Black women's community work. This assumption works far better in societies where individual rights are legally protected than they do in societies that lack this history or where, as is the case in the United States, citizens do not receive equal protection under the law. Take, for example, the standard response to domestic violence within advanced Western societies. Women who are beaten by their husbands and partners are encouraged to go to shelters where they will be protected until they can start a new life. This strategy means that women must leave all of the relationships in their lives to gain freedom from violence. As feminist advocacy groups point out, even middle-class White women with the rights of first-class citizenship often have great difficulty leaving their husbands and partners. If deciding to leave is difficult for this group, it becomes even more difficult for women in societies where family and ethnic ties mandate group solidarity. Cleage's entreaty that the so-called domestic violence within African American communities be reclassified as "male crimes against women" and censured by the community stems from this ethos of trying to get the community to change so that Black women will not be forced to leave. Where would Black single mothers with children go in a society that still discriminates against them?

In this context, Black women's actions in everyday life typically are not categorized as resistance, activism, or political. Often called "maternal politics" within Western feminism and misunderstood within that framework, Black women's activism that is catalyzed by community work is often categorized as a lesser form of women's politics.[58] Take, for example, Julia Wells's perceptions of what she calls the "maternal politics" that she claims characterize both the South African women's anti-pass campaigns of the 1960s and the protests that began in 1979 when mothers of the Plaza de Mayo in Argentina demanded to know the whereabouts of their disappeared children. According to Wells, maternal politics refers to "political movements which are rooted in women's defense of their roles as mothers and protectors of their children."[59] Suggesting that such movements develop because many women view their maternal roles as the driving force behind public political actions, Wells then distinguishes between "maternal politics" and "feminism":

> Maternal politics are clearly not to be confused with feminism. Women swept up in mother-centered movements are not fighting for their own personal rights as women but for their custodial rights as mothers. Since concepts of the sanctity of motherhood are so deeply entrenched in the social fabric of most societies, this strategy often proves effective where other attempts to generate social change fail. So potent has been the traditional discourse on motherhood that husbands, families, and government officials all tend to acknowledge and respect the heartrending claims of mothers, giving women an unusual amount of political space in which to organize. Significant allies are easily won over, strengthening the political clout of such movements. Nevertheless, these movements must be recognized as limited in scope, duration, and success in achieving their goals and, above all, should not be mistaken for political maturity.[60]

This type of thinking sets up a hierarchy of women's political activism whereby women's gender activism that fights for their "personal rights as women" constitutes a more authentic feminist politics than women's gender activism that occurs through community-development initiatives. Within this logic, forms of women's activism associated with mothering or with advocating on behalf of men seemingly lacks the "political maturity" of bona fide feminist activism. This type of thinking also assigns a secondary status to Black women's community work. Black women's community work becomes portrayed as a "politically immature" vehicle claimed by women who fail to accept the analysis of the family as the fundamental site of women's oppression or personal advocacy in one's own self-interest as a more mature form of politics.

Left unchallenged, these norms can obscure forms of Black women's politics that do exist. Much of Black women's political activism often remains unrecognized, and this lack of recognition leaves women unaware of their own political power. Since most discussions of politics assume self-interest as a motivation for participation, actions that derive from altruism or from a concern for collective good are rarely incorporated into contemporary political analyses. One study reports that Black and Puerto Rican women community workers in low-income neighborhoods were reluctant to identify their actions as "political."[61] As Nancy Naples points out, "Most of the workers did not define themselves a political people, feminists, radicals, or socialists. They simply believed that they were acting to protect their communities."[62] A similar study of a group of elderly Black women who ran co-op buildings in Harlem found that the activities of women in co-ops linked domestic life and cooperative organization. Leaders and tenants in successful co-ops likened their building to a family in which elderly Black women became leaders not only because of their special abilities but also because of their membership in longstanding social networks that they relied on for survival.[63] But because the women's behavior in both of these cases could not be coded within dominant norms of political self-interest, their actions were not defined as political activism.

Unfortunately, Black American women who reject Western feminism because it derogates their community work can also throw out ideas that might benefit them. For example, Black ministers, sons and daughters, grandchildren, and partners rarely think to ask whether the African American women who cook endless church diners, provide free baby-sitting for their grandchildren, give money to their unemployed children, and show up for low-paying, dead-end jobs are exploited. Certainly, many African American women pay a high price for their involvement in the lives of their own children and in those of the community's children—for example, the range of stress-related illnesses that afflict large numbers of Black women. The line between altruism and exploitation can be a fine one, indeed. For example, Pauline Terrelonge contends that a common view within African American communities is that African American women can handle abuse mainly because of their "fortitude, inner, wisdom, and sheer ability to survive."[64] Connected to this emphasis on Black women's strength is the related argument that African American women play such critical roles in keeping Black families together and in supporting Black men that a responsibility for the status of the race rests more heavily on Black women's shoulders than on those of Black men. These activities have been important in offsetting the potential annihilation of African Americans as a "race." As a result, "many blacks regard the role of uniting all blacks to be the primary duty of the black woman, one that should supersede all other roles that she might want to perform, and certainly one that is essentially incompatible with her own individual liberation."[65]

Terrolonge, Cleage, and others who describe the harm done to African American women by these expectations point out how adhering to Black solidarity at all costs can promote a paradigm of individual sacrifice that borders on exploitation. They suggest that frameworks of Black women's community work encourage African American women not only to see their own needs as simultaneously joined with those of Black families and communities, but also to view their needs as *always* secondary to this larger, more significant political struggle. Because issues identified as being women's issues are seen as always being less important than the greater needs of the Black community overall, speaking out about overtly feminist issues such as comparable worth, reproductive rights, and domestic-violence initiatives becomes difficult. African American women's resistance to personal advocacy can run so deep that many dismiss any political action labeled "feminist," even if it is in their own best interests. Persuaded to view personal advocacy as synonymous with being selfish, many Black women instead appear much more comfortable couching women's issues within the egalitarian, collectivist ideological framework of Black women's community work.[66] Yet if such work routinely exploits them, this is a selflessness that ultimately may harm them.

Black Nationalist Interpretations of Black Women's Community Work

Nationalism has risen in importance within global politics of the past fifty years. In particular, many anticolonial social movements that catalyzed new nation-states in Africa and Asia used nationalist ideologies as part of their struggles for political independence. The core themes of nationalist ideology—namely, the quest for self-definition, self-reliance, and self-determination—shaped a range of social movements that brought Black leaders to power over nation-states with large Black majorities.[67] Influenced by these trends, nationalist ideology also took root within the borders of the United States, Great Britain, France, and other advanced industrial societies whose labor needs fostered their growth as multiethnic, multiracial societies. For example, within U.S. society, participants in the Black Power Movement saw Black nationalism as a logical reaction to the deeply entrenched racial segregation that African Americans faced.[68]

For several reasons, the core ideas of Black nationalism appeal to African Americans of different social classes, genders, ages, and regions of the United States. As opposed to viewing African Americans as a minority group whose interests must always be framed in terms of broader social agendas that are endorsed by a larger and unsympathetic White public, Black nationalist projects unashamedly center their agendas on the self-defined interests of Black people. Sometimes these interests do match those of wider society, but often they do not. Also, as a political philosophy, Black nationalism reflects longstanding norms of Black solidarity that reflect the religious/spiritual ethos of lived

African American experience. Moreover, faced with the seeming failures of racial integration, Black nationalism often seems to be the only
game in town that explicitly focuses on poor and working-class African
Americans.[69]

It is important to remember that various forms of nationalism exist:
some progressive, others clearly reactionary, and most occupying a
position in between. Nationalist ideology can be used by groups on
both sides of state power to mobilize populations for specific political
agendas. For example, global politics at the turn of the twenty-first
century are quite different from those that framed post–World War II
anticolonial struggles, as well as Black Power and other social movements within the United States. We now know that many of the new
nations established via anticolonial struggles have recast their progressive nationalist ideologies into nationalisms that support reactionary state policies. One need only look at the troubled history of Haiti,
the first Black-run republic in the Western hemisphere and currently
one of the poorest nations in the world, to see that replacing White faces
with Black ones at the helm of government may not be the answer.

The fact remains that, when it comes to African Americans, other
people of color, and non–White immigrant populations in the United
States, American national identity functions as a form of unstated
"White nationalism." With Whiteness and the ability to speak standard
American English serving as the markers of first-class citizenship in the
American nation-state, being of the right biological stock (not of African descent) and possessing the values seemingly cherished by the
dominant culture (families organized around two-parent heterosexual
couples who speak standard American English) matter greatly.[70]

The fact that many African American women see value in Black nationalism does not mean that Black nationalism has been uniformly good
for Black American women. For example, influenced by the gender
politics of Black cultural nationalism, Afrocentric projects within
American higher education have routinely ignored women's issues and
have not taken gender and sexuality seriously as vital for Black community development.[71] Other expressions of Black cultural nationalism
have been empowering for African American women. For example,
Carolyn Rouse's important study *Engaged Surrender: African American
Women and Islam* documents how poor and working-class African
American women have built a Sunni Muslim community that supports
them in their troubled neighborhoods. These same women might have
placed all of their efforts in working for public-school reform or trying to

elect candidates to office. Yet they chose this Black nationalist-influenced path, drawing on religious beliefs as a core part of culture.[72] In this context, assessing how various expressions of Black nationalism have interpreted Black women's community work, as well as evaluating the broader issue of the gender politics of Black nationalism, are empirical questions, not definitional ones. Is patriarchy so prominent within Black nationalist politics that such politics are irreparably compromised? How have women been viewed within Black nationalist frameworks?

Black nationalism's recognition of group solidarity as the basic unit of political action stems from the persistence of racial segregation and of Black women's community work in confronting it. The theme of women of African descent as cultural workers reappears throughout the African diaspora where Black women thwarted European and White American efforts to eliminate African-derived cultural frameworks.[73] In the context of the internal and external racisms associated with the treatment of Black people in America, efforts to preserve Black identity and Black culture become highly significant.[74] Identity and culture can shield individuals against an everyday racism that is so routinized that it is often taken for granted by both Black and White Americans.[75] Yet its purpose is to destroy not just actions that resist, but the very ideas that might stimulate such resistance. Black women's actions as cultural workers thus become radical through the struggle to conserve Black group cultural traditions.

This theme of Black women as cultural workers is a more focused form of Black women's community work that upholds the significance of traditional culture within the nationalist projects of oppressed groups. Women have been central to a variety of nationalist projects on both sides of nation-state power. Many nationalist projects in the colonial world celebrated their traditional ethnic or religious cultures as a part of opposing European domination and saw women as significant in this cause. In the African diaspora, thinkers such as Amilcar Cabral and Frantz Fanon identified the significance of Black culture, a dynamic and changing entity that they saw as part of a complex network of social practices, ideas, and actions that were intertwined within political struggle.[76]

This view of Black women as *cultural workers* should be distinguished from the related idea of Black women as *culture bearers*. Over time, more political views of Black culture such as those expressed by Cabral and Fanon shifted to views of culture as a packet of rules and rituals that are replicated from one generation to the next, with great implications for women. Within this more conservative view of culture, the status of women serves as a marker of traditional culture.[77] In nationalist projects where colonialism subordinates Black populations but does not strive to suppress traditional cultures, women serve as symbols of the traditional culture that act as a base of resistance. Efforts to clothe women in traditional garb, keep them sheltered from the incursions of Western culture, have them remain at home to teach children the proper culture, and make them symbols of the nation exemplify using women as culture bearers. With views of culture as an ahistoric, unchanging packet of rituals and beliefs, women are expected to bear the culture by giving birth to it and nurturing it. This notion of women as culture bearers is one dimension of nationalism that is often criticized by feminists.[78]

The problems that Black cultural nationalism encountered in the United States concerned a misreading of the difference between Black women as culture bearers and as cultural workers. Afrocentric projects routinely aimed to turn women within African American nationalist projects into culture bearers of an imagined African past and a hoped for future.[79] Afrocentrists tried to construct a new Black identity to replace the one seemingly destroyed by American slavery. They created new national myths of the golden age of Africa where women and men enjoyed a gender complementarity that disappeared in the face of capitalism. These nationalist programs may have espoused gender complementarity for Black men and women in the past, yet when it came to contemporary gender relations, they remained wedded to patriarchal norms of the West. Such projects were unable to unpack the negative effects of gender ideology on their own political practice. For example, the glorification of middle-class White mothers as those who are best "fit" to become mothers of the nation defines such women as culture bearers for Western civilization itself.[80] When faced with this situation, Black cultural nationalists tried to put the women of their race on a similar yet equally confining pedestal. Thus, Afrocentric projects may have recognized the importance of Black women's community work to the Black freedom struggle, but their focus on interpreting Black women's actions as culture workers through the framework of Black women as culture bearers simultaneously fostered the gender exploitation of Black women.

Proponents of Black cultural nationalism may have understood the significance of Black solidarity and Black women's community work in sustaining it, yet as the culture-bearer argument suggests, their uncritical approval of the Western family ideal misunderstands and misuses Black women's community work. Just as fathers should be the natural heads of families, African American gender norms place the concerns of Black men above those of Black women. This unexamined gender hierarchy (which is naturalized by family rhetoric) fosters a gendered construction of racial victims that sees Black men as being more victimized by racism than Black women. As Devon Carbado points out, "As a result of this focus on Black men, without a similar focus on Black women, Black men are perceived to be *significantly* more vulnerable and *significantly* more 'endangered' than Black women."[81] The uncritical acceptance of these gender roles fosters a mother glorification that can subordinate Black women to Black men, all the while praising women for their submission.

These norms of Black solidarity that rely on an unexamined and therefore naturalized family language not only harm African American women. They also damage women's relationships with African American men, the relationships among Black men, and the relationships with Black lesbian, gay, bisexual, and transgendered (LGBT) people.[82] They also affect the very workings of Black women's political actions. Because African American women's political involvement routinely occurs within Black organizations, primarily church and religious communities, such organizations serve as the primary site for Black women's political engagement. In this context, Black women's community work garners recognition and praise because of its value for Black American survival, yet at the same time, if these same organizations uncritically accept prevailing norms of family and community, they too can foster the subordination of Black women who are single mothers, who are lesbian or bisexual, who are sex workers, who have criminal records, who are HIV positive, or who in some way violate the norms of Black respectability.[83] For example, when Black male leaders of churches and other community organizations remain so focused on saving Black manhood, they have difficulty seeing Black women as leaders and persist in viewing Black women primarily as supporters of Black men. This situation discourages women of African descent from identifying their own everyday actions as competent and important, if not indispensable, forms of political resistance and further obscures the significance of community work. As Gilkes points out, "White women have trouble seeing black women as agents of culture and community; black men do not want to admit that black women are effective agents of culture and community; black women themselves, knowing that their efficacy contradicts the dominant culture's expectations of women, often refuse to acknowledge openly their own ability to make a difference."[84]

Some Black women manage to avoid the selfless toil on behalf of Black community that refuses to acknowledge Black women's "ability to make a difference." Sounding like a contemporary Fannie Lou Hamer, the self-defined hip-hop feminist Joan Morgan puts forth a contemporary version of a humanist vision that has long characterized Black feminism. Responding to queries about her commitment to Black feminism, Morgan says:

> Since my sexual preference could not be of any relevance to you, whatcha really wanna know is how I feel about brothas. It's simple. I love black men like I love no other. And I'm not talking sex or aesthetics, I'm talking about loving y'all enough to be down for the drama—stomping anything that threatens your existence. Now only a fool loves that hard without asking the same in return. So yeah, I demand that black men fight sexism with the same passion they battle racism. I want you to annihilate anything that endangers sistas' welfare—including violence against women—because my survival walks hand in hand with yours.[85]

Morgan strikes a hard bargain: The much touted gender complementarity in Black communities is possible only if "black men fight sexism with the same passion they battle racism." Morgan is not alone in her criticism of these gendered norms within African American communities. Because Black women in the hip-hop generation are uniquely positioned to see the contradictions of a Black nationalism that relies so heavily on African American women's labor yet refuses to fight sexism, they challenge any norms of Black solidarity that are predicated on their subordination.

Morgan has been far from alone in her call for contemporary Black women to put down the mantle of the Strong Black Woman (SBW) that has long been associated with Black women's community work. Cleage's demand that African American men and women value Black women and girls foreshadows the increased willingness of African American women within the hip-hop generation to challenge "domestic" Black community practices that harm women and girls. Because they have been hurt by many of these practices, they can argue in their own behalf.[86] One visible example of this willingness to refuse to sacrifice Black women to the greater good of the Black community can be found in grassroots Black feminist work against rape and sexual violence.[87] For example, Aishah Simmons's feature film "*NO!*," which chronicles the problems of sexual assault within African American communities, breaks with Black community norms that Black women should not criticize the actions of Black men. Instead, this ground-breaking work creates needed space to debate the issue of how violence against women harms Black women and those who love them.[88]

Moreover, the emergence of a hip-hop feminism among women of the hip-hop generation uses the genres of hip-hop popular culture—namely, rap, autobiography, film, and magazines—to challenge misogynistic ideas and behaviors of their Black male counterparts and Black community norms. Alice Walker, Toni Morrison, and Ntozake Shange, among others, used Black women's fiction to raise issues of misogyny within African American communities. Queen Latifah, Salt-n-Pepa, Missy "Misdemeanor" Elliott, and other Black women artists raise similar issues within the terrain of popular culture. The public nature of their protest makes many Black women uncomfortable, but the choice of venue is understandable. Because young Black women are so maligned within Black popular culture, it stands to reason that young Black women and girls will defend themselves in this public arena. Ironically, their decision to become visible female players within rap, a genre that has been influenced by Black nationalist ideology, signals a feminist challenge to Black nationalist frameworks that say men should always be in charge.[89]

Black Women's Community Work and Feminist Nationalist Frameworks

The continuing refusal by many African American women and girls to engage in personal advocacy on their own behalf, even though they may face physical, sexual, and emotional violence, early motherhood, negative media images, and other significant problems that stem from gender oppression, stems from the absence of sustained debate of feminist ideas *within* African American communities. Cleage's work on violence against women may be popular in some mainstream feminist circles, but the real significance of her fiction is that she writes to African American women and men in the hope that they will rethink their ideas about gender and sexuality. Unlike the attention paid in the 1970s and 1980s to the serious fiction and essays of Alice Walker, Audre Lorde, Toni Morrison, Ntozake Shange, Paule Marshall, June Jordan, and other major Black women writers, the onslaught of visually oriented mass media, coupled with the poor quality of public education, makes it difficult for serious writers to reach African American audiences.[90] In this climate, mass-media images and messages such as those of women in rap music become even more significant.[91] Without such interventions, African American women and girls who reject feminism by claiming that it is for White women lack access to important critiques of prevailing gender politics.

Because African American communities remain so segregated, the vast majority of African American women and girls lack access to the types of educational experiences that give them access to feminism. Their work and family responsibilities make it very difficult to engage in grassroots political activism of any sort, especially multiracial feminist coalitions. In this context, Black nationalist-influenced traditions persist among African American women and men, often uncritically accepted, including the much criticized sexist dimensions of some strands of Black nationalism. In essence, the very constituencies most in need of dialogue concerning the issues they face as Black women have been shut out of debate. Farah Jasmine Griffin puts her finger on the problem: "Black feminists tended to retreat from the hostility and homophobia they often encountered when they tried to raise feminist concerns in all-black settings, be they black churches or cultural nationalist venues. Black women academics and critics continued to talk and to argue with white feminist and black male scholars, but they have not continued the dialogue among black women who shared different gender politics."[92] In this context, mass media becomes the default site for negotiating Black gender politics.

Currently, not only is it difficult to find social locations for these much-needed debates; it is also difficult to find interpretive paradigms that explain contemporary African American women's social and political realities. By themselves, Western feminist and Black nationalist perspectives hold partial perspectives on Black women's community work generally, and on Black feminist nationalism/Black nationalist feminism in particular. Positioning one group of activist Black women within the camp of feminism and another within the framework of Black community politics misreads the activism of both groups and mandates the impossibility of Black feminist nationalism/Black nationalist feminism. These seeming contradictions between feminism and nationalism erase the radical visions of women such as Hamer, Bambara, and Cleage, whose politics do not fit comfortably within the assumed binary of nationalism and feminism. In contrast, rather than viewing feminism primarily as a critique of nationalism, and vice versa, feminism and nationalism may reinforce each other.[93]

American insularity gets in the way of understanding these potential connections. Americans in general are woefully uninformed about the rest of the globe, and Black Americans are no exception. In this regard, African American women have much to learn from women who do not live in the United States. In the global context, the vast majority of women of color who are opposed to gender oppression see themselves not as unencumbered individuals, but as members of historically con- stituted families, communities, racial/ethnic groups, or religious groups. As African, Asian, and Latin American women, they participate in a third space—namely, that of *feminist nationalism*.[94] Because global space is segmented by race and class (rich White nations of the North juxtaposed to poor black and brown ones of the South), this feminism within nationalist spaces reappears transnationally: "Various types of feminist and nationalist movement activists on both a grassroots and elite level work today for the identification with their national group— be it based on shared history, culture (language, religion, ethnicity, styles, fashions, tastes), sense of place (the region), or kinship—while simultaneously fighting for what they define as the rights of women within their cultural contexts."[95] In essence, women of color are re- constructing meanings of both nationalism and feminism within cul- turally specific contexts produced within postcolonialism and racial desegregation.[96]

Rethinking Black American women's community work within a global feminist nationalist framework yields several potential bene- fits. First, interpreting African American women's community work through a framework of feminist nationalism not only counteracts this tendency to view feminism and nationalism as antithetical to each other, but it also creates space for needed dialogue among Black American women who are differently positioned within both areas. This tension between nationalism and feminism has long affected Black American feminism. For example, Toni Cade Bambara's 1970 an- thology *The Black Woman*, a founding text of modern Black feminism, was situated "at the nexus of two oppositional discourses—Black na- tionalism and feminism—both of which were profoundly limited by their failure to acknowledge sexism and racism respectively."[97] Nu- merous Black American women have spoken about the difficulty of choosing race or gender (nationalism or feminism) and about how these false choices hurt African American women. The critical race theorist

Kimberlé Crenshaw provides an especially compelling example of this conflict by showing how competing discourses of race and gender affected the outcome of the 1992 confirmation hearings of Supreme Court justice Clarence Thomas. In the hearing, narratives of lynching (race) and rape (gender) were presented in such a way that one left no room for the other. The losers were Black women whose experiences straddled both.[98]

In contrast to these views, I suggest that politically active African American women are located within a fluid and often contested border zone between mainstream Western feminism that advances a political agenda framed by ideas about the significance of individualism, class privilege, and claiming first-class citizenship rights, and a deeply entrenched (albeit typically unnamed Black nationalism) that continues to shape Black community politics grounded in respect for collective political action, class disadvantage, and an ethos of resisting being treated as second-class citizens because of racial identity. This border zone of Black nationalist feminism/Black feminist nationalism contains at least two groups of Black women who engage in different expressions of collective identity politics and who far too often perceive each other as being in separate camps. Together, these two groups might connect, in the words of Radford-Hill, "theories of gender oppression with a renewed grassroots activism that resurrects black cultural power to rebuild black communities."

One group consists of the self-identified Black feminists who populate the ranks of women of color within the hip-hop generation and who refuse to be silenced within contemporary Western feminism and Black nationalism. For example, the college-educated women in *Colonize This! Young Women of Color on Today's Feminism*, whose emerging collective-identity politics I describe elsewhere in this anthology, constitute women whose formal training in feminist theory and politics enables them to challenge Western feminism.[99] Women writers in so-called Third Wave Black Feminism also contribute to this new expression of a Black feminist nationalism/Black nationalist feminism. Lisa Jones's collection of essays in *Bulletproof Diva: Tales of Race, Sex, and Hair*, Joan Morgan's essays in *When Chickenheads Come Home to Roost: My Life as a Hip-Hop Feminist*, and Veronica Chambers's memoir *Mama's Girl* are all examples of writing that challenges the politics of Western feminism and Black community norms that have been the bedrock of Black nationalist agendas.[100] Black women whose venue is Black popular culture also are important in addressing the antifeminist trends of rap especially, and within hip-hop culture more generally. These are the female rappers whose disruptions of the misogynistic practices of rap are analyzed at length in Gwendolyn Pough's *Check It While I Wreck It: Black Womanhood, Hip-Hop Culture, and the Public Sphere*.[101]

The other group within this border zone of Black nationalist feminism/Black feminist nationalism consists of African American women concerned about racial oppression who engage in the type of Black women's community work described earlier. In some ways, there appears to be a generational divide between women who carry the burdens of reproductive labor and those in the hip-hop generation, because the visible spokespeople of each group are clearly in different generations. It is important to remember, however, that Black women activists of all ages can be found in both groups, whereas the issues and styles of activism of the hip-hop generation are primarily specific to their cohort. More important, each group holds an important piece of the puzzle for empowering Black women. Both negotiate a distinctive politics of race, gender, class, and sexuality that may be better understood through a framework of feminist nationalism/nationalist feminism than through feminism and nationalism in their current form. Moreover, both craft a collective Black identity politics that involves a gender-consciousness in that both care about the status of Black women and girls.

Placing diverse patterns of African American women's activism within the border zone of Black feminist nationalism/Black nationalist feminism in the United States, as well as within a broader, global framework of feminist nationalism, might accomplish several things. For one, it might create space for much needed dialogue among Black women activists, who often perceive themselves as standing on opposite sides of a generational divide, as well as alliances with other groups of racial ethnic women. African American women do not live in a vacuum. The issues that they face also confront other racial/ethnic women in the United States. Thus, recognizing the various forms that feminist nationalism can take among American women can start to put some political teeth into the term "women of color." Like Black American women, Chicanas, Puerto Rican women, and women from indigenous groups have similar yet distinctive histories of struggle in the United States that originate with the founding of the American nation-state itself.[102] Women from these diverse groups confront distinctive patterns of being viewed as culture bearers or cultural workers within their respective racial/ethnic group; as a result, their activism as women resembles that of African American women. For example, Chicana feminism has followed a path similar to that of Black feminism, with its focus on family and community tempered with the history of the effects of colonization rather than the legacy of slavery.[103] Some Native American women express a similar sensibility about what I describe here as feminist nationalism around issues of culture and territorial sovereignty. Take, for example, Maria Anna Jaines Guerrero's challenge to Western feminism: "Any feminism that does not address land rights, sovereignty, and the state's systematic erasure of the cultural practices of native peoples, or that defines native women's participation in these struggles as non-feminist, is limited in vision and exclusionary in practice."[104] Moreover, women of color from these groups have traditions of community work where they are expected to sacrifice for their families and communities. Class differences may mediate these histories, but the challenges that confront those who are non–White in America, as well as the social norms that accompany being part of racial/ethnic groups, do share a great deal.[105]

A second potential benefit of situating Black women's community work within global feminist nationalist frameworks concerns opportunities to link Black American women's politics with important trends in global feminism. Instead of viewing African American women's community work as the labor of a minority within a minority—the current treatment of African American women within the American race-relations framework—Black women's community work more accurately reflects similar struggles by women worldwide. The changing contours of women's community work across diverse societies suggests that the particular combination of capitalism, nation-state policies, cultural frameworks of dominant society, cultural frameworks within racial/ethnic groups, and the citizenship status of women and men produce similar yet diverse challenges for women and, by implication, for women's resistance.

Across diverse societies, many of the themes raised by women negotiating the contradictions of feminist nationalism resonate with those of African American women engaged in community work in New York, Detroit, Birmingham, and Oakland. Cultural differences of religion, language, and customs can mask the similarities between African American women and women who occupy similar structural positions in other societies, especially non–Western societies.[106] Cases in which the status of women within the racial/ethnic group is linked to the overall empowerment of the group itself resemble the social conditions that confront African American women in that women see themselves as cultural workers who are engaged in community work. For example, women's involvement in Palestinian nationalist struggles illustrates one specific history with feminism, nationalism, and a feminist nationalist political space. One would expect that a similar set of social conditions might catalyze comparable reactions among women. This seems to be the case. For example, young Palestinian women's participation in their national liberation struggle seemingly catalyzed a "feminist" consciousness. Like African American women, many Palestinian women activists refuse to be identified as "feminists," often giving the same reasons that African American women give—namely, the need to struggle in solidarity with men against a common enemy. Yet unlike Black American women, the Palestinian women's movement has aligned itself with international women's movements.[107] Unlike Western women, Black and White, Palestinian women and women in similar political, economic, and social contexts can tell the difference between a nationalism that oppresses and one with liberatory aspirations.

Successful nationalist movements that capture the power of the nation-state run the risk of installing conservative ideology about women as culture bearers at the center of the new nation-state's national identity. When backed by the power of religion and politicized within governmental policies, this version of nation-state organization can catalyze social policies that may appear to protect women but that may actually do more harm than good.[108] As a mature democracy that also found its roots in revolution, the United States rallies around an American national identity grounded in Whiteness and Christianity that reserves a special place for White women as the mothers of the nation. This ideology was a major factor in stimulating White women's rejection of domesticity and the women's movement that ensued. In a similar fashion, Muslim women's reactions to the growth of Islamic fundamentalism that captures state power (for example, in Iran and Afghanistan) may also catalyze a feminist nationalism that shows a commitment to protecting Islam, the nation-state, and women's equality within both. Drawing on the same overarching religious beliefs in Islam as Palestinian nationalism, women not only contest Western views of Muslim women as routinely downtrodden, they also resist notions of women as passive culture bearers who need not to be educated and whose interests should be subordinated to those of the men of the group. The Iranian feminist Haideh Moghissi captures these contradictions when she challenges the widespread use of the treatment of women under Islam in the Western media as an example of Islamic backwardness by developing a more nuanced analysis of feminism within Islamic societies. At the same time, Moghissi refuses to become an apologist for Islamic fundamentalism. Her text, written at the intersection of feminism and nationalism, provides a provocative view of the negotiations between these systems of thought. It also provides a model for the type of criticism internal to racial/ethnic communities.[109]

Feminist nationalist frameworks applied to the specific issue of understanding the African diaspora also shed light on African American women's political activism (or seeming lack thereof), this time within the more specific antiracist, transnational context. Here the experiences that link women of African descent provide another important piece of how Black American women's community work might be reinterpreted. When it comes to issues of work, family, and economic status, women of African descent throughout the African diaspora have much in common. For example, the attacks on the social-welfare state within domestic American politics, which have had a negative effect on poor African American women and their children, resemble the structural-adjustment policies backed by U.S. foreign policy that have had similar effects on women in Africa and the Caribbean.[110] These structural changes in turn affect the contours of Black women's politics. For example, in her study of women in West African societies, Filomina Chioma Steady describes a process of losing traditional sources of community power under Westernization that bears strong resemblance to Sheila Radford-Hill's thesis that African American women have become less empowered under conditions of racial desegregation. As opposed to seeing Westernization as inherently good for women because it brings stronger individual rights, Steady posits that African-derived models of strong, resilient women-centered networks can also be eroded by urbanization and its effects on traditional ways of life. In her discussion of women and collective action, Steady suggests that in the African context, "female models" of organization provide a base for mobilization and women's solidarity. In her work on female secret societies among the Sande people of West Africa, for example, Steady found that some traditional female sanctions were far more effective in controlling male aggression than modern law enforcement. Women complained to Steady that traditional forms of women's collective action better controlled domestic violence—in rural areas, censure consisted of tying a violator's hands and feet and letting him roll down a rocky hill. This was no longer possible in urban areas. Because they have been disrupted by Western interventions and misunderstood in the West, the effectiveness of practices such as these have declined.[111]

This focus on the African diaspora can also shed light on structural similarities that shape African American women's community work and that of women of African descent across different nation-state configurations. Patterns of Black women's activism within South Africa reflect the differences within South African society as well as the common struggle that Black South Africans pursued for a protracted freedom struggle. Black women in post-apartheid South Africa (1994) confront issues of nation-state development, a lingering racial ideology of White supremacy, and a social structure with many Black female-headed households.[112] Black South African women not only face the loss of traditional power; they also are part of a growing global urban population in which Black women as single mothers bear a heavy responsibility for child care. Sindiwe Magona's novel *Mother to Mother*, a fictionalized account of the actual tragic event of the murder of a young White woman who went to South Africa to help rebuild its society, describes women's work in South African townships where women have to work and leave their children unsupervised. Using the format of "mother to mother," in which the mother of a young Black man accused of the murder speaks to the mother of the young White woman who has been killed, Magona refuses to individualize the struggle of the Black mother. Instead, we see how the violence that permeates the nation itself unfolds through this personal tragedy.[113] This is Bambara's notion of how a community that is "penned up in a concentration-camp horror" engenders the seemingly irrational violence of this murder, as well as the more familiar, familial domestic violence.

Black British feminists demonstrate yet another pattern of how "Black" women negotiate the contradictions of nationalism and feminism, this time within the boundaries of a democratic, advanced industrial nation-state with a policy of embracing multiculturalism. Immigrant populations from former British colonies in the Caribbean, continental Africa, Pakistan, and India, craft new racial/ethnic identities as minorities within Great Britain, even though they were majorities within their postcolonial nation-states. Resembling the creation of a new collective identity around the term "women of color," the first task for Black British women was to craft this as a feminist political identity.[114] Julia Sudbury's important empirical study of Black British feminist organizations in the 1980s examines notions of race that go beyond the static racial authenticity models that have characterized African American scholarship and politics. Black British women also did community work, but they did so with a much greater acceptance of feminist sensibilities. At the same time, the issue of sexuality, and of lesbianism in particular, operated as a major stumbling block for organizational effectiveness.[115] In *The Family*, the Nigerian novelist Buchi Emecheta describes the trials of Gwendolyn, a young Jamaican migrant, and how she negotiated issues of family and motherhood. Despite the similarities of work and family, the "Black" British women were first- and second-generation immigrants, a status that differs from that of populations with long histories of internal racism within a nation-state. The racial/ethnic community closest to that of African American women may not be immigrant women of color, but the Irish population, the "Blacks" of Great Britain whose history has been described as one of internal colonialism. The specific form that Irish feminism has taken in this political context provides an important piece of feminist nationalism that might inform the political activism of African American women.

The contemporary Brazilian context provides another example of how working for community can expand into more formal political activism—this time, a feminist nationalist space within a more established democracy that contains elements of many other places. Brazil illustrates the problems of citizenship rights in a nation-state that has a large Black population, that continues to discriminate against people of African descent, but that seemingly celebrates an official policy of racial democracy. The autobiography of the Black Brazilian political official Benedito da Silva provides a textbook case of how community work can provide the foundation for political development. Da Silva's decision to help change her *favela* (inner-city neighborhood) by running for office catalyzed a political activism that embraced feminism, nationalism, and anticapitalist class politics. Not only does da Silva examine the contradictions of being a dark-skinned Black woman in a country that seemingly does not recognize race, but her autobiography maps the path from community work to community activism to more formal politics.[116]

In the face of persistent racial segregation, substantive structural change for African American women can occur only by revitalizing traditions of Black women's community work in a context that is cognizant of the mass-media environment that affects young Black women and girls. African American women political activists in the border zone of Black nationalist feminism/Black feminist nationalism have not yet found a way to infuse this global feminist nationalist sensibility into a revitalized Black women's collective identity politics that in turn might catalyze effective political responses to the new racism.

When it comes to Black women's political resistance, where you stand, what you can see from that vantage point, and what you stand for matter greatly. Versions of the political put forward by any group can offer only a partial perspective on definitions of feminism, nationalism, or any form of Black women's politics. No matter how significant any view may be, elevating one version of women's political activism over other forms and declaring it to be the "best" or most "authentic" approach redefines a partial perspective as a universal truth. More complex conceptualizations of political activism that combine ideas about individualism, personal dignity, and citizenship rights with conceptions of social justice that take into account group-based, historically specific experiences require new models of doing intellectual and political work. In this sense, Fannie Lou Hamer's ideas of social justice for the group; the connections among struggles against multiple, intersecting oppressions; and the significance of empowering individual women and men in the context of their everyday lives provides a beacon for such an analysis. Mrs. Hamer insisted on working for social justice for all people who were disenfranchised. As she once observed, "Whether you have a Ph.D., D.D., or no D., we're in this bag together."[117]

6 Is the Personal Still Political?

The Women's Movement, Feminism, and Black Women in the Hip-Hop Generation

> White girls don't call their men "brothers" and that
> made their struggle enviably simpler than mine. Racism
> and the will to survive it create a sense of intra-racial
> loyalty that makes it impossible for black women to turn
> our backs on black men—even in their ugliest and most
> sexist moments. I needed a feminism that would allow us
> to continue loving ourselves and the brothers who hurt
> us without letting race loyalty buy us early tombstones.
>
> —*Joan Morgan*

In her much discussed book of essays *When Chickenheads Come Home to Roost: My Life as a Hip-Hop Feminist* (1999), Joan Morgan claims feminism but wants a feminism that will allow Black women "to continue loving ourselves and the brothers who hurt us without letting race loyalty buy us early tombstones." In this quest, Morgan lays bare the contradictions that confront not only African American women but those in racial/ethnic groups whose histories have been shaped by racial oppression. Quite simply, for Black women and other women of color, is there space for the fusion of feminism (loving ourselves) and nationalism (race loyalty) that Morgan asserts as crucial for the feminism that she needs? If so, how might this space be crafted within contemporary politics that have marked the end of the Black Power Movement and the explosive growth of hip hop?

Beyond the substance of these core questions, Morgan's book of personal essays is also significant because it is written for a nonacademic readership. In her choice of substance and style, Morgan joins a growing list of African American women in the hip-hop generation who bypass scholarly venues and other traditional outlets for feminist thought. Instead, they express their feminist politics through mass media and popular culture venues of hip-hop culture—namely, collections of personal essays, fiction, rap music, and spoken-word poetry.[1] Lisa Jones's collection of essays *Bulletproof Diva: Tales of Race, Sex, and Hair* (1994), Veronica Chambers's memoir *Mama's Girl* (1996), and Morgan's book constitute three key texts from African American women in the hip-hop generation. All three volumes deploy this format of personal essays or fiction for the masses as a way to examine Black women's relationships in a space of nationalist race loyalty and feminist self-love.[2]

One striking feature of the feminist politics expressed by African American women in the hip-hop generation who use these publishing venues seems to be a renewed focus on the "personal is political." Their version of both the "personal" and what constitutes the "political" resembles yet differs dramatically from that expressed by feminists of the 1960s and 1970s. In this sense, these women may be the most visible face of the contemporary U.S. women's movement. Despite mass-media predictions of its imminent demise, the modern U.S. women's movement as a social movement persists. The movement has, however, gone through several stages: that of mobilization (1960s and 1970s); decline (1970s and 1980s); abeyance (1980s–present); and, perhaps, another mobilization by women in the hip-hop generation (1990s–present).[3] In a similar fashion, the initial meaning of the feminist slogan "The Personal Is Political" has also undergone change, reflecting the needs and constraints of each stage of the modern women's movement. Ironically, the women's movement and the paths that it has taken since the 1960s and 1970s have left many African American women unfamiliar with its accomplishments and ideology. Yet Morgan, Jones, Chambers, and other racial/ethnic women in the hip-hop generation who do manage to find feminism increasingly carve out a space that simultaneously accepts and rejects the tenets of feminism and nationalism. Specifically, they may be transforming the core feminist ideology that the personal is political in response to the challenges that confront them.

The Women's Movement Mobilizes: "The Personal Is Political" within Feminist Politics

We believe that the purpose of male chauvinism is primarily to obtain psychological ego satisfaction, and that only secondarily does this manifest itself in economic

> relationships. . . . The political oppression of women has its own class dynamic; and that dynamic must be understood in terms previously called "non-political"— namely the politics of the ego.
>
> —*New York Radical Feminists (1969)*[4]

> The most general statement of our politics at the present time would be that we are actively committed to struggling against racial, sexual, heterosexual, and class oppression and see as our particular task the development of an integrated analysis and practice based upon the fact that the major systems of oppression are interlocking. The synthesis of these oppressions creates the conditions of our lives.
>
> —*Combahee River Collective (1982)*[5]

The views of the New York Radical Feminists and the Combahee River Collective reflect the analyses of two important women's collectives that are widely accepted as important within the modern women's movement during its second-wave mobilization. The structures of each group, as well as their embrace of identity politics as a powerful tool for women's empowerment, may have resembled each other, yet their perspectives on feminism differed dramatically. In their 1969 position paper "The Politics of the Ego: A Manifesto for New York Radical Feminists," members of the New York Radical Feminists locate women's oppression in an overarching structure of patriarchy. They identify the work of psychological extraction from patriarchal assumptions and practices as fundamental to women's political activism. Through their focus on the politics of the ego, they felt that understanding and challenging women's subordination to men in everyday life constituted political activism. In this endeavor, they advocated consciousness-raising within small groups as an important strategy for women's empowerment and embraced the slogan "The Personal Is Political" as emblematic of feminist politics.

During the same period of women's mobilization, African American women, especially those from the working class, expressed far less allegiance to feminism and to this particular feminist slogan. Self-described as a collective of Black feminists who had been meeting since 1974, the women in the Boston-based Combahee River Collective did not reject feminism but staked a different claim in it. Grounding their feminism within Black women's community work, the collective claimed that "contemporary black feminism is the outgrowth of countless generations of personal sacrifice, militancy, and work by our mothers and sisters."[6] They pointed out that racism remained such a pervasive force in the lives of Black women that it limited Black women's ability to "look more deeply into our own experiences and define those things that make our lives what they are and our oppression specific to us."[7] They clearly saw their work as expanding the feminist principle that the personal is political. The collective unapologetically argued that working on their own behalf was not disloyal to the "race"; nor did it indicate that they had sold out to White feminists. Instead, they claimed, "We realize that the only people who care enough about us to work consistently for our liberation is us."[8] The collective's members declared that identity politics constituted the most valid form of politics for them because the most radical politics came from working on their own behalf from their positions honed at interlocking oppressions that so constrained their lives.

During this period of mobilization, the New York Radical Feminists, the Combahee River Collective, and similar groups that connected the personal experiences of women to a broader system of male domination made invaluable contributions in heightening awareness of women's oppression. Initially, radical feminist groups who argued that their personal experiences as women were not just personal problems but, instead, had broader political implications, adopted the slogan "The Personal Is Political."[9] The slogan is most often associated with consciousness-raising, a technique of intensive, group-based discussions about their experiences as women. The overall strategy of consciousness-raising was to (1) heighten individual women's awareness of gender oppression in their lives; and (2) organize this group of individuals into a collectivity that would jointly design and implement action strategies that resisted women's oppression. Consciousness-raising aimed to help individual women see the links between their personal experiences with male domination and larger structures of patriarchy. Thus, consciousness-raising created group consciousness about common problems.[10]

Outsiders often considered consciousness-raising among women therapy, yet women involved in consciousness-raising activities insisted that their activities emphasized building theory, not finding personal solutions to personal problems. Moreover, these early consciousness-raising sessions were not seen as precursors to political action. They were political action. As Carol Hanisch points out, "These analytic sessions are a form of political action. It is at this point a political action to tell it like it is, to say what I really believe about my life instead of what I've always been told to say."[11] Conceiving of consciousness-raising for women as political in and of itself, Hanisch also discusses how personal issues are political: "One of the first things we discover in these groups is that personal problems are political problems. There are no personal solutions at this time. There is only collective action for a collective solution."[12] The British feminists Liz Stanley and Sue Wise take a similar position: "The radical feminist understanding of feminist theory is that 'the personal' truly is the political, and that there is both a direct and necessary relationship between theory and practice. 'The revolution' is within each and every one of us and it will come about—and is coming about—as a result of many 'small revolutions', many small changes in relationships, behaviours, attitudes and experiences."[13]

The strategy may have been the same, yet it readily became apparent that the actual women in consciousness-raising groups often brought vastly different personal problems to group meetings. Because White middle-class American college students who cut their teeth in leftist politics predominated in early feminist groups, the issues that they raised reflected the standpoint of this group. Despite the homogeneity of this recognized group of founders, it would be a mistake to underestimate the significance of consciousness-raising by seeing it as a strategy embraced solely by middle-class, White American women or by radical lesbian feminists. Grassroots groups from this period typically left few records, yet racial/ethnic and working-class women also found a compelling argument in the idea that women's personal lives had larger social meaning and that the everyday could serve as a crucial place for feminist politics. Several Black feminist groups emerged during this period, among them the Third World Women's Alliance, the Black Women's Liberation Group of Mount Vernon/New Rochelle, the National Black Feminist Organization, the National Alliance of Black Feminists, Black Women Organized for Action, and the Combahee River Collective.[14] Because these groups were influenced by the broader ideas of feminist mobilization, their agendas and operating styles drew on a similar personal politics.

The National Black Feminist Organization (NBFO) was one of the best-known Black feminist organizations. Although its tenure was short lived (1973–75), it launched a frontal assault on sexism and racism. In its statement of purpose, the NBFO criticized practices of stereotyping Black women, treating Black men's issues as more important than those that faced Black women, and negatively viewing Black women's accomplishments. The NBFO was equally feminist in criticizing practices within Black community politics. It cautioned that African American communities needed to cultivate Black female leadership and stop using Black women for domestic duties. The organization aimed to raise the consciousness of African American women concerning these issues and their needs and rights. To do this, they pledged to work on specific issues, such as child-care centers, unemployment, job training, domestic workers' rights, addiction, abortion rights, welfare rights, and health care. As it did for the National Organization of Women (NOW), consciousness-raising constituted the NBFO's principal organizing tool.[15]

Black feminists may have used similar tools of consciousness-raising, but the issues that they talked about were quite different. When asked about the content of Black women's consciousness-raising groups, Brenda Eichelberger, chairperson of the NBFO's Chicago chapter, identifies a list of topics that grew from Black women's social location within interlocking systems of oppression. For example, Eichelberger points out that African American women were troubled by the "Black man–White woman phenomenon" in which Black men dated and married White women when there were so few Black men to begin with. She also identifies the politics of appearance, especially the effects of skin color and hair texture on Black women's self-images and how others treated them, as prominent in Black women's consciousness-raising groups. Black women in consciousness-raising groups brought up other themes that were important to them—for example, the greater mobility of White women in job settings, the lack of housing, the prevalence of rape and crime in Black communities, the burdens of the matriarchy thesis, and the myths of Black women's promiscuity.[16]

The demise of avowedly Black feminist national organizations with distinctive Black women's agendas did not mean that their impact disappeared. The NBFO, for example, catalyzed the creation of at least two important Black feminist organizations that outlasted it. In Chicago, the National Alliance of Black Feminists (NABF) survived until 1979. In the Boston–Cambridge area, the Combahee River Collective struck out on its own, in part because of the NBFO's stance on sexuality. Black Women Organized for Action (BWOA), organized in the San Francisco Bay area in the 1970s, had connections both to the NBFO and to NOW. Collectively, these groups took Black feminism into African American communities and broadened feminism's base by establishing rape-crisis centers and battered women's shelters.[17]

The limitations of consciousness-raising lay less in the technique itself than in other factors. For one, when compared with the heady period of women's mobilization, the conservative backlash against the entire women's movement that came to fruition during the twelve years of the Reagan and Bush administrations (1980–92) sent the women's movement into decline or abeyance. The use of violence by a growing antiabortion movement in the United States exemplifies this process. During this period, the broad-based reproductive-rights movement initially advanced by the women's movement became stigmatized by media images of selfish, careerist feminists who wanted the personal freedom (and lack of personal accountability) to have abortions on demand. Feminists involved in struggles to address a broad array of reproductive-rights issues found their time and energy sapped by the overarching issue of protecting women's right to choose. For another, the race and class segregation of neighborhoods, churches, and schools within American society divided women, limiting the degree to which individual women could generalize their personal issues to the larger population of women. Consciousness-raising groups had difficulty transcending the limitations of the homogeneity of their members' personal experiences because they also lacked access to groups that differed from themselves (for example, between groups such as the New York Radical Feminists and the Combahee River Collective). Because early consciousness-raising groups run by middle-class White women failed directly to address how race and social-class relations fostered their homogeneity, little impetus existed within such groups to arrange dialogues among groups or examine the assumptions about their own group that militated against diversity.[18] As is the case today, deeply entrenched racial segregation coupled with social-class stratification that divided the American population into homogeneous groups militated against developing a broad-based movement that fostered a collective identity for women that encompassed diverse groups.[19]

The Women's Movement in Decline and Abeyance: The Changing Contours of the Personal and the Political

Despite these pressures, the women's movement neither prevailed nor disappeared. Instead, it moved into a period of decline or abeyance that simultaneously ensured continuity of the movement and created the conditions for future mobilization. During periods of abeyance, values, identity, and political vision can be sustained through internal structures that permit organizations to maintain a small, committed core of activists and focus on internally oriented activities.[20] It is important to note that the version of politics suggested by "The Personal Is Political" constitutes one important emphasis within the U.S. women's movement. Women's political activism took many forms in the 1970s and 1980s that have been expressed via a wide range of ideological perspectives and activist agendas.[21] Groups that stressed the importance of advancing women's rights within political and economic structures—for example, the liberal feminism of NOW—constituted another emphasis within the U.S. women's movement.

Despite considerable heterogeneity within the women's movement, some forms of women's political activism came to prevail as emblematic of *feminist* political activism whereas others either languished as lesser forms of women's politics or lacked recognition as feminist politics at all. In the face of the decline of visible women's mobilization, and in an increasingly conservative social context, the slogan "The Personal Is Political" became increasingly symbolic of *feminist* political activism.[22] A hierarchy of what counts as feminist political activism now exists, with forms of women's activism that more closely approximate the actions of the New York Radical Feminists and, secondarily, those of the Combahee River Collective, deemed more authentically "feminist" than activism that takes other forms. Within an often unstated hierarchy of women's political activism, the actions of women whose ideology or actions reflect the personal politics suggested by the personal as political find it easier to claim the mantle of "feminist" than women who advocate on behalf of children, men, racial/ethnic groups, or social issues. Moreover, the slogan "The Personal Is Political" remained visible, yet the identity politics associated with it, the kind described by the Combahee River Collective, changed dramatically. Despite the heterogeneity that continued to characterize the women's movement, even in abeyance, the personal politics associated with a narrow understanding of the personal as political developed an enduring quality that began to eclipse its competitors.

Several factors influenced this situation. First, the apparent successes of liberal feminism in gaining basic political rights for American women diverted attention from the political economy as a fundamental site of women's oppression. As a result of liberal feminism's mobilization, women gained much needed rights in the United States. Legislation that prohibited sexual harassment, employment discrimination, and housing discrimination against mothers, coupled with reproductive-rights guarantees and affirmative-action policies, helped define the state as a champion of women's rights instead of as a source of women's oppression. Women who chose not to identify their political activism as explicitly feminist often spearheaded these actions. For example, in the early 1970s women lobbyists tried to work within the system and emphasized women's rights rather than women's liberation. Responding to the sexism and injustice in organizations in which they already volunteered or worked, their actions combined their professional work with activism on behalf of women. Overwhelmingly White and middle class, these women were interested in "building power—their own as well as that of the movement—through establishment channels."[23]

By the 1980s, this "unobtrusive mobilization" of women within higher education, foundations, social services, the media, the professions, the armed forces, churches, and other core institutions of American society garnered considerable success as a strategy during a period of movement abeyance.[24] But because many women's rights advocates avoided using the term "feminist," in part to escape the stigma attached to the term, their actions typically were not seen as feminist political activism but, rather, as a more palatable women's political activism. By stigmatizing the term "feminism," mass media facilitated this process. In describing feminist images in the media, Deborah Rhode points out that media coverage "encourages individuals to believe that they can meet all challenges individually—by choosing the right attire, the right degree of assertiveness, the right time-management skills, and so forth. In this journalistic universe, feminism's aspirations to equality are widely shared, but its call for collective action is widely ignored."[25] Ironically, the legislative successes and political sophistication of these career feminists in extracting institutional gains apparently left many U.S. women feeling that women's equality had been achieved. If the American media is to be believed, by the 1990s most American women thought they had arrived, with some women launching a backlash against a feminism that was seen as dated, strident, and out of touch with contemporary issues. Liberal feminism's success in gaining women's rights ironically undercut the broader feminist movement.

The prominence of a feminism organized around personal politics as compared with a feminism highlighting political and economic arguments endured for a second reason. Within American civil society, conservative Republicans prevailed in diverting attention away from structural causes of social inequality and toward personal failure as the cause of social problems. In this context, the status of women who were not doing well—namely, single women heading families; women working in low-paid, dead-end jobs; women on welfare; and racial/ethnic women—was increasingly explained not as a feminist issue but as caused by their flawed values and bad personal decisions. The behavior of individual women, especially in relation to the seeming failures of the American family, gained increased scrutiny. For example, when former Vice President Dan Quayle used the term "family values" near the end of a speech at a political fundraiser in 1992, he apparently touched a national nerve. Following Quayle's speech, close to three hundred articles using the term "family values" in their titles appeared in the popular press. Despite the range of political perspectives expressed on family values, one thing remained clear: Family values, however defined, were vital for America's future, and women were central in upholding or destroying traditional family values. The family values debate thus constituted a touchstone, a phrase that apparently tapped much deeper feelings about the significance of ideas about both family and values to an increasingly conservative American public.

In this political climate, the malleability of the slogan "The Personal Is Political" (as well as the actual slippage in meaning tilting toward the conservative) meant that it could be reformulated to mean that personal sources of social change should take precedent over structural versions. The notion of the personal as political resembled existing ideological structures of American individualism, personal efficacy, individual talent, hard work, and moral and cultural values as defining features of economic success and political power. Psychological models of explaining not only social inequality but also social phenomena of all types remain more compatible with deep-seated values permeating American social institutions. In contrast to structural interpretations that stress political power and capitalist development, personal attributes such as intelligence, motivation, moral training, and family background have long dominated American explanations for social inequality.[26] From this perspective, social problems are best remedied not through collective action, but through individual initiative and ingenuity. What are essentially systemic social issues become relegated to the terrain of the psyche, where working on oneself becomes sufficient in addressing social problems. The element of the personal, especially if affiliated with an individualized notion of the political, thus resonates with U.S. cultural norms.

Socialist feminist thinkers proved to be no match for the convergence of the seeming success of liberal feminism in gaining women's rights, conservative forces that preached family values, and shifting messages of personal responsibility that stigmatized individuals for their failures. Such thinkers criticized the effects of globalization and transnationalism on the status of women. Yet in the United States, they could neither organize or form coalitions of working-class and poor women who were adversely affected by capitalist development nor appeal to the largely middle-class leadership and student populations in American universities who benefited from the social-class system.[27] Socialist feminism in the United States faced several barriers. For one, since the 1950s individuals and social movements that espoused radical philosophies had been suppressed allegedly in response to the exigencies of Cold War politics. Because a large segment of the American population believed that socialism and communism were antithetical to American interests, they supported public policies that banned these ideas from public debate. This historical erasure impoverished American radicalism.[28] For another, the collapse of the Soviet bloc in 1990 and the demise of socialist states in the 1990s left socialism in disarray. Capitalism emerged as the global economic system, leaving socialist states as vestiges of an anachronistic past. For yet another, liberal feminism's success in gaining concessions from the U.S. nation-state ironically helped create a context in which more hard-hitting analyses of the economy seemed out of touch. Moreover, despite the fact that working-class women were politically active during this period, their activism typically was not identified as feminist. For example, even though the Southeast Women's Employment Coalition, a multiracial women's organization founded in 1979, addressed the economic disadvantage experienced by working-class women of all races, organizations such as this one continue to be seen primarily as class-based activism.[29]

Collectively, the social context made it increasingly difficult for the women's movement to see, let alone analyze, the eroding meaning of the personal as political within its practices. Internal debates about the meaning of personal politics took energy away from challenging broader structural forces and eventually fractured the movement into two camps. The tensions within mainstream feminism concerning sexuality, especially lesbian identity politics, illustrate these internal debates about two versions of personal politics, both of which had important implications for American feminism. Lesbians were an important part of the emergence of the women's movement during the period of mobilization. Lesbian identity politics constituted a natural extension of the personal politics that characterized the type of American radical feminism proposed by the New York Radical Feminists and the Combahee River Collective.

On the one hand, over time lesbians not only claimed a personal politics that politicized sexuality as an important category of identity, but lesbians became more openly identified as the visible representatives of feminism itself. Radical feminists by default became lesbians, and vice versa, and feminism, especially in the academy, became identified as advancing a lesbian agenda. On the other hand, this very same focus on sexuality coupled with the emergence of queer theory in the 1990s fostered a feminist politics organized around more fluid notions of identity that reintroduced ideas of individual choices of identities. The emergence of a renewed focus on plural sexualities, multiple genders, and socially constructed identities not only failed to challenge the market-based choice models of individual identity so celebrated in mainstream consumer culture, but they inadvertently supported conservative notions of personal politics. Moreover, they also fostered a new version of personal politics that ironically offered up critiques of lesbian identity politics. Thus, the feminism that became overly associated with one segment of the women's movement—namely, the consciousness-raising groups of radical feminism—became unsettled by internal critiques that saw lesbian, group-based politics as suppressing individual personal freedom. By the 1990s, radical feminists were redefined as radical lesbian feminists whose apparent radicalism was out of step with queer theory's allegedly transgressive behaviors. Moreover, all of this occurred under the watchful eye of an American public that had been coached to view both the women's movement and lesbian, gay, bisexual, and transgendered (LGBT) movements as being at best unnecessary, and at worst anti-American.

Queer theory did little to disrupt the growing emphasis on individualism within American culture, the assumed Whiteness of the individual subject and assumptions of citizenship rights that buttressed the new queer politics of transgression, not to mention old-fashioned racism and poverty. In describing the links between notions of the personal as political and the sexual politics that emerged in analyses of sexuality as a system of oppression, the British cultural critic Kobena Mercer observes that "sexual politics is narrowed down first to sexuality, then to the self. It strikes me that this 'self-centeredness' is a characteristic of white sexual politics, or rather it is an interpretation of 'the personal is political' which is made in a highly individualistic manner that tends to exclude questions of race because it is so preoccupied with 'self' at the expense of the 'social.' "[30] The new personal identity politics associated with queer theory reinforced the significance of individual voice and narrative, often at the expense of collective identity politics that have been so effective in bringing about social change.

Personal Politics and Women's Studies

The slogan that linked the personal with the political enabled activist women who embraced its increasingly conservative meanings to extract some much needed reforms from American social institutions. The notion of personal politics increasingly invoked norms of personal responsibility and individual programs for social change. This accounts for its appeal to bureaucracies whose mission is to work with individuals, not groups. But the success of this version of personal as political came at a price because it simultaneously laid the foundation for incorporating a less robust version of feminist politics into bureaucracies of the state, especially social-service–delivery agencies, and into academic bureaucracies, primarily through women's studies programs and women's studies scholarship.

The tension between invoking the original meaning of "The Personal Is Political" as emblematic of feminism while effectively negotiating the rules and regulations of social-service and academic bureaucracies remains a challenging issue for the U.S. women's movement. Identifying wife-battering, reproductive rights, sexual harassment, and rape as important issues emerging from consciousness-raising activities, many early feminist groups organized within their local communities to meet the needs of their members, friends, and families. These grassroots groups saw helping women through service delivery and pressuring appropriate state agencies as part of their mission. Over time, feminist groups spawned by the women's movement that developed into feminist organizations encountered a new set of challenges.

Their success led them to seek government funding and inclusion under the umbrella of government-supported social-service–delivery agencies. This incorporation not only included them within pre-existing social-service bureaucracies; it also changed the initial mission of many feminist grassroots organizations. The vast array of feminist organizations reflect varying responses to this basic dilemma of maintaining their position as social-movement organizations—illustrated here via consciousness-raising and the accompanying slogan of "The Personal Is Political"—as well as the benefits that accompanied being within mainstream, professional service organizations.[31] Case studies of feminist organizations reflect the contested nature of these relationships in battered women's shelters and rape-crisis centers.[32] Over time, many groups shifted their focus from empowering women to becoming social-service agencies that service the personal needs of women.[33]

The record remains mixed on how African American women and other women of color fared under the creation of these new bureaucratic services to women. On the one hand, many women of color with appropriate training and skills got jobs helping women. But, as some activist women of color point out, "the 'browning' of America has yet to serve as a wakeup call for feminist organizers."[34] More than thirty years after the feminist movement encountered charges of racism and elitism, the executive directors of women's organizations and their senior staffs are still overwhelmingly White. As the feminist activists Daisy Hernández and Pandora L. Leong point out, an increasingly professionalized nonprofit world that has internalized corporate expectations has deepened racial and class divides. Women who cannot afford to work for free remain marginalized and, in pursuit of mainstream acceptance, "organizations are losing touch with the grassroots that could revive feminism."[35]

Women's studies programs in American colleges and universities confronted the same pressures to shed their women's movement origins for an opportunity to bring women's issues into the academy, with similar results. In an intriguing article titled, "Academic Feminism against Itself," Robyn Wiegman takes on the question of how women's studies is faring within contemporary colleges and universities and how this placement in turn frames feminist scholarship. She describes the origins of academic feminism in the early 1970s as being "a renegade knowledge, one whose illegitimacy demonstrated the movement's central political claim concerning women's oppression and systematic exclusion."[36] When compared with its origins, by bureaucratic norms, contemporary women's studies is doing quite well. The expanding numbers of majors, the creation of doctoral programs, requirements within general education programs, and the growth of departments with tenure lines signals that academic feminism is no longer a "renegade knowledge." Yet Wiegman also points out that this seeming success has been accompanied by an "increasing uneasiness among many feminist scholars, sometimes overt despair, over the future of academic feminism."[37]

Interestingly, Wiegman's take on this seeming problem is to resist the impulse to try to "fix" the problem by striving to infuse academic feminism with a grassroots, social-movement ethos. Instead, she focuses on the challenges that confront academic feminism in positioning itself within academic debates concerning disciplinary and interdisciplinary knowledge production.[38] Academic feminism most certainly should *study* feminist social movements, but it cannot be the intellectual spearhead for feminist politics. Wiegman also points out that women's studies "has increasingly turned to a living subject as the methodological and epistemological center of its knowledge project. Whether in the language of standpoint theory or in the ethnographical register of witnessing and autobiography, whether linked to a cultural studies emphasis on the everyday or as part of an interpretive social analytic geared toward the authority of experience, the live subject is the most cited, most highly regarded form (and formula) for linking the real world to women's studies scholarship."[39] In other words, the personal politics within women's studies classrooms, one that is the legacy of the initial personal as political, has overshadowed other forms of knowledge creation and knowledge validation. This classroom-based personal politics is now emblematic of feminist scholarship, yet it should remain unconnected to collective social movements.

Claiming legitimacy as the repository for feminist theory, women's studies projects in the academy that fail to question these trends can easily shift from a discourse on patriarchy, domination, and women's oppression to an increasing emphasis on an apolitical difference. Advocating the significance of attending to difference, postmodern social theory eschews centers and unitary knowledge in favor of multiple knowledges and deconstructs groups of all types, including feminist ones.[40] Unfortunately, the type of "voice" developed in academic settings fostered a separation of theory from activism. The process of bringing women to voice and in incorporating many voices may bear surface resemblance to early grassroots feminist consciousness-raising, but endless conversations about difference in the rarefied climate of academe do little to unsettle the hegemonic power relations that bar working-class and racial/ethnic women from universities themselves.

The African American thinker Sheila Radford-Hill describes the contradictions of the severing of ideas and action, all the while retaining the illusion that they remained connected: "Much of the feminist thought from the mid-1980s through the early 1990s ... labored over precise explanations about whose perspective a work represented (for example, lesbians, Jews, Latinas, or queers) or whose point of view it was intended to express. This preoccupation with the connections between political identity and particular strands of feminist theorizing is more reflective of feminism's self-absorption with the politics of its own identity than of the identity and empowerment dilemmas of women as individuals or as members of social groups."[41]

The need to protect and develop academic feminism is a compelling argument, but I wonder what this rupture might mean for Black feminist thought. African American female scholars encounter similar pressures to sever Black feminist thought as an academic discourse from social movement politics of a nascent Black feminism and Black women's community work. Many Black academic women who saw how their work was being used within women's studies offerings reacted with alarm. Barbara Christian was one of the first Black scholars to identify how African American women's literature was increasingly recast as a set of texts in the "race for theory" within the academy. Christian bemoaned the fate of a literature that served as a legitimate voice for African American women's thought that had become reduced to texts for academic analysis.[42] How ironic—a room full of White girls writing papers on Toni Morrison's *Beloved* and wishing they had somebody whom they deemed to be authentically Black to talk to about it. Recognizing the costs of Black feminists' success, Farah Jasmine Griffith revisited Toni Cade Bambara's *The Black Woman: An Anthology* (1970) and observed, "At its inception black feminist thought (including fiction, literary criticism and theory, the social sciences, and polemics) claimed a relationship to political struggle."[43] Her essay provides a provocative analysis of why the rich debates within Black feminism that were published in Bambara's volume have largely disappeared. Unfortunately, Black feminist activists who uncritically accept the tenets of mainstream feminism and its agenda can fail to see the contradictions that have plagued feminism itself. Thus, the outpouring of essays, fiction, and other personal narratives that lack any sustained attention to social structures or to the struggles of African Americans illustrate how a Black feminism safely contained within the academy suffers from the same problems as mainstream feminism.[44]

At the same time, the attention paid to Black feminism in the academy and, more broadly, the version of personal identity politics within women's studies often overshadow other forms of women's political action that do not carry the imprimatur of feminism. For example, womanism as practiced by Black female theologians brings a needed critique and praxis to African American church communities, one important location within African American civil society where women constitute approximately 70 percent of church members. Because Black churches remain important sites for Black political opinion and for social activism, working within these institutions, as opposed to standing outside and criticizing their practices, constitutes an important dimension of Black women's political activism. Someone has to join the Black church to garner the credibility to change it from within. In this sense, using womanist philosophies (thus avoiding the troubled history associated with the term "feminist") enables African American women to build on yet challenge traditions of Black women's community work.[45]

These unresolved issues within Western feminism concerning who owns feminism and how that perceived ownership shapes the very definition of the term helps explain a recurring contradiction within African American women's politics. On the one hand, African American women consistently reject the term "feminism" and routinely claim that they do not support feminism.[46] Many African American women share Taigi Smith's view of the feminism that she studied in college:

> I declared myself a womanist when I realized that white women's feminism really didn't speak to my needs as the daughter of a black, single, domestic worker. I felt that, historically, white women were working hard to liberate themselves from housework and childcare, while women of color got stuck cleaning their kitchens and raising their babies. When I realized that feminism largely liberated white women at the economic and social expense of women of color, I knew I was fundamentally unable to call myself a feminist.[47]

Many Black American women openly reject feminism to the point at which they have been accused of fearing feminism and lacking political consciousness. At the same time, opinion polls indicate that African American women support issues that have long been central to a global feminist agenda—namely, access to good jobs and equal pay for doing them; policies against sexual and domestic violence; a comprehensive reproductive rights agenda that provides women with quality health-care services; equal schooling for girls and boys; adequate family policies, especially child care for working mothers; and strong social-welfare support for poor women, especially housing and public safety. How is it that African American women can embrace the ideas of a global women's movement yet reject the term "feminism" that seemingly catalyzed that very same agenda in the United States? What exactly is it about American or Western feminism that Black women seemingly reject?

Personal Identity Politics and Western Feminism: How Race, Class, and Nation Matter

Race, class, and nation matter in definitions of women's political activism generally and in American feminism itself. Political strategies that assume that the fundamental unit of political organizing consists of an *individual* with rights gain meaning primarily in a context of racial privilege and its accompanying notions of individuality situated in a social-class system that allows middle-class individuals both individuality and privacy. Within a context of possessive individualism, political rights become viewed as commodities that American citizens possess or own as individuals. When tied to a racial system that writes off large numbers of people who are seen not as individuals but as members of groups, this possessive individualism also fosters an irresponsible individualism. Because women in the United States all participate in the same society, but from vastly different social locations, these American values affect women's politics. In this context, race, class, and nation frame understandings of the personal, the political, and the place of both personal identity politics and collective identity politics in U.S. society.

As *individuals*, African American and White American women are remarkably diverse. Yet hierarchical power relations in the United States routinely sort individual women into racial and social class *groups* that in turn generate distinctive experiences for women as first-class, second-class, and non-citizens. For example, racial segregation of neighborhoods, schools, and occupations continues to foster separate and largely unequal opportunity structures for African American, Latina, working-class, and immigrant women and girls. Individual women may express divergent reactions to these structural constraints—for example, the difference between middle-class White women who buy into the status quo and who choose to become "race traitors." Yet few can erase different opportunity structures such as those of largely affluent and middle-class White suburban neighborhoods and their largely working-class Black and Latino inner-city counterparts by acting up and transgressing personal boundaries. Despite these differences, however, White and African American women have in common American citizenship, a shared assumption that erases questions of how belonging to the American body politic matters. Issues of citizenship are not absent; rather, they are refracted through a framework of first- and second-class citizenship, such that being White and middle-class garners first-class treatment whereas being Black and poor or working-class merits second-class status.

Racism is socially constructed in the United States by using racial classifications to allocate individuality to first-class class citizens and to deny it to second-class and non-citizens. Whites typically view themselves as being "raceless," yet they perceive Blacks, Latinos, and indigenous peoples as having a "race" or an ethnicity.[48] Whites and Blacks thus represent two ends of a racial continuum, with one end populated by un-raced White *individuals*, and the other occupied by an intensely raced Black *group*. Latinos, Asians, and racial/ethnic immigrant groups jockey for a place between these two poles, forced to position themselves between the social meanings attached to White and Black—in this case, the beneficial treatment afforded individuals and the discrimination and stigma attached to Blacks as a derogated racial group. Across these different racial formations, one commonality is that the closer one approaches Whiteness, the more likely one is to be seen as an individual and to be granted the rights of first-class citizenship. Racism as a system of power obscures its own workings in creating differential treatment based on race. Whether the historical practices associated with America's one-drop rule of classifying individuals as either White or Black, or the more fluid racial formations of Brazil, Puerto Rico, and other Latin American societies, or the still emerging American racial order in response to sizable Asian and Latino immigration, individual treatment is linked to group status.[49]

White privilege enables White Americans to avoid confronting how being members of a racial group generates the privileges they enjoy—in this case, individuality itself. In this context, White Americans are routinely encouraged to racialize social problems—for example, to attribute higher rates of joblessness and poverty and poor health that affect Black Americans to so-called racial characteristics of Black people. Using a dizzying array of biological and cultural arguments to explain African Americans' group conditions, they simultaneously fail to apply this same logic to their own situation of privilege. Instead, Whites routinely attribute their own success not to unfair advantage emanating from their group classification as Whites in a racial formation that privileges Whiteness, but to their *individual* attributes, such as ability, talent, motivation, self-discipline, and hard work. Within this logic of irresponsible individualism, they are not responsible for anyone but themselves. This is not a new argument. The erasure of Black individuality and the creation of Blacks as a racial group originated in the political economy of slavery that legally classified Black people as chattel and property, and not as human beings. What is new is the ability of Whiteness to continue to obscure its own workings in the context of the greatly changed social conditions of the new racism.

This ideology of irresponsible individualism has palpable effects on Black people and other oppressed groups that in turn influence feminist politics. Consider Siobhan Brooks's description of how acceptance of this belief system fostered normalized violence in the poor African American neighborhood in San Francisco where she was raised: "It was as if issues of abuse had nothing to do with us, that only white people were worthy of naming abuse. Suffering and systematic abuse in communities of color was so normalized. We often didn't even know we were oppressed. Some of us thought suffering was just a part of being Black."[50] Only White individuals have the benefits of claiming individual harm; members of historically oppressed groups should simply endure. Erica González Martinez offers another view of how American notions of individualism play out differently in Puerto Rican communities with a history of daughters who are expected to be dutiful community builders: "As a politically conscious, single woman, I have the internal critic as well as the external cultural judge evaluating whether I'm acting like a selfish, individualistic *gringa* or a community-building and respecting Latina."[51]

A feminist politics that fails to criticize the image of the "selfish, individualistic *gringa*" will remain limited in becoming a broad-based women's movement. Refusing to engage these issues of a racialized individualism confronts a collective identity politics of African American women who see how negotiating one at a time can yield very modest results for Black women as a group. This narrow view of feminist politics may be effective within assumptions of liberalism, but for those who historically have been denied the benefits of individuality, this stance can aggravate the pre-existing racial order. At the same time, Martinez is equally critical of what is now seen as the obverse of irresponsible individualism: the type of politics advanced by the "community-building and respecting Latina" who is encouraged to subordinate her needs as an individual to the perceived needs of the group. These two views of individuality need not be contradictory, yet they are often perceived that way.[52]

Race intersects with class to such a degree in the United States that race often stands as proxy for class. Yet social class also produces fundamental group-based differences that are often masked by the inordinate attention paid to racism. Classes represent bounded categories of the American population who have different interests growing from their positions within capitalism.[53] For example, affluent Americans have a vested interest in eliminating social-welfare programs that they see as supporting irresponsible people or upholding a bloated federal government that is riddled with waste (but not corruption). Globalization typically helps this population, in that lowering trade barriers and tariffs creates greater opportunities for investment. This population benefits from the mobility of capital. In contrast, working-class and poor Americans seek education, jobs, and basic human services. Lacking accumulated wealth as a cushion against capitalist marketplaces, they look to government institutions to protect them from the worst aspects of development. Globalization typically harms this population. Its jobs disappear and are moved to foreign nation-states. The tax bases that supported schools, created jobs, and provided basic human services shrink, leaving this population with high medical bills and no health insurance.

Just as the right to individualism accrues to those who are White, the right to privacy constitutes one class privilege associated with being middle class. Beliefs in the sanctity of private property reflected in the ability to purchase a home in the suburbs—fundamentally private space juxtaposed to the public space of public housing, public transportation, and public schools—allows middle-class families to enjoy the lack of intrusion by neighbors, colleagues, and government regulation. For members of the middle class, class privilege purchases privacy from state intervention in their nuclear-family households. Idealized family rhetoric projects middle-class homes as havens from the public sphere, places of nurturance where individual family members garner the support that enables them to contribute to the public sphere. Class privilege also procures protection of one's individuality in public space—namely, the use of police power to protect the interests of middle-class individuals who find themselves in contact with working-class people. Together, these connections between these notions of family privacy and the protection of the rights of middle-class individuals in public spaces foster a distinctive orientation toward individual rights. Grounded in the notion of the citizen as a human being who possesses individual rights, the assumption of individual rights remains fundamental to democratic politics.

In the United States, middle-class White women's location within this racial and social-class context explains how this group is treated within American public policy.[54] It also explains the initial saliency of the personal-as-political model for this group and why the absence of race and social-class analysis fostered an individualistic gender analysis within American feminism. As Barbara Ellen Smith points out, "Gender-specific strategies tend to be highly individualistic, in part because . . . gender in the United States does not create territorial communities of women."[55] Feminist analyses of the links between the personal and the political reflect this individualistic bias. Whiteness and middle-class privilege allegedly provided the freedom to be an individual in the privacy of one's home and protection as an individual within the public sphere, yet gender excluded middle-class White women from fully enjoying either of these privileges. Specifically, feminist analyses of the family critiquing male domination within the home did not view the private sphere of the home as a location for personal expression and freedom. White women's fathers and husbands prevented them from getting educations, aspiring to meaningful employment, and controlling their own reproductive capacities. Rather than being a location that fostered White women's individuality, the private sphere of the home came to symbolize the location suppressing individual rights of personal expression. Issues such as the rights-based discourse of reproductive choice grounded in the individual woman's rights to control her own body emerge from this interpretive context. Similarly, fear of rape limited safe access to the public sphere of the streets; sexual harassment retarded access to the workplace; and cultural representations of White women as fragile, weak, and dependent worked against the emergence of women's independence.

These individualistic aspirations to exert power and control within private and public spaces reflect the White middle-class privileges that accompany first-class citizenship—working-class, racial/ethnic, and immigrant women of color have been afforded much less privacy and individuality. For example, African American women struggled to maintain rights in both the private sphere of family life and dual public spheres of Black civil society and White-dominated governmental, employment, and social institutions. African American women thus stand in a different relationship to the social-class system and to these notions of family privacy and protection of those seen as individuals within public space. Like middle-class White American women, Black American women experience male domination in the home and harassment in the public sphere. But at the same time, distinctive views on individualism emerging from a comparable convergence of race and class fostered a different perspective for Black women, one eschewing individual approaches to social issues in favor of collective responses.[56]

These belief systems retard Black women's ability to develop a robust politics that is fully responsive to the needs of women who are not middle-class, White American citizens. Take, for example, Black women's need for a new Black sexual politics. The personal politics of feminism seen through the lens of irresponsible individualism and rights to privacy, coupled with the transgressive personal politics spurred by queer theory, leaves little space for a new Black body politics that would provide Black women with a degree of sexual autonomy and honest interpersonal relationships.[57] One important contribution of the increased attention to sexuality is the emergence of a rights-based body politics that argues that women have the right to control their own bodies, especially their sexuality and fertility. The difficulty lies in reconciling this rights-based body politics with the context in which it originated: a rights-based individualism where rights derive from individual property rights. Within this logic, bodies become property to be disposed of as one wishes. This language of ownership of one's own body reflects the language of property associated with American slavery and with historical patterns of viewing women and children through the lens of men's property. When combined with the seemingly unfettered individualism of transgressive queer politics, these personal politics do little to challenge the racism and social-class exploitation that so proscribes African American women's lives.

Overall, initial notions within Western feminism of the personal as a metaphor for more transgressive ideas about women's empowerment have given way to a version of personal politics that is increasingly narcissistic and amenable to annexation by conservative political forces in the United States. Moreover, notions of the political that initially focused on women's poverty as a window to class inequalities in the

United States have also evolved into demands to find a niche within pre-existing systems of class stratification. Black women's politics, as well as those confronting women from subordinate race, class, and ethnic groups, faces the same pressures.

Finding Feminism: Black Women in the Hip-Hop Generation

> I used to think I had missed my time. I thought the flame lighting the hearts of activists had been snuffed. . . . But liberating my definitions of activism from the constraints and constructs of the sixties opened up my mind to a whole new world of work and progressive thought. Now I draw strength from the knowledge that people have been actively combating sexism, racism and other intersecting oppressions for a long time. Many of those icons I respect are still on the scene actively doing their thing for us. That knowledge is my ammunition as I join with them and my peers to continue fighting those battles and the other fronts unique to our time. We can't get complacent. The most important thing we can do as a generation is to see our new positions as power and weapons to be used strategically in the struggle rather than as spoils of war.
>
> —*shani jamila*[58]

Born to the generation that came of age after the women's mobilization in the 1960s and 1970s, the hip-hop generation Black feminist shani jamila thought that she had missed her time. From what she saw, the "flame lighting the hearts of activists had been snuffed." But just as jamila came to see that the icons that she respected continued their political work, we now see that the women's movement did not fade away. Because the need for feminism certainly has not disappeared, jamila's search raises questions concerning the agendas and strategies of the U.S. women's movement. Is the women's movement entering a new phase of mobilization, one that requires active participation, if not leadership, from Black women in the hip-hop generation? How will the women's movement respond to challenges to its existing focus on individual rights to the exclusion of group-based social-justice projects, to its framework that treats rights as possessions that women own and control, and to conservative pressures to annex market-based notions of personal politics to conservative political agendas? Black women seemingly reject certain expressions of feminism, not because they disagree with the main ideas of feminism, but because they reject feminist principles as refracted through American relations of race, class, and nation. Moreover, when it comes to the feminist sensibilities of Black women in the hip-hop generation, is the personal still political?

Here I will focus on themes that I think address new forms of mobilization among African American women in the hip-hop generation, as well as how reformulations of the personal as political affect them. One theme concerns the process of how African American women and other racial/ethnic women find feminism in the first place. Women who attend colleges and universities with women's studies programs and who choose or find themselves in such classes are more likely to find feminism than women who lack education or whose lives are spent wholly within the confines of racial/ethnic communities. This path is significant because poor and working-class racial/ethnic women in the United States face barriers to attending college, let alone enrolling in women's studies courses. Access to today's feminism is rationed: It is no longer public. Instead, it is increasingly privatized.

African American women's first exposure to feminism may occur in women's studies classrooms, yet because many sense the prevailing contradictions between Black nationalism and Western feminism, they come to question classroom assumptions concerning what counts as feminism. Like other social movements in the United States, women's studies has reacted to pervasive pressures to reduce systemic, structural issues of oppression to the level of individual personal problems. Taming and safely containing feminist radicalism of the 1960s and 1970s within women's studies classrooms fosters attenuated notions of personal politics as emblematic of feminist political activism. Preoccupied with notions of the "self" at the expense of the "social," many classrooms as a result embrace an impoverished personal identity politics of simple storytelling that mimics the personal politics of wider American society, one where working on one's own personal problems *is* politics.

This situation whereby Black women's first exposure to feminism occurs within women's studies classrooms raises several questions. Can an academic feminism that lacks a link to a women's movement and that is hobbled by its position on race, class, and nation serve African American women and other racial/ethnic women beyond helping them explore their personal issues? Here the term "women of color" can obscure more than it reveals. Terms such as "African American," "Chicano," "Puerto Rican," "Vietnamese," "Jamaican," and "indigenous people" refer to racial/ethnic groups with identifiable histories with racial or national oppression. In contrast, the term "color" lacks this historical context and is more easily attached to the individual bodies that are so celebrated within postmodern frameworks. In a climate where one woman of "color" is just as good an another, the radical potential of racial/ethnic women who bring a critical perspective not just on gender, but also on issues of race, class, and nation, can easily be eliminated from college generally, and from women's studies class-rooms in particular. These young women have much of value to say, but if they are appointed the spokespeople of "colored feminism," in what ways might they be furthering the goals of the new racism and its focus on colorblindness? They are "color" conscious, but are they ra-cially/ethnically conscious? Conversely, the very marginality of racial/ethnic women within women's studies creates a new collective identity—ironically, that of "feminist women of color"—that is posi-tioned between both the collective identity politics of racial/ethnic communities (nationalism) and the individual-rights agendas of wom-en's studies projects (feminism).

Given these contradictions, in women's studies classrooms, holding fast to the personal as political may be the salvation for African American women, Chicanas, Puerto Rican women, and racial/ethnic immigrant women from working-class and poor communities. The few who find their way to women's studies classrooms use the consciousness-raising assumptions of their own personal politics to challenge the equally personal politics of their classmates. Siobhan Brooks, an African Amer-ican women's studies major, describes how these dynamics play out in many classrooms: "Women's studies classes do not have to be a struggle for power between white women and women of color, yet that is often what they are because of white women's racism. . . . It is not constructive for white women to tell us that our anger is making it hard for them to relate to us, that our anger makes them feel uncomfortable, that we are not willing to find common alliances with them. This is a classic example of white women's racism."[59] Moreover, women's studies classrooms that abandon feminist praxis in favor of a narcissistic personal politics run the risk of misreading important ideas that women of color may bring to those settings. Take, for example, Paula Austin's description of the kind of "everyday feminism" that she learned from her mother:

> My mother taught me everything I know about "feminism" even if she
> didn't think she was teaching me. She taught me to work hard, to be hard,

to fight mean, to fear love (to question love). She taught me the meaning of honor and retribution and fear, and pain that goes way back. She taught me what she knew. She taught me about desire and sex and sensuality. How to flirt, be coy and demure. How to be femme, a high diva, show off my cleavage. How to be looked at, how to be invisible and afraid. How to survive, to stay alive. She taught me what she could. About women's power and authority.[60]

This is a very different political sensibility expressed by the very same women whose more privileged classmates are encouraged to see them as voiceless, marginalized subalterns who cannot speak.

Fortunately, women of color with an emerging collective identity as "feminist women of color" have decided not simply to turn their voices inward within such classrooms but also to seek to turn their voices outward and provide a more comprehensive analysis of contemporary consciousness-raising. Take, for example, the recurring themes in *Colonize This! Young Women of Color on Today's Feminism*, a book of essays that tells us much about the ideas of women of color who find feminism in college.[61] For one, the women of color writing these essays came to feminism not through family, community politics, and/or social movement experience, but through being exposed to it in college. For many women, initially the feminism within women's studies classrooms felt liberating. As Paula Austin points out, "In many ways this was an idyllic time: social activism and diversity work in a relatively safe environment. I wouldn't know the real impact of patriarchy and its intersection with racism, sexism, and homophobia until I left school."[62] At the same time, something was missing. As one African American woman succinctly points out, "The everyday feminism that I grew up with was missing from my classes; the women had the theory but not the practice."[63] The editors describe this process in their own lives: "Like so many other women of color, the two of us first learned the language of feminism in college through a white, middle-class perspective, one form of colonization. Feminism should have brought us closer to our mothers and sisters and to our aunties in the Third World. Instead it took us further away."[64]

Another recurring theme in *Colonize This!* concerns the tension between the "liberating" stance of White feminism and the women's desire to remain connected to the women of color who had nurtured their feminism. Several claimed that their mothers (and, in a few cases, fathers) had raised them to be strong, self-reliant women. Mothers played an important part in many narratives, not in the mother-blaming fashion of some White feminist literature, but through recognition of how their mothers' lives had affected their own. Martinez's description of her feminist sensibilities is common: "My first real understanding of feminism came through the women who looked like me and who spoke to me culturally and politically. They were committed to liberation, of a colony or of one's self. As a Puerto Rican, these questions of race, class and national liberation were critical to me."[65] This "everyday feminism" took many forms. For some, their mothers were migrants whose struggles to provide for their children had given their daughters the gift of opportunity and the will to "migrate" away from home and into the White spaces of higher education. Others admired their mothers' will but not their values. None learned to name the behavior of the women in their lives as "feminist" until they encountered the term within formal women's studies programs. They knew that the women who had raised them encouraged their resilience, yet little space seemed to exist within what counted as feminism for their mothers, sisters, aunts, and neighbors. As a result of this tension, many of the authors also expressed varying degrees of comfort and discomfort with what they learned about feminism. They clearly embraced its main ideas yet remained ambivalent about its applicability to the women in their lives.

The choice of personal-identity narratives as the preferred method of discussing feminism is one of the most striking themes of *Colonize This!* On one level, these young feminists deploy the feminist slogan "The Personal Is Political" not within the confines of consciousness-raising groups but, rather, in the space of contemporary popular culture. At the same time, few of the authors write *inside* the traditional collective identities of racial, ethnic, religious, or citizenship groups, even those who grew up within them. Instead, they rely on the memories of home spaces, as well as the lessons learned on journeys outside these accepted collective identities. From these outsider spaces of personal-identity narratives, virtually none of the essays cast a sustained external gaze on the social conditions that affect women in the United States and beyond.[66] There is virtually no discussion of population policies, welfare reform, comparable worth, family policy, or women's grassroots organizations unless such discussions are tied directly to the personal experiences of the author. Instead, not only does their politics grow from their personal lives; it does not seem to go much further than this. The authors clearly understand and have progressive views on racism, sexism, heterosexism, and class exploitation, but their narratives do not examine the structural foundations of how these systems affect women as well as women's organized responses to them (for example, the women's movement). Feminist social issues permeate the narratives—abortion, HIV infection, the drudgery of women's unpaid housework, the challenges of motherhood with no money, and so on—and the impact of reading the individual narratives as a collectivity is powerful. At the same time, the social-movement context of feminism remains a backdrop for more personal issues.

I cite the essays in *Colonize This!* because the ideas and experiences of women of color in the hip-hop generation signal a significant break with earlier paths to feminist politics by racial/ethnic women. Contemporary women of color seemingly follow a different personal path to find feminism from that taken by African American, Chicana, Puerto Rican, and other women in the 1960s and 1970s; they also confront a different political reality when they find it. During this earlier period, a rich social-movement context played an important role in shaping all segments of the women's movement. Describing the effects of this context on feminist politics, Benita Roth argues that Black, Chicana, and White women followed "separate roads to feminism" that reflected and shaped the multiplicity of feminisms of the times.[67] In contrast, conservative, right-wing Republican governments of the 1980s to the present have led the way in criticizing and ridiculing not just the women's movement, but also the aspirations of unions, civil-rights groups, sexual minorities, immigrant groups, and poor people. Moreover, the kinds of women of color who identify themselves as feminists may be less likely to have sustained ties within established racial/ethnic communities where another kind of "everyday feminism" that is linked to a collective identity politics may be practiced.

I am deeply concerned about any group of women that encounters feminism as a so-called radical ideology through a process that rations education to the privileged few. Few spaces within American higher education are radical: They are progressive, perhaps, and liberal on occasion, but they are definitely not radical. "Tenured radical" is an oxymoron. Radicalism is not tolerated within elite institutions, the types that contain the most visible women's studies programs, because true radicalism would take aim at the very social conditions that produce these classroom structures and the dynamics that they engender. The most "radical" women I have met within American colleges and universities work at community colleges, where they define their mission as uplifting working-class students, especially students of color.

Their work is theoretically informed, yet because they teach five courses per quarter or semester, they have little time to publish, let alone engage in extended debates about the meaning of difference.

There is also the important question of what constitutes the feminist canon within women's studies classrooms. Young Black women are often not aware of the many works by Black feminist writers and theorists and certainly are not getting information about these women in their undergrad women's studies classes. Most undergraduate women's studies classes introduce a few major names—for example, Audre Lorde and bell hooks—and at best assign a few of their works as the Black feminist canon. Within largely White feminist/women's studies spaces, the complexities of Black feminist thought becomes constructed in one of two ways: either as the "Earth/Mother/Goddess" soul of the discipline (as illustrated in the works of Audre Lorde) or as the "moral police" of women's studies (bell hooks' early work) that critiques the discipline's exclusion of the voices of women of color. Works by Black feminists that link Black women's personal narratives to social hierarchies of race, class, and nation and that use varying Black experiences to unmask and critique social structures of inequity and domination are excluded from the core curriculum. Black women and other racial/ethnic women in such classrooms often write from personal experience without explicit connections to structural realities, often because this is what they have been offered as the Black feminist canon. As one perceptive women's studies student contends, "The creative energy of black feminist thinkers, and its products, are still presented in manners in which they are in service to white women's greater goals and not primarily to highlight the realities of black women's lives."[68]

It is important to stress that African American women (and many men) reject not the ideas of feminism but the label of feminism. I have found that in my own African American studies classrooms, Black women are open to discussing Black feminist ideas because they see the potential benefits to themselves and their communities. Black men who are brave enough to join them also demonstrate far less resistance to Black feminist ideas than pervasive media images of hypermasculine, Black men's sexism would have us believe. Given this receptivity, the lack of knowledge about Black feminism even among women who have had access to college educations is troubling. Whether Black women and other women of color call themselves "feminists" is not important. The power of a stigmatized label to shut down radical protest and keep young Black women from learning their own history for fear of being labeled "feminists" is a much larger problem for African Americans as a collectivity than the continued racism or elitism of any individual White American feminist.

The second theme that affects Black women in the hip-hop generation concerns how they use knowledge gained through consciousness-raising within women's studies classrooms, especially the importance of the personal as political. Ironically, while uncomfortable to live through, the contradictions that African American women, Chicanas, Puerto Rican women, and other racial/ethnic women experience may be a good thing. They see the incongruity of learning about feminism in their college classrooms, yet their response lies not in becoming academics who broker commodified knowledge within the academic marketplace. Rather, many choose to engage a different marketplace— namely, the terrain of popular culture. Many certainly advocate or support the kinds of grassroots politics that have been the bedrock of racial/ethnic women's collective identity politics. Yet as the earlier discussion of the work of Joan Morgan, Lisa Jones, Veronica Chambers, and the authors in *Colonize This!* suggest, educated women of color also choose films, music videos, fiction, spoken-word poetry, magazines, and other dimensions of popular culture as venues for their feminist politics. Stated differently, in contrast to feminist mobilizations of the 1960s and 1970s, their women's movement mobilization occurs not within bureaucracies of the state or higher education but within popular culture and mass media.

Hip-hop culture reaches far more women than the relatively small number of women of color who manage to find women's studies classrooms within colleges and universities. Hip-hop culture is itself a response by Black and Latino youth who were denied access not just to college educations, but to schooling, adequate housing, recreational activities, and music lessons. Instead of being defeated and disenfranchised, these young people created new art forms from the fragments that they inherited.[69] For Black and Latino youth who have been denied high-quality educations, school is no longer the place where they learn literacy and politics. Rather, for many, mass media has become their classroom. The creation and persistence of this generational culture represents not only the resilience of Black and Latino youth. It also speaks to themes of alienation of a global youth population. In particular, rap music is a global phenomenon that transcends the provincialism of American academe and that has influence far beyond the Black and Latino neighborhoods where it first appeared in the 1980s.

This does not mean that hip-hop culture, and rap in particular, are unproblematic. Rather, as an art form rap can accommodate all measure of ideas—some provocative, some mediocre, and some quite dangerous. Recognizing the power of this new forum simultaneously to oppress and liberate women, many women of color choose mass-market venues to express feminist sensibilities. This stands to reason, given the misogyny that is routinely expressed by some rap artists. For African American women in particular, the links seem clear. Black women at the turn of the twentieth century saw their images reviled within an emerging mass media; contemporary Black women in the hip-hop generation face a similar challenge. Mary Church Terrell and other middle-class clubwomen organized a Black women's movement to grapple with the status of Black women, and one important part of their agenda was to refute negative representations of Black womanhood. Contemporary African American women find themselves under similar attack. Those Black women who have managed to develop a feminist analysis recognize the need to use the art form of rap as a forum to reach young women who have no other means of finding feminism.

If hip hop is the voice of this generation, it should come as no surprise that this venue may become a critical area for the emergence of a hip-hop feminism. Some feel that, because these young Black feminists choose media avenues for hip-hop feminism over more traditional activities of grassroots Black community politics or integrating academe, their politics are misguided. But another view is that these women are using public space in ways that are new and needed. Examining the work of Morgan, Chambers, and Jones, Kimberly Springer categorizes the themes within the work of Black hip-hop feminists as: (1) Black women's relationships to their personal and political histories; (2) relationship to self; and (3) relationships to Black men.[70] Working within a different venue, Gwendolyn D. Pough's *Check It While I Wreck It: Black Womanhood, Hip-Hop Culture, and the Public Sphere* (2004) claims that Black women rappers demonstrate a feminist sensibility when they disrupt, or "wreck," misogynistic representations of Black women within their music.[71] Specifically, hip-hop–influenced writers and rap or rhythm-and-blues artists such as Salt-n-Pepa, Lauryn Hill, Queen Latifah, India/Arie, and Alicia Keyes routinely argue that Black women have the right to be respected, to be loved by their families and partners, to express themselves freely (artistically and sexually), and not to be mistaken for the stereotypes that have been applied to them. Black women artists encourage Black girls and women to embrace their individualism and personal expression. This is a personal politics but one that seems quite different from the intense, consciousness-raising groups of the Combahee River Collective era.

These women challenge prevailing norms within African American communities that counsel Black women to place their needs and desires as individuals in service to the allegedly greater needs of the Black community. African American women within the hip-hop generation seem much more likely to challenge the image of the strong Black woman and argue in their own behalf than women in prior genera-tions.[72] In particular, these hip-hop Black feminists perceive the refusal on the part of so many African American women to engage in personal advocacy on their own behalf or on the behalf of Black women as a group as a major stumbling block for African American political and economic development. How can any group progress if half of its members remain oppressed?

This new version of personal politics expressed within popular-culture venues is important, but representations that remain untethered to actual social movements make it difficult for popular-culture con-sumers to tell whether they are participating in an important new form of feminist politics or merely being entertained by it. For exam-ple, structural issues and social problems are noticeably absent from Springer's schema of the content of hip-hop feminism. Moreover, Springer suggests that a generational divide now characterizes Black feminists, one in which the generation that came of age during the period of mobilization has somehow failed to provide for the current generation.[73] Beverly Guy-Sheftall takes Springer's accusations seri-ously yet also contends: "I am not as convinced as Springer that young Black feminists are carrying on the legacy left by nineteenth-century abolitionists, antilynching crusaders, club women, Civil Rights orga-nizers, Black nationalist revolutionaries, and 1970s Black feminists, though I would like to embrace her argument."[74]

This accusation brings me to my final theme—namely, investigat-ing the connections between trends within hip-hop feminism and the extensive need for developing new grassroots feminist organizations within African American communities and infusing churches, recrea-tional activities, and civil-rights organizations of Black civil society with a feminist sensibility. There is a need to make the links between the types of community work that builds institutions and the inroads made by Black women within popular culture. The themes of feminism as articulated by this next generation of Black feminists need to be heard within African American communities and should inform Black women's community work. In essence, one might ask whether Black women in the hip-hop generation are beginning to make these important connections between the power of mass media and the need for grassroots political organization, even though the connections may not be readily apparent. Conversely, a similar question concerns how open Black women working within grassroots organizations are to the beachhead of Black women in popular culture.

I see this split between Black women and women of color working within popular culture and those within grassroots organizations less as a generational divide than as reflecting the absence of analysis that conceptualizes these expressions of Black women's activism as intersecting versus parallel spheres of activity. For example, feminism need not be central to, or even listed within, an organization's activities for feminist politics to be present. Just because an individual or an organization refuses to claim feminism does not mean that African Americans women's empowerment is being neglected. For example, in *Stand and Deliver: Political Activism, Leadership, and Hip Hop Culture* (2004), Yvonne Bynoe says relatively little about feminism but clearly infuses her analysis of the need for revitalized grassroots leadership with a feminist sensibility. In her chapter "Lessons from Our Political Grandmother: Ella J. Baker," Bynoe claims the leadership styles and grassroots politics of Black female foremothers as crucial for women and men in the hip-hop generation. Most significant, Bynoe's volume is not written *about* the hip-hop generation but *for* it.[75]

The small but growing number of Black feminist projects that oppose rape and violence against women speak to intersections of grassroots and media modes of activism. African American women are far less likely to sacrifice their own personal safety and that of their daughters in service to an elusive Black solidarity. On the one hand, Black women are clearly involved in grassroots organizations to challenge issues of sexual assault.[76] At the same time, other women strive to make inroads into media. Take, for example, the tireless efforts of Aishah Simmons to raise money to fund her documentary *"NO!"* an exposé of the realities of rape and sexual assault within African American communities. Simmons has no interest in starring in her production. Her goal is not personal fame. Rather, her personal politics around the issue of sexual assault, as well as her background within television, catalyzed her activism: She aims to control the content and distribution of her intellectual production. Her goal is that *NO!* be shown to Black youth to raise awareness in Black communities.[77]

Old binaries no longer work—if in fact they ever did. Books such as *When Chickenheads Come Home to Roost* and *Colonize This!* remind us that U.S. feminism is not now, nor has it ever been, the exclusive property of White, middle-class, or affluent women. Then and now, the U.S. women's movement has attracted women from diverse backgrounds who find feminist ideas to be powerful in explaining and helping to change their lived experiences with gender inequality. The fact that African American women are more likely to reject what many perceive to be a Western feminism that has incorporated, often uncritically, hallmarks of American society such as individualism, materialism, and personal choice without accountability, provides an important corrective to what currently counts as feminism. Yet because African American women are also members of American society, like their mainstream counterparts, they simultaneously accept these ideas that stem from a common, overarching ideological framework of liberalism and capitalism. The materialism of the hip-hop generation belies any collective, humanitarian, socialist spirit. In this regard, Black American kids are American—they want rap CDs, gym shoes, and fancy baby clothes for their children just as much as their White American counterparts do. All of these groups hold American citizenship and thus incorporate prevailing ideas of American national identity into their politics. Extracting these and other expressions of women's political activism from American ideologies of race, class, and nation not only creates new frameworks for analyzing Black women's political activism in particular. It also creates new opportunities to revitalize American feminism.

Black women and other women of color in the hip-hop generation do seem to be striking out in a different direction, and for the most part I like where they seem to be going. Take, for example, Silja Talvi's discussion of third-wave feminism where "women on the edge" speak out most strongly about the intersections of racism, classism, homophobia, and sexism. These are women who push and pull at the "inner and outermost definitions of femininity, feminism, and womanhood" and who rebel not just against dominant culture, but against a "feminist culture that can be just as proscriptive in defining what is 'normal.'" Talvi points to how these women demand change, but this time much of the change is happening on a personal level. As she claims, "The personal, to revisit the second wave feminist phase, is still political. . . . [T]hese are young women who refuse to allow anything (or anyone) to dictate to them how they should look, act, or think. They are not dropping out from society or tuning out the concept of feminism, but instead continuing to engage with their communities on their own terms."[78] The rap diva Queen Latifah describes a similar sensibility: "I don't act the way society dictates that a woman 'should.' I am not dainty. I do not hold back my opinions. I don't stay behind a man. But I'm not here to live by somebody else's standards. I'm defining what a woman is for myself. Simply put, I am not interested in subscribing to what society has decided for half of humankind. I am an individual."[79] Talvi and Queen Latifah both express a new personal politics that creates space for free women who reject the definitions that do not work for them. The same personal politics of boldness graces *Fierce* magazine, a new publication for women who are "too bold for boundaries."

How wondrous and fearful it must be to step out into that space of possibility where you define yourself on your own terms, to craft a new multiethnic, gender-bending, biracial, sexually dynamic, fluid personal identity that is seen and respected by all sorts of people who seem so different from oneself. The responsibility and potential freedom that this promises are boundless. Yet it is obvious that these new personal identities can never occur without fundamental structural change that makes such identities possible for everyone. This is the message of the women in *Colonize This!* They seem to be struggling for new identities in which they can be "too bold for boundaries," but they refuse to go it alone and leave their loved ones behind. When Joan Morgan says, "I needed a feminism that would allow us to continue loving ourselves and the brothers who hurt us without letting race loyalty buy us early tombstones," she describes this path that women of color in the hip-hop generation hope to blaze.[80] When the Black hip-hop feminist shani jamila states, "We can't get complacent. The most important thing we can do as a generation is to see our new positions as power and weapons to be used strategically in the struggle rather than as spoils of war," she issues a clarion call to women of color in the hip-hop generation.[81] If the contributors to *Colonize This!*, Silja Talvi, Queen Latifah, the editors of *Fierce* magazine, Joan Morgan, and shani jamila have their way, growing numbers of young women who find feminism will find a new freedom. If this does come to pass, then a needed new movement nurtured in the spaces of the women's movement in abeyance is truly under way. If so, then the "flame lighting the hearts of activists" has not been snuffed. Shani jamila has not missed her time. Instead, she's right on time.

Notes

Introduction

Epigraphs: Shakur 1993, 69; Trebay 2000; Souljah 1999, 192–93; Latifah 1999, 126–27.

1. Kitwana 2002, xiii.

2. Neal 2002, 3.

3. All data are taken from McKinnon 2003, 108–10. One need only trace the resegregation of American public education since 1954 to understand how White and middle-class Americans have refused to send their children to school with Black American youth. Young urban African American men are also incarcerated at alarmingly high levels.

4. It is important to distinguish between the actual hip-hop generation—youth from diverse racial, ethnic backgrounds who are distributed across an increasingly heterogeneous social class structure—with the creation and commodification of Black hip-hop culture within popular culture. In mass media, the hip-hop generation becomes reduced to a specific segment of Black youth who have access to "authentic" Black culture, a phenomenon that becomes further defined as the cultural production of selected artists. Thus, despite hip-hop culture's growth at the crossroads of many influences, it remains marketed as the "authentic" culture of poor Black youth and serves as a site of reproduction and contestation for the new racism that appears in gender-specific forms.

5. For a discussion of Black images, see Turner 1994.

6. P. Williams 1995, 25.

7. Guinier and Torres 2002, 35.

8. Bauman 1998, 9.

9. For a thorough analysis of how globalization shapes contemporary racial formations, see Howard Winant's analysis of the United States, South Africa, Brazil, and Europe in the post–World War II era: Winant 2001. Feminist analysis has also produced a broad literature on globalization and women's economic status, some of it focused on racism, sexism, and issues of globalization. For representative theoretical work in this tradition, see Alexander 1997; Mohanty 1997. African American scholars have also focused more attention on the global political economy. For representative works in this tradition, see Brewer 1994; Squires 1994; Wilson 1996.

10. Integrationism is situated in a much larger discourse of liberalism. Committed to individualism, liberalism takes as basic the moral, political, and legal claims of the individual over and against those of the collective and seeks universal principles that are applicable to all human beings. Liberalism seeks to transcend

particular historical, social, and cultural differences by concerning itself with broad identities that unite people on moral grounds. Issues of race, class, gender, and the like, as well as groups formed around these identities, are deemed to be problematic because these entities divide people. Liberalism's commitment to equality leads to political programs such as colorblindness and tolerance of individual differences: Goldberg 1993, 5.

11. It is difficult to find reliable empirical tests of African American attitudes toward Black nationalism generally and ideas about self-determination or Black autonomy in particular. In his study of how ideas about race and class shape the political views of African Americans, Michael C. Dawson (1994) recognizes these difficulties. Dawson uses the following four questions from a National Black Election Panel Study of 1984–88 to construct a measure of Black autonomy: (1) Blacks should give their children African names; (2) Blacks should always vote for Black candidates; (3) Blacks should have nothing to do with Whites; and (4) Blacks should form an independent political party. African American responses to these four questions provide evidence for African American attitudes toward Black autonomy.

12. See, for example, criticisms in Lubiano 1997; White 1990.

13. Hip-hop culture also emerged as a terrain of Black nationalist expression. See my discussion of feminism and women of color in the hip-hop generation in chapter 6 of this volume.

14. For one of the most accessible analyses of socialism and communism and their influence on African American social and political thought, see Kelley 2002. See also Kelley's historical work on the Black working class, especially his discussion of how working-class Black youth responded to the deindustrialization of Los Angeles through hip-hop culture: Kelley 1994, 183–227.

15. Roth 2004, 76–128.

16. Dawson 1994.

17. As Dawson (1994) argues, whereas African Americans are more class stratified than in prior eras, they continue to vote as a block mainly because there are so few options in a "truncated" American political spectrum.

18. For a book-length treatment of critical social theory, see Collins 1998a.

19. See, for example, Anthias and Yuval-Davis 1992; Enloe 1990; West 1997a; Yuval-Davis 1997.

20. See, e.g., Lorde 1984.

21. Crenshaw 1992, 434.

22. Mercer 1994, 284.

23. Here I collapse a large and complex body of literature to two main focal points. The first, described as the "power-as-domination" model, draws on Marxian sociology and conflict theory as well as Weberian sociology's attention to bureaucracy and large structures of power. The second, described as the "resource-mobilization" approach, draws on collective movement theory as well as models of "micropower" advanced by the French philosopher Michel Foucault.

24. Foucault's more fluid notion of power as something that is continually constructed and contested sparked increased interest in the social construction of power. For a discussion, see Foucault 1980. James Scott analyzes this resource mobilization model of resistance to illustrate how individuals empower themselves in everyday life: See Scott 1985, 1990. For a discussion of empowerment, see James 1993, 51.

25. For an introduction to Black women's issues in a transnational context, see Nnaemeka 1988; Pala 1995.

26. The term in no way describes an essential Black woman who has certain inherent or natural traits. Rather, as used here, the phrase "Black women" is a political identity that has cultural or biological roots. By using this expansive definition of Black women, I recognize the danger of potentially privileging Black American women's experiences by using those of women throughout the African diaspora to help explain Black American women's realities. This is not my intent.

27. Cohen 1999, 8–160.

28. This essay draws on the main tenets of standpoint theory. For summaries of the main ideas of standpoint theory, see Harding 1986; Hartsock 1983. For an expanded treatment of the notion of group standpoint, see commentary by Nancy Hartsock, Sandra Harding, Dorothy Smith and Patricia Hill Collins in the forum on standpoint epistemology published in *Signs* 22, no. 2 (1997).

29. West 1997b, xii.

30. Latifah 1999, 126–27.

Chapter One

Epigraph: Childress 1986, 1–2.

1. Harris 1986.

2. First issued in book form in 1956 by a small publisher, this important collection of Alice Childress's writings remained virtually neglected for two decades. Recognizing how Mildred's monologues provide provocative African American feminist analyses of issues of race, gender, and class in the United States, the literary critic Trudier Harris succeeded in having the collection reissued in 1986 under the title *Like One of the Family*, also the title of the first piece in the volume. Despite Harris's efforts, Childress's work remains largely unrecognized.

3. In exploring these connections, it is important to distinguish among the terms "nation," "nation-state," and "nationalism." These terms are often used interchangeably, yet they refer to different things. A "nation" consists of a group of people who have come to believe that they have been shaped by a common past and are destined to share a common future. That belief is usually nurtured by common cultural characteristics, such as language and customs; a well-defined geographic territory; the belief in a common origin and history; assumptions that closer ties exist among members of the nation than with outsiders; a sense of difference from groups around them; and mutual hostility toward outside groups. The specific content of a group's language, culture, and belief systems constitutes its national identity. "Nationalism" is the ideology deployed by such groups who aim to gain or maintain political power for their nation. Finally, when a national group acquires sufficient state power to realize its goals, it controls a "nation-state." For extended discussions of these concepts, see Calhoun 1993; Yuval-Davis 1997.

4. Collins 1998a, 44–76.

5. Collins 1998b.

6. Balibar and Wallerstein 1991.

7. Significant differences of opinion exist concerning what to call indigenous peoples. Various groups have used terms such as "American Indians," "Indians,"

"Native Americans," and "native peoples." In this chapter, I settle on "Native Americans" as the term of choice, even though I realize that it is far from perfect.

8. Omi and Winant 1994.

9. Calhoun 1993.

10. See Anthias and Yuval-Davis 1992; Yuval-Davis 1997, 26–29.

11. Ignatiev 1995.

12. Sacks 1994.

13. Baldwin and Mead 1971, 67–68.

14. Andersen 1991; Thorne 1992.

15. Ibid.

16. Collins 1998b, 2000a.

17. Oliver and Shapiro 1995.

18. B. Williams 1995.

19. Collins 1999.

20. Young 1995.

21. Goldberg 1993.

22. Gould 1981.

23. For the popular use of the term "American apartheid," see Massey and Denton 1993.

24. Baldwin and Mead 1971, 70.

25. McClintock 1995.

26. Waters 1996.

27. Jackson and Penrose 1993.

28. Anthias and Yuval-Davis 1992; Calhoun 1993.

29. Childress 1986, 2.

30. Collins 2000a.

31. Ibid., 173–99.

32. Childress 1986, 2–3.

Chapter Two

1. Haller 1984, 78.

2. Gilroy 1987, 43.

3. Andersen 1991. I present a more comprehensive analysis of these ideas in chapter 1 of this volume.

4. Coontz 1992.

5. Anthias and Yuval-Davis 1992.

6. Proctor 1988, 286.

7. Haller 1984.

8. See, for example, ibid.

9. Discussions of these concepts can be found in Anthias and Yuval-Davis 1992; Bock 1984; Bridenthal et al. 1984; Gilman 1985; Proctor 1988.

10. Berry 1994.

11. See, e.g., Massey and Denton 1993; Omi and Winant 1994.

12. Racial formations in the United States demonstrate a shift from theories of race based on the racist biology that characterized nineteenth-century science and toward a cultural racism more useful in defending current racial practices. But this

means neither that racism based in biology has atrophied nor that it may not take on new forms. Troy Duster offers an unsettling argument concerning the re-racialization of genetic arguments in contemporary American scholarship. Duster argues that advances in genetic research show that genetic disorders are distributed differently through different racial/ethnic groups. Duster (1990, 3) queries, "The importance of race and ethnicity in cultural history has refueled the old logic to give rise to a new question: If genetic disorders are differentially distributed by race and ethnicity, why aren't other human traits and characteristics?"

13. Omi and Winant 1994. Scholarship on the welfare state reveals how state policies reflect race-, class-, and gender-specific concerns. For analyses of how social policies have had differential impact on different groups, see Gordon 1994; Mink 1990; Nelson 1990. For analyses of how race frames American social-welfare state policy, see Brewer 1994; Gilkes 1983.

14. This process is neither historical nor confined to the United States. For discussions of similar population policies, see work on Singapore in Heng and Devan 1992 and on South Africa in Kuumba 1993.

15. As quoted in Haller 1984, 11.

16. As quoted in ibid., 139.

17. Ikemoto 1996.

18. Nsiah-Jefferson 1989; Roberts 1997, 264–72; Rowland 1987.

19. Solinger 1992.

20. Squires 1994.

21. See, e.g., Teresa Amott's discussion of African American women and Aid to Families with Dependent Children in Amott 1990.

22. Roberts 1997, 3.

23. For a discussion of such images, see Lubiano 1992. Middle-class African American women occupy a peculiar place in the nexus of population policies targeted toward African American women as a group. On the one hand, these women clearly have the economic resources to care for their children. In this sense, African American middle-class children will not be a drain on nation-state resources. But on the other hand, these children are not of the "right" genetic stock to become symbolic of the nation. They compete with the "rightful heirs" of the nation—its White children—for resources. The analogy between the king's rightful heir and the king's bastard son seems apt here: Both are seen as being part of the royal family, but their status is not the same.

24. Omolade 1994.

25. Chang 1994, 263.

26. Ibid.; Dill 1988; Glenn 1992.

27. Raymond 1993; Rowland 1987.

28. Katz 1989, 127.

29. Roberts 1997, 294–312; Ross et al. 2002; "Two Mission Statements" 1999.

Chapter Three

1. For sample work on the contours of the new racism, see Bonilla-Silva 1996, 2001; Essed 1991; Ferber 1998; Gilroy 2000; Jhally and Lewis 1992; Memmi 2000; Miles 1989; Neubeck and Cazenave 2001; Van Dijk 1993. John Calmore's analysis

of the new demography of multiracial America is especially intriguing (Calmore 2001).

2. Massey and Denton 1993.

3. Orfield and Ashkinaze 1991.

4. Davis 1997; Miller 1996; Pinar 2001.

5. For discussions of this logic of colorblindness, see Crenshaw 1997; Bonilla-Silva 2001; Guinier and Torres 2002.

6. I rely on the sociologist Eduardo Bonilla-Silva's distinction between race and ethnicity as different bases for group association. Unlike ethnicity, racialized social systems contain power hierarchies that distinguish between superiors and subordinates. I use the term "racial/ethnic" groups to refer to the interaction between racial/ethnic group assignment by the nation-state and racial/ethnic identification as constructed by individuals and groups within it (Bonilla-Silva 1996). Using a similar language of "ethnoracial assignment" and "ethnoracial identity," Karen Brodkin (2000) points out the conceptual distinction between the two. Tracing the history of U.S. census classifications of residents into racial categories and into citizenship categories of native-born versus immigrant, Brodkin examines the changing patterns of racial/ethnic assignment within U.S. society. In contrast to this classification process, individuals and groups construct racial/ethnic identities, but do so within the context of their racial/ethnic assignments. I capitalize the terms "Black" and "White" because both refer to specific racial/ethnic groups in American society. African Americans use the terms "African American" and "Black" interchangeably to self-describe this racial/ethnic identification. If national identities such as "French," "Italian," or "British" can be substituted for "Black," then I capitalize the term. Capitalizing "White" is more troublesome, precisely because Whites reject an ethnic identification as "Whites."

7. Robinson 2001.

8. Moses 1978; Pinkney 1976; Van Deburg 1997.

9. Dawson 1994.

10. Collins 2001.

11. I present a comprehensive analysis of these issues in chapter 1 of this volume.

12. Bellah 1992, 169–73.

13. Via a set of cultural ideas, symbols, and practices, American civil religion encourages members of American society to worship the "American way of life." Two of the sacred texts of American civil religion, the Declaration of Independence and the U.S. Constitution, are in conflict. The declaration encompasses the ideas of a republican form of government with clear attention to a deity, whereas the constitution represents the liberal democratic state of the Enlightenment (Bellah 1992). Within American civil religion, the so-called Founding Fathers can be seen as demigods; American presidents serve as high priests; and citizens who die in service of democracy (warfare) become the martyrs. This religious ideology also resembles the rhetoric of family that shapes both American national identity and the public policies of the nation-state. See the essays in Part I of this volume.

14. Pieterse 2004.

15. Brodkin 2000, 103–37.

16. Robinson 2001, 104–17.

17. Cone 1972; Hood 1994; Paris 1995.

18. Lincoln 1999, xxiv.

19. Berry 1994.

20. Massey and Denton 1993.

21. Collins 1998a, 82–83.

22. For a discussion of Jews and whiteness, see Brodkin 2000, 144–53. For Asians, see Tuan 1998.

23. Lincoln 1999, 91–92.

24. Robinson 2001, 118.

25. Ibid.

26. For a comprehensive discussion of how ideas about family shape American national identity, see chapter 1 in this volume.

27. See, for example, Lee 1996.

28. In this section, I distinguish between the narrow concept of Afrocentrism advanced by selected academics within U.S. higher education (Asante 1990), and a broader definition of Afrocentrism that references African-influenced customs among African Americans. It is important to note that African Americans may deploy the ideas of Black consciousness or Afrocentrism without using this terminology to describe their beliefs and/or activities.

29. Collins 1998a, 155–83.

30. Sobel 1979.

31. Richards 1990.

32. Patillo-McCoy 1998.

33. Ibid., 767.

34. Ibid., 768.

35. West 1993, 19.

36. Senghor 1995, 45; italics in the original.

37. Asante 1993, 43.

38. Asante 1990, 2; italics in the original.

39. Senghor 1995, 46; italics in the original.

40. The seven principles of the Nguzo Saba seem designed to provide guidance for African American behavior in everyday lived experience. They are *Umoja*, or unity; *Kujichagulia*, or self-determination; *Ujima*, or collective work and responsibility; *Ujamaa*, or cooperative economics; *Nia*, or purpose; *Kuumba*, or creativity; and *Imani*, or faith (Karenga 1995). In the way that formal religions identify articles of faith used to guide their everyday behavior, the Nguzo Saba fulfills a similar function. Together, the seven principles outline a way of life for true believers and specify a framework within which African Americans can express Black solidarity via Black consciousness.

41. Karenga 1995, 276.

42. Paris 1995; Patillo-McCoy 1998.

43. Dyson 1993; Lubiano 1997.

44. Asante 1993, 143.

45. Baldwin 1980.

46. For a discussion of this conversion process and Black identity, see Cross 1971.

47. Collins 1998a, 90–91, 155–57.

48. Ibid., 97–105.
49. See, for example, Lefkowitz 1996.
50. Lubiano 1997.
51. Cross 1971.
52. Lusane 1993; Zook 1992.
53. Collins 1998a, 174–79.
54. Robinson 2001, 119.

Chapter Four

Epigraph: Baldwin and Mead 1971, 24.
1. Asante 1987, 1990; Karenga 1978, 1982, 1995; Karenga 1990; Welsing 1991.
2. Gates 1992; Gilroy 1992, 1993; Karenga 1982; Marable 1993; Ransby and Matthews 1993; West 1993; White 1990. Molefi Asante's volume *The Afrocentric Idea* (1987) is most often credited with introducing the term "Afrocentrism." Asante's *Kemet, Afrocentricity, and Knowledge* (1990) and Maulana Karenga's *Introduction to Black Studies* (1982) are considered foundational texts in Afrocentrism. For an insider's overview of Afrocentrism written by an Afrocentric practitioner, see Kershaw 1992. For an outsider's overview that succinctly summarizes its scope and actual practices, see Marable 1993, esp.119–22. Marable distinguishes between "scholarly" and "vulgar" Afrocentrism, viewing thinkers such as Asante as scholarly and media figures associated with political issues as vulgar. Marable does not simply juxtapose scholarly and vulgar as variations of positive and negative; he also critiques inconsistencies in scholarly Afrocentrism. Barbara Ransby and Tracye Matthews (1993) also offer a discussion of the resurgence of Black cultural nationalism in African American communities. They link Afrocentrism to interest in Malcolm X and rap music within hip-hop culture.
3. Van Deburg 1992.
4. Massey and Denton 1993; Squires 1994.
5. Souljah 1994.
6. Lusane 1993.
7. Darlene Clark Hine (1992) classifies Black studies scholarship into three paradigmatic orientations: traditionalist, feminist, and Afrocentrist. Individual scholars often cannot be classified easily within one paradigm and may move among all three. Hine argues that Black studies practitioners reflects diverse racial backgrounds and can be found across a range of academic disciplines. However, while Black studies units house practitioners of all three paradigms, the Afrocentrist paradigm is found almost exclusively within Black studies programs and departments. Hine's view differs from other taxonomies. For examples, see essays in T. Anderson 1990, especially the introductory essay, "Black Studies: Overview and Theoretical Perspective."
8. Gould 1981; McKee 1993; Tucker 1994.
9. For contrasting interpretations of the history of Black studies programs in higher education, see Conyers 1995; Huggins 1985, esp. 45–46. The former Black Panther Elaine Brown (1992) provides a political analysis of Karenga's Black cultural nationalism and its impact on Black studies formation at the University of California, Los Angeles. Henry Louis Gates (1992) offers an interesting

comparison of the different paths taken by Black studies and women's studies and their impact on Black women's studies. Gates notes that the Black arts movement of the 1960s generated Black studies but did not have an impact on the traditional university curriculum. In contrast, White women in the academy and the women's studies programs they created have influenced the general curriculum and in turn are part of the revitalization of Black women's studies.

Explaining the appeal of Afrocentrism to some Black academics in higher education is another issue. Describing the relationship of British Black social workers to their clients, the Black British sociologist Paul Gilroy speculates about how the contradictory location of Blacks working on behalf of Black issues in White-supported institutional settings heightens the appeal of Black consciousness approaches such as Afrocentrism to this constituency: "It is possible to see the invocation of racial identity and culture in the mystic forms of kinship and blood characteristic of cultural nationalism as the means with which black professionals in these institutions have sought to justify the special quality of their relationship with their black clients. These ideas provide a superficially coherent ideological reply to the contradictory position black professionals occupy" (Gilroy 1987, 66–67). In short, Afrocentrism may provide a mechanism for remaining ideologically connected to Black civil society when practitioners find themselves distanced by being in White-controlled institutions.

10. For standard works on Black nationalism and its place in African American politics, see Franklin 1992; Jones 1997; Karenga 1978; Moses 1978; Pinkney 1976; Robinson 2001; Van Deburg 1997. For an analysis of Afrocentrism as a civil religion, see chapter 3 of this volume.

11. Hine 1992.

12. Yuval-Davis 1997.

13. For discussions of Black cultural nationalism, see Franklin 1992; Moses 1978; Pinkney 1976.

14. Gayle 1971; Van Deburg 1992.

15. See, for example, Goldberg 1993; Gossett 1963; Gould 1981; Jordan 1968; McKee 1993.

16. Crenshaw 1993.

17. Smitherman 1977.

18. Asante 1987, 1990.

19. See, for example, Diop 1974.

20. Fanon 1963; Karenga 1978. In this effort, Black cultural nationalism is not an aberration; instead, it resembles the nationalist aspirations of comparable groups. Analyzing Chicano nationalism, the theorist Genero M. Padilla observes, "What we see repeated again and again, whether it be in nineteenth-century Hungary or Czechoslovakia, the Irish nationalist movement, the African anti-colonial uprisings, or even the French Canadian autonomy drive ... is a close relationship between a people's desire to determine their own political fortunes and their passion to report their own cultural myths, a vital psychic component of national identity which gives energy and purpose to their political struggle" (Padilla 1989, 113). Black cultural nationalism aims to give a similar purpose to Black political struggle—namely, the purpose of self-definition and self-determination. As Padilla points out, "Without heroic dreams and cultural symbols of mythic

proportion . . . the material aims of a nationalist movement may lack the spiritual center which sustains struggle" (Padilla 1989, 114).

21. Dubey 1994; Gayle 1971.

22. For a more comprehensive discussion of "soul," see Collins 2004, 282–89.

23. Baldwin 1980.

24. Cross 1971.

25. Ibid.; Fanon 1967; Nobles 1972.

26. Anderson 1983.

27. Ben-Jochannan 1972.

28. For an analysis and historical context for this approach and its ties to prior racial analyses, see Appiah 1992. The chapter "Ethnophilosophy and Its Critics" is especially useful, especially his critique of Diop (ibid., 101) and the links between pan-Africanism and Black cultural nationalism.

29. Asante 1987, 1990; Karenga 1982; Myers 1988. Invoking African-derived frameworks to explain and interpret Black life and culture originated much earlier (Herskovitz 1990). For example, William E. B. Du Bois's work on the Negro American family explicitly addressed the African origins of such family life (Du Bois 1969). Du Bois's situation illustrates how political factors have shaped the contours of Afrocentrism. Du Bois could not find a position as an academician and turned to political activism as the primary orientation for his intellectual production. As a result, while he may have pursued Afrocentric scholarship had he been able to find the resources to do so, he turned to political activism outside of academe (Broderick 1974; Green and Driver 1978). Thus, the issue is less the longevity of Afrocentrism as a theoretical orientation guiding scholarship than the lack of institutional resources available for Afrocentrism's development.

30. For classic works in these areas, see Diop 1974; Mbiti 1969; Serequeberhan 1991; Thompson 1983.

31. Holloway 1990; Herskovitz 1990.

32. For discussions of self, see Myers 1998; on concern for harmony as a fundamental principle of community organization where individuals find their worth in relationship to a community and to nature, and in relationship to some supreme idea or being, see Asante 1987; on the relationship between the spiritual and material aspects of being and for a cyclical versus linear conception of time, change, and human agency, consult Richards 1980.

33. Asante and Asante 1990; Holloway 1990.

34. Brodhead 1987; Diop 1974.

35. Asante 1990; Karenga 1990.

36. For discussions of family, consult Dickerson 1995; Sudarkasa 1981. On Black religious expression and spirituality, see Hood 1994; Mitchell and Lewter 1986; Sobel 1979. On Black cultural production, see Asante and Asante 1990; Cone 1972; Thompson 1983. On language, consult Smitherman 1977.

37. Cabral 1973; Fanon 1963; San Juan Jr. 1992.

38. Asante 1990.

39. Wallace 1990, 19.

40. See, for example, Welsing 1991.

41. Akbar 1991, 36.

42. Baldwin 1980; Myers 1988; White and Parham 1990. For representative scholarship in Black psychology, see articles by Wade Nobles, Na'im Akbar, and William E. Cross, among others, in the special issue "Psychological Nigrescence," *Consulting Psychologist* 12, no. 2 (April 1989). Also, the *Journal of Black Psychology* routinely examines issues of Black identity.

43. Gilroy 2000.

44. Winant 1994.

45. Ransby and Matthews 1993, 59.

46. For a discussion of strategic essentialism, see Spivak 1993, 1–25.

47. Cabral 1973; Fanon 1967.

48. Diawara in Dent 1992, 289.

49. For an extended discussion of how American national identity has been built from the traditional family ideal and how public policies are influenced by this process, see the essays in Part I of this volume.

50. Yuval-Davis 1997.

51. Andersen 1991; Thorne 1992.

52. Coontz 1992; Zinn 1992.

53. Collins 1989. See also Collins 2004, 181–85.

54. See the essays in Bambara 1970.

55. Brown 1992.

56. Davis 1974.

57. Baraka 1970, 8. Baraka has since gone through substantial changes of political philosophy. Smitherman reports that Baraka had the following reaction to the 1995 Million Man March on Washington: "Some Blacks, such as 1960s activist and writer, Amiri Baraka, took issue with the March because it did not include women. Baraka remarked that if he were going to war, he wouldn't leave half the army at home" (Smitherman 1996, 105).

58. Yuval-Davis 1997.

59. For discussions of eugenics and race, see Duster 1990; Haller 1984. See also Davis 1981, 202–21.

60. For a discussion of the Tuskegee experiment, see Jones 1993.

61. Collins 2000a. See also Collins 2004, 119–48.

62. For an extended discussion of these issues, see "Prisons for Our Bodies, Closets for Our Minds: Racism, Heterosexism, and Black Sexuality" in Collins 2004, 87–116.

63. See, for example, Cleaver 1968.

64. Anthias and Yuval-Davis 1992.

65. Gates 1992, 79.

66. For a critique of gender complementarity in African American communities, see Collins 2004, 119–212.

67. Davis 1994, 37.

68. Terborg-Penn et al. 1987.

69. Reagon 1987; Sudarkasa 1981.

70. Tate 1983.

71. For a discussion of this issue, see Jordan 1981.

72. Dubey 1994.

73. Welsing 1991.
74. Ransby and Matthews 1993, 59.
75. White 1990, 75.
76. Asante 1987, 1990; Madhubuti 1990; Myers 1988.
77. Asante 1990, 9.
78. Ibid., 10.
79. On violence, see Collins 1998c; Crenshaw 1991; Hall 1983; Harris 1984; West 1999; White 1985. On Black women's political activism, see Avery 1994; Collier-Thomas and Franklin 2001; Gilkes 2001; Reagon 1987; Rouse 2004; Springer 1999; Terborg-Penn et al. 1987; White 1999. On gendered analyses of work and family, see Dill 1988; Franklin 1997. On reproductive rights, see Hartouni 1997; Kuumba 1993; Nsiah-Jefferson 1989; Springer 1999. On heterosexism and homophobia, see Battle et al. 2002; Clarke 1983; Cohen 1999; Cohen and Jones 1999; Smith 1998. And on intersectional analyses of Black political economy, see Brewer 1994; Collins 2000b; Omolade 1994.
80. Bambara 1970.
81. For histories of the social movement politics of Black feminism, see Roth 2004, 76–128; White 1999, 212–56. I also discuss Black feminism in the context of the modern women's movement in chapter 6 of this volume.
82. For a discussion of how the Black arts movement affected Black feminism, see Dubey 1994.
83. West 1993.

Chapter Five

Epigraphs: In Lerner 1972, 611–12; Bambara 1996, 95; Cleage 1995, 431.
1. Despite overlapping and competing meanings assigned to the term "community," this term remains central to African American politics. Two uses are common. First, the term can refer to a neighborhood or similar specific geographic locations. This sense of community invokes a home place, a homeland, and a home base. Among African Americans, this use of "community" often refers to both the Southern rural communities that provide home places for the majority of African Americans and urban neighborhoods that served as points of arrival for Black migrants. Even when working-class and middle-class Black Americans move away from these initial Black neighborhoods, they symbolize the heart of Black community. This geographic concept also characterizes uses within contemporary hip-hop culture. The use of the term "the 'hood" and messages about "keepin' it real" and "don't forget where you came from" speak to the importance of place among inner-city Black youth. In a second use, the term "community" can also refer to a population group that is not tethered to specific geographic locations. Here, "community" becomes a euphemism for Black ethnic group, Black nation, Black collectivity, or Blacks as a race. In this sense, the term "community" describes the social organization and cultural practices of Black civil society, especially its families, churches, fraternal groups, and grassroots organizations, as well as its cultural production music, dance, literature, film, and art. In both of these usages, "the notion of the 'community' assumes an organic wholeness. The community is a 'natural' social unit. It is 'out there' and one either belongs to it or not" (Anthias and Yuval-Davis 1992, 163).

2. As the twentieth child in a sharecropping family, Hamer, like other Black Mississippians before the 1960s, was denied an education and went to work as a timekeeper on a plantation. After eighteen years on this job, she attended a mass meeting on voting and was so inspired by the speeches that she agreed to be one of seventeen African Americans who would try to register to vote. Hamer's recognized political activism began with this act and led to activities such as heading a delegation at the Democratic Party's National Convention that challenged the party's exclusion of African American representatives and organizing a food cooperative that was open to poor Blacks and poor Whites (Crawford et al. 1990).

3. Toni Cade Bambara's essays and fiction examine all aspects of African American experiences, especially the significance of Black artists and intellectuals for Black community development. For representative works, see Bambara 1992, 1996; Bambara 1970.

4. *What Looks Like Crazy on an Ordinary Day* (1997) and *I Wish I Had a Red Dress* (2001), Peal Cleage's two books of fiction, examine gender politics within African American communities. In these novels, she not only speaks out against violence against women and girls but is one of the few authors to take on issues of sexuality and HIV/AIDS.

5. Sociologists have turned to the concept of collective identity to fill gaps in social movement literature. The concepts of resource mobilization and political process have been especially helpful in examining how and why social movements emerge and function. For an analysis of this literature, see Polletta and Jasper 2001.

6. Ibid. 2001, 285. One key feature of collective identities is that, for individuals within such groups, collective identity carries with it positive or negative feelings for other members of the group.

7. This collective-identity framework has been used to study feminism. See, for example, Verta Taylor and Leila J. Rupp's application of the framework to the twentieth-century international women's movement (Taylor and Rupp 1993).

8. For a close reading of community work, see Gilkes 2001, 15–20. See also Collins 1994.

9. I present an extended analysis of this issue in Collins 2000a, 201–25.

10. For an extended discussion of how the themes of individualism, rights, and property affect Western feminism, see chapter 6 of this volume.

11. Gilkes 2001, 4.

12. Brown 1994, 125.

13. Berry 1994.

14. The longevity and scope of negative depictions of Black people within the media has generated a comprehensive body of literature. For selected work within this tradition, see Bogle 2001; Entman and Rojecki 2000; Gray 1995. For a discussion of how contemporary African Americans have used the media to express alternative points of view, see Neal 2002. For an analysis of how race, class, gender, and sexuality intersect within contemporary popular culture, see Collins 2004, 119–80.

15. Hord and Lee 1995.

16. For an extensive discussion of this term, see Higginbotham 1993. See, also, Reagon 1987 for a description of how this concept intersected with African

American women's activities as cultural workers. For a comprehensive historical overview of Black women's organizations, see White 1999.

17. Higginbotham 1993.

18. Hine 1993, 343.

19. Cannon 1988. Within African American theology, issues of racial justice have been cast within frameworks of social justice. One major issue faced by Black feminists has been extending this framework to issues of gender and, most recently, continued extension of this logic to questions of sexuality. Womanist theology examines these contradictions. See Douglas 1999.

20. Higginbotham 1993.

21. Much discussion centers on the patterns and significance of Black women's self-naming practices—in this case, issues of feminism and womanism. Here I use feminism, although much of what I argue in this essay would be recognizable to many African American women as womanism. For a summary of these debates, see Collins 1998a, 61–70.

22. Adler 1992.

23. Crawford et al. 1990.

24. Barnett 1993; Sacks 1988.

25. Collins 2000a. I think that contemporary Western feminism has traveled some distance in incorporating these ideas into its rhetoric. In part, this may reflect the sustained critiques of its race and class politics raised by racial/ethnic women who find themselves within minority groups in the United States, Canada, Great Britain, and other advanced Western societies. These shifts also result from the greatly changed demographics of the women's movement in the global context, where the diverse groups of women in postcolonial societies have catalyzed new issues within the women's movement and have challenged some of the prevailing assumptions of Western feminism.

26. Gilkes 2001, 4.

27. Feldstein 2000, 86–110.

28. Anderson-Bricker 1999.

29. See Evelyn Brooks Higginbotham's study of women's leadership in Baptist churches (Higginbotham 1993).

30. For information on the status of the African American population, consult *The Black Population in the United States: March 2002*, available at www.census.gov/prod/2003pubs/p-20-541.pdf.

31. For an insightful analysis of these trends in the mass media, see Neal 2002.

32. Radford-Hill 2000.

33. For overviews of racial desegregation in housing, see Massey and Denton 1993; Orfield and Ashkinaze 1991. For a discussion of how racial segregation persists among Black middle-class families, see Patillo-McCoy 1999.

34. For representative work on the contours and significance of changes in African American social class structure, see E. Anderson 1990; Dawson 1994; Graham 2000; Kelley 1994; Patillo-McCoy 1999; Wilson 1978, 1987, 1996.

35. Squires 1994.

36. For discussions of neighborhood change and its effects on African American neighborhoods, see E. Anderson 1990; Brewer 1995; Brooks 2002; Franklin 1997;

Glasgow 1980; Simon and Burns 1997; Small and Newman 2001; Wilson 1987, 1996.

37. For analyses of Black women as single mothers, see Brewer 1995; Dickerson 1995; Franklin 1997; Geiger 1995; Jarrett 1994; Okongwu 1993. For analyses of Black women's work, see Amott and Matthaei 1991; Dill 2002; Glenn 1992; Jones 1985.

38. Radford-Hill 2000.

39. Avery 1994.

40. For an introduction to womanist ethics and its potential and actual role in Black community politics, see Cannon 1988; Douglas 1999; Grant 1989. For a discussion of how the religious ethos in Black civil society shapes African American politics, see Lincoln 1999; Patillo-McCoy 1998. See also my discussion of the intersections of religion, ethnicity, and Black nationalism in chapter 3 of this volume.

41. For an analysis of why some African American women supported the march, see Smitherman 1996; Smooth and Tucker 1999.

42. Tait 1999.

43. Amott 1990.

44. Siobhan Brooks (2002, 115) uses this term to describe the women in her working-class African American neighborhood. Here I present community work as historically having organizational bases in Black neighborhoods, yet Brooks describes a similar ethos that is not attached to community institutions. For discussions of how women within racial/ethnic communities express this ethos of "everyday feminism," see Hernández and Rehman 2002.

45. Radford-Hill 2000, xi.

46. Ibid., xiii. I share Radford-Hill's concerns but think that she gives modern Black feminism far more power that it actually has. Black feminism constitutes one factor in a broad array of negative forces that have eroded the status of women and girls in the post–Civil Rights era. The task is less one of connecting theories of gender oppression to grassroots activism than of analyzing how such theories became cut off from grassroots activism. One critical factor has been the lessening of grassroots activism in a media-saturated environment. Ironically, the successes of the Civil Rights and Black Power movements positioned grassroots organizations for co-optation. Black grassroots organizations and civil-rights organizations faced the challenges of their apparent successes. These challenges have taken forms as diverse as having the power of Black radical language co-opted by the state to individuals being offered jobs within the growing prison industry, social-welfare bureaucracies, and community colleges that track African American students into technical-degree programs. As the anthropologist Steven Gregory observes, "Depoliticizing of race in local activism can be viewed in part as the result of a harnessing of the public sphere of African American neighborhood life to state sponsored mechanisms of political participation, established in the wake of civil rights era activism and urban unrest" (Gregory 1994, 149). For a discussion of co-optation, see Omi and Winant 1994. The task identified by Radford-Hill is critical. It is equally important to recognize the pressures on both Black intellectual production, in this case Black feminist thought and grassroots political activism—namely, Black women's community work.

47. Cole and Guy-Sheftall 2003; Collins 20004.

48. There is a huge body of literature on Western feminism, and I make no effort to summarize it here. Instead, see the following works for perspectives on how Western feminism and Black feminism are related: Bannerji 1995; Caraway 1991; Collins 2000a; Hernández and Rehman 2002; Roth 2004. For my own close reading of the intersections of Western feminism in the United States and Black feminism under the new racism, see chapter 6 of this volume.

49. See, for example, Andersen 1991; Collier et al. 1992; Thorne 1992.

50. For extended discussions of how family serves as a template for naturalizing hierarchy, see Collins 1998b, 2001. See also chapter 1 of this volume.

51. For a multicultural analysis of women and work in the United States, see Amott and Matthaei 1991. For an overview of Black women and work, see Jones 1985. For an extended discussion of the family as a naturalizing and normalizing institution for intersecting systems of oppression, see chapter 1 of this volume.

52. Gilkes 2001, 11.

53. Elsewhere, I have written extensively on Black women and motherhood. For an early version of the argument presented here, see Collins 1994. For a general overview of African American women and motherhood, see Collins 2000a, 173–99.

54. For work on African influences in African American families, especially the significance of extended families and consanguineal family networks, see Gutman 1976; Sudarkasa 1981. For representative work discussing the significance of attacks on African American families within U.S. public policy, see Coontz 1992; Collins 1989; Franklin 1997, 153–214; Moynihan 1965.

55. For two overviews and critiques of these group-based traditions among African Americans, see chapters 3 and 4 of this volume. Both essays stress the importance of collective identity politics for African American survival. Both essays also examine some of the internal contradictions that affect these politics.

56. For a discussion of the distinctions between civic and ethnic nationalism, see Calhoun 1993.

57. In some European traditions, for example, the construction of nation is viewed as grounded in patriarchy (Kaplan 1997, 7–8).

58. Wells 1998, 251.

59. Ibid., 251.

60. Ibid., 253.

61. Naples 1991.

62. Ibid., 491.

63. Saegert 1989.

64. Terrelonge 1984, 557.

65. Ibid. Pauline Terrelonge's ideas were an opening volley of Black feminist criticism that increasingly identified Black women's working for community not as a sign of strength but as evidence of exploitation. More recently, the self-defined hip-hop feminist Joan Morgan identified and rejected this icon of the "Strong Black Woman" (Morgan 1999).

66. Matthews 1989; Poster 1995.

67. For general works on the significance of nationalism, see Anderson 1983; Calhoun 1993; Enloe 1990; Kaplan 1997; Mosse 1985; Yuval-Davis 1997.

68. Black civil society exists in large part due to persistent racism organized via racial segregation. Longstanding efforts to keep Blacks separate in turn have stimulated a historical Black nationalist-influenced political program within Black civil society. It is important to remember that among African Americans, Black nationalism is not merely an academic theory but has palpable political repercussions. Black nationalism has long been widespread among a significant segment of African Americans, and its influence has been felt among Black people who do not identify themselves as nationalists. For general works on Black nationalism, see Franklin 1992; Karenga 1978; Moses 1978; Van Deburg 1997. For an overview of Black nationalism in the post–Civil Rights era, see Robinson 2001.

69. I discuss these ideas in depth in chapter 3 of this volume. See also Franklin 1992; Moses 1978; Pinkney 1976; Robinson 2001; Van Deburg 1997.

70. For further discussion of these ideas, see chapter 1 of this volume.

71. See chapter 4 of this volume. For related criticisms of the gender politics of Black culture and Black nationalism, see Dubey 1994; Lubiano 1997; Ransby and Matthews 1993; White 1990.

72. Rouse 2004.

73. Thiam 1978. For a discussion of African American women as cultural workers, see Reagon 1987.

74. Internal racism and external racism constitute two interrelated forms of social control that have both been targeted toward African Americans. Internal racism occurs when powerful racial groups subordinate less powerful racial groups within one society, typically because they need such groups to maintain their standard of living. External racism occurs when powerful racial groups aim to remove less powerful groups from schools, jobs, neighborhoods, regions, nation-states, or social spaces that more powerful groups perceive as being their property or birthright. Designed to maintain the racial homogeneity of the neighborhood, school, occupational category, or nation-state, such racism aims to purify geographical or social space of the threat that inferior races seemingly represent. For a discussion of these racial formations, see Balibar and Wallerstein 1991.

75. For a detailed study of the practices of everyday racism, see Essed 1991. For research on practices used by White Americans to minimize racism, see Bonilla-Silva 2001.

76. Cabral 1973; Fanon 1963; San Juan Jr. 1992.

77. The new Black-run nation-states grounded in principles of Western democracy have also incorporated legacies of customary laws that subordinated women and children. Take, for example, the case of Unity Dow in Botswana. Dow was born in Botswana to two citizens of Botswana. When Dow became a single parent, her child was granted Botswanian citizenship. Yet when Dow married a White American and had two additional children, who were also born in Botswana, the two children whose father was American were denied Botswanian citizenship. In Botswana, citizenship descended through the father; even though the children were born to a Botswanian mother in Botswana, they were not considered citizens. Dow, a lawyer, sued and won. Despite women's participation in nationalist and class struggles, as well as their possession of formal rights under new national laws, gender inequality in the domestic sphere persists (Steady 1993).

78. For an accessible summary of these ideas, see Yuval-Davis 1997. Also, the distinction that I make here between cultural workers and culture bearers may also function as one important criterion for categorizing forms of Black American nationalism itself.

79. See, for example, views of the role of women within traditional Mexican society and how this affected Chicano nationalism in Padilla 1989. See also how these ideas framed Chicana feminism in Roth 2004, 129–77.

80. For an extended analysis of how ideas about women are important to American national identity, see my discussion of how a logic of eugenics frames contemporary population politics in chapter 2 of this volume. For work that examines this process in an international context, see Enloe 1990; Kaplan 1997; Yuval-Davis 1997.

81. Carbado 1999, 4.

82. For an extended discussion of these issues, see Collins 2004.

83. For an extended discussion of the class and gender politics of Black respectability and Black authenticity, see ibid., 71–75, 121–48.

84. Gilkes 2001, 5.

85. Morgan 1999, 44.

86. For example, Morgan (1999) criticizes harm done to Black women by the image of the Strong Black Woman.

87. Pierce-Baker 1998; West 1999; White 1985.

88. As of this writing, Simmons is still raising money to complete this important film.

89. For a discussion of these issues, see Pough 2004.

90. Because publishers have realized the power of Black women's consumer dollars, there is, however, a growing mass market for romance novels targeted to Black women. In some cases, African American authors have managed to ride the crest of this publisher-driven trend and carve out a third space between so-called high fiction and tabloid journalism. I am thinking here of the success of Terri MacMillan's books, several of which have been made into movies, and the visibility of Black LGBT issues in the works of E. Lynn Harris.

91. Pough 2004.

92. Griffin 2002, 122–23.

93. West's edited volume contains case studies of feminist nationalist movements in Europe, the Middle East, Africa, Central and East Asia, the Pacific Islands, and the Americas. West suggests that academe has not yet adequately defined women in actual political struggles. She notes that in much of the discourse on nationalism, women remain invisible, subsumed under the "fraternity" of nation; they constitute another variable to be studied within predefined nationalist movements; or women are analyzed primarily through the lens of cultural nationalism. In response, West argues, "Not only must we begin with the women's standpoint on nationalism and feminism, we must move to an understanding of the construction of nationalism as an inherently 'gendered' phenomenon" (West 1997b, xiv).

94. The definitions here are difficult. This group could be seen as women who have been harmed by Western racism—in other words, women of color. Alternatively, I am thinking here of women of the South versus those in the North. The term "Third World" also aims to encapsulate this population of women of color.

What places them in this third space is not their ethnicity or color per se, but the history of their group with racism that in turn has fostered nationalistic responses.

95. West 1997b, xiii.

96. Within a nationalist feminist framework, Western feminism itself exists as a form of "White feminist nationalism" whereby Whites have control over the nation-state apparatuses and the feminism expressed by White women in particular has been constructed within nationalist assumptions associated with race. Feminist nationalist frameworks remind us that whiteness is also a "race," and one that is just as central to the feminism produced by White women in the West as by Black women in continental Africa, Latin America, the Caribbean, Europe, and North America. The issue with Western feminism lies less in its content than in the Western tendency to elevate it to the status of a universal feminism rather than see it as one standpoint in a particular social and political context. For an extended discussion of this theme, see chapter 6 of this volume.

97. Griffin 2002, 117. E. Frances White's criticism of some of my earlier work in this area points out the difficulties of the type of synthesis that I attempt here (White 1990). At the time, it was less clear to me that I was trying to synthesize nationalism and feminism. White dismisses any potential success for such a project, mainly because she is so closely wedded to the assumptions of Western feminism that it is difficult for her to imagine a Black feminism that is so closely intertwined with Black community-development strategies that it transforms existing notions of Black nationalism. I see ideologies and social practices as being much more malleable and historically contingent.

98. Crenshaw 1992.

99. See chapter 6 of this volume.

100. Chambers 1996; Jones 1994; Morgan 1999.

101. Pough 2004.

102. Here I make a distinction between women of color whose history within the United States predates the massive wave of immigration since 1965. Vietnamese, Cambodian, and Pakistani immigrant groups from Asian societies and Caribbean and African immigrants from African diasporic societies enter into these issues, but in different ways. For a discussion of the original racial triangle and how it has framed race in America, see chapter 1 of this volume.

103. For work on Chicana feminism, see Alarcón 1999; Garcia 1997; Roth 2004, 129–77; Sampaio 2002.

104. Guerrero 1997, 101.

105. White ethnic women face similar pressures. Scholarship that examines the process of Americanization by claiming Whiteness has not yet addressed how this may be a gender-specific process. See, for example, Sacks 1994 on the whitening of Jews and Ignatiev 1995 on how the Irish became White. Work on immigrant women of color best captures these intersectional dynamics among ethnicity (here discussed in its politicized form as a national identity), racism, and citizenship. Work on Asian and Latina immigrants investigates issues of negotiating gender expectations of racial/ethnic migrant communities, the labor needs of domestic work, and assimilation into American society (Americanization).

106. This is a vast literature, and I make no attempt to summarize it here. For a solid theoretical overview of the myriad issues that affect women of color in

a global context as presented by women of color, see Alexander and Mohanty 1997 as well as essays in their edited volume. For articles on the connections between feminism and antiracism in a transnational context, see Twine and Blee 2001.

107. Gluck 1997.

108. In a global context, this theme reappears across numerous societies within scholarship that examines how new nation-states are deeply gendered endeavors. For work in this tradition, see works by Kaplan 1997 on Europe; Heng and Devan 1992 on Singapore; and Bacchetta 2001 on India. For a complex analysis of these issues, see Alexander 1997.

109. Moghissi 1999.

110. Emeagwali 1995.

111. Steady 1993, 92–93.

112. Fester 1998; Mangaliso 1997.

113. Magona 1998.

114. For a range of essays by Black British women who struggled to craft this new identity, see Mirza 1997.

115. Sudbury 1998.

116. Benjamin and Mendonca 1997.

117. Lerner 1972, 613.

Chapter Six

Epigraph: Morgan 1999, 36.

1. Other women of color demonstrate similar choices. For example, *Colonize This! Young Women of Color on Today's Feminism* (Hernández and Rehman 2002), a book of personal essays by a diverse collection of young women of color, engages these issues of feminism and nationalism through the use of personal narratives.

2. Springer 2002.

3. The next section relies on social movement theory—in particular, work on the women's movement. Recent social-movement research focuses on the continuity of movements during times of abeyance, times when collective action is less visible. For extended analyses of these ideas, see Taylor 1989; Taylor and Rupp 1993; Taylor and Whittier 1992.

4. New York Radical Feminists 1969, 442.

5. Combahee River Collective 1995, 13.

6. Ibid., 233.

7. Ibid.

8. Ibid., 234.

9. For an overview and historical treatment of the centrality of the personal as political for feminist theory, see Stanley and Wise 1993. They identify three defining features that they see as central to feminist theory: (1) women are oppressed; (2) the personal is the political; and (3) feminist consciousness is essential for women to gain an understanding of the first two features. The actual origins of the idea of the personal as political remain contested. Rae Chow (1993) attributes the concept to consciousness-raising during the Chinese Revolution, where peasants were encouraged to "speak bitterness" against the old regime. Barbara Omolade attributes the popularity of the concept in the United States to Ella

Baker's use of it during the Civil Rights Movement in the 1950s (Omolade 1994). Charles Lemert takes a different view, attributing the intellectual origins to the populist tradition of C. Wright Mills within sociology (Lemert 1995). This all raises the question of how the realm of "private expressions" relates to consciousness-raising as feminist method and to individual and collective consciousness. For example, Catherine McKinnon claims consciousness-raising as a *feminist* method of theorizing. In contrast, as Chow, Omolade, and Lemert suggest, this form of praxis was not invented by feminism and was not intended as an academic exercise. Rather, severing this method of theorizing from its initial political mooring results in an impoverishment of politics. In the case of Western feminism, abandoning praxis left both the personal and the political vulnerable to cooptation.

10. Sarachild 1978.

11. Hanisch 1978, 204.

12. Ibid.

13. Stanley and Wise 1993, 57.

14. For a discussion of these organizations, see Roth 2004, 76–128.

15. White 1999, 242–53.

16. Ibid., 243–45. The Black Women's Liberation Group of Mount Vernon/ New Rochelle, a collective meeting in the late 1960s that consisted primarily of African American and poor women, also used consciousness-raising tactics to identify issues that were important to group members. They initially met to discuss their personal experiences as Black women. But over time, this group became an outspoken critic of women's oppression and a militant advocate of women's liberation. The history of the National Welfare Rights Organization (NWRO), also composed primarily of poor and African American women, relied on consciousness-raising as an important tool of political organizing.

17. Roth 2004, 118–27; White 1999, 256.

18. Benita Roth suggests that White feminists striving to build a movement that was autonomous from the New Left decided not to try to build coalitions across race and class. For a similar analysis of the race and class politics of the women's movement, see Caraway 1991.

19. Many women's groups may have used consciousness-raising as a style of political organizing, but this tactic also has certain key assumptions that may not be shared across diverse racial, ethnic, or social class groups. Strategies typifying the participatory democracy of radical feminist consciousness-raising groups—the lack of formal group structure, an emphasis on participation by everyone, deliberate sharing of tasks among group members, and the exclusion of men as a precondition for women's healing—were not uniformly endorsed by other progressive movements. For example, one study of the group-building practices of two grassroots environmental movements revealed divergent approaches to community that reflected cultural differences of the membership of each group. One group—largely White, middle-class, and college-educated—constructed a personalized movement community that accented individual responsibility and individual voice within a collective effort. In contrast, the other group—primarily low- to moderate-income African Americans—created a local communitarian movement that emphasized the collective effort of a united membership. While both groups supported a comparable environmental agenda, differences in what each group saw as appropriate

political communities interfered with their ability to work together (Lichterman 1995).

20. Taylor 1989; Taylor and Rupp 1993; Taylor and Whittier 1992.

21. For example, Chicana feminism has grappled with issues of women's poverty, citizenship status, and norms within Chicano communities (Garcia 1997). Puerto Rican feminism has engaged the issue of the effects of Puerto Rico's status as a pseudo-colony of the United States on women's issues—in particular, reproductive issues and labor status.

22. Other models existed from the inception of modern feminism. For example, the Combahee River Collective advanced an intersectional model of feminism in the early 1980s (Combahee River Collective 1995). This group identified race, class, gender, and sexuality as intersecting categories of analysis. They counseled a feminism that was grounded in inclusiveness. However, because so few Black women or women of color found positions of leadership within mainstream feminism, groups such as these found themselves in a border zone of "explaining" the absence of Black women and other women of color within White feminist organizations.

23. Daniels 1991, 592.

24. Katzenstein 1990.

25. Rhode 1995, 703.

26. Katz 1989.

27. See, for example, Fox-Genovese 1979–80.

28. An example is African American radicalism that took root in the 1930s that might have offered effective racial critiques of American capitalism yet was suppressed (Kelley 2002). This tradition might also have advanced a class analysis of women's place in American political economy that was more evident in British and French feminist work unencumbered by this suppression.

29. Smith 1995.

30. Mercer 1994, 148.

31. For a discussion of feminist organizations, see, for example, Martin 1990.

32. Fried 1994; Matthews 1989; Rodriguez 1988.

33. In her comprehensive overview of feminist organizations, Patricia Yancey Martin (1990) distinguishes between a feminist group and a feminist organization as a relatively enduring group of people that is structured to pursue goals that are collectively identified. My argument refers to the point at which feminist groups become institutionalized as feminist organizations. As Martin notes, "Feminist organizations that combine the qualities of social movement organizations and mainstream, professional service organizations are criticized as having been coopted.... In actuality, few feminist organizations reflect a pure or ideal type, and scholars should use caution in labeling mixed types as coopted, institutionalized, or no longer part of the women's movement" (Martin 1990, 186).

34. Hernández and Leong 2004.

35. Ibid. 2004.

36. Wiegman 2002, 18.

37. Ibid. Two factors stand out as causing this concern. One is the persistent fear that gender studies has emerged as an alternative to women's studies,

undermining women as the focus of study and thus weakening the historical link between the U.S. women's movement and the institutionalization of feminism in the academy. The other concerns the costs of bureaucratization. When coupled with the careerist, consumer-oriented reconfiguration of colleges and universities, many of the pedagogical emphases of early women's studies have been lost.

38. For a comprehensive treatment of this theme, as well as a good survey of the history of women's studies in the United States, see Buker 2003.

39. Wiegman 2002, 29.

40. Collins 1998a, 124–54.

41. Radford-Hill 2000, xvii–xviii.

42. Christian 1988.

43. Griffin 2002, 116.

44. I present an extended discussion of this argument in Collins 1998a, 44–76. See also Sheila Radford-Hill's analysis of the changing contours of Black women's empowerment within African American communities (Radford-Hill 2000, xvii–xviii).

45. Expressions of Black women's community work that struggle with the contradictions raised by intersections of feminism and nationalism also potentially address the ruptures of theory and activism that have characterized much academic feminism.

46. Other women of color in the United States as well as women in non–Western societies express a similar disdain for the term "feminism."

47. Smith 2002, 62.

48. For an analysis of the strategies that White Americans use to construct these raced and unraced identities, see Bonilla-Silva 2001.

49. For a discussion of how this process has operated in the United States, see chapter 1 of this volume.

50. Brooks 2002, 108.

51. Martinez 2002, 153.

52. I analyze these seeming contradictions as stemming from the ways in which Western feminism and Black nationalism are constructed as opposites. I suggest that a framework of feminist nationalism may be one promising path toward political and theoretical synthesis. See chapter 5 of this volume.

53. Concentrations of economic power (ownership of income-producing property), political power (direct supervisory authority in workplaces coupled with dominance in governmental arenas), and ideological power (managerial functions and control over the schools, media, and other forms of representation) distinguish the middle class from the working class. In contrast to models of social status reflecting beliefs in individualism, social-class approaches remain grounded in notions of group positionality (Higginbotham and Weber 1992). In contrast to group-based social-class models, education, prestige, and income represent social statuses—hierarchically structured relative rankings along a ladder of economic success and social prestige. Positions along these dimensions are not established by social relations of dominance and subordination but, instead, as rankings on scales representing resources and desirability. Reliance on social-status categories reinforces the tendency to see social issues in individualistic terms, while social class

fosters a collective orientation. This distinction between individual and group shapes discussions of individual and group standpoints, as well.

54. For a discussion of how this differential treatment frames U.S. population policies, see chapter 2 of this volume.

55. Smith 1995, 692.

56. I discuss these ideas at great length in Collins 2000a.

57. This denial of individuality and privacy also helps explain why Black LGBT people have not uniformly embraced the seemingly transgressive politics of queer theory. Black LGBT people have a distinctive position within these social relations that shapes their politics. For an extended discussion of this theme, see Collins 2004, 105–14. For a survey of Black LGBT opinions, including the unwillingness to claim the term "queer," see Battle et al. 2002.

58. Jamila 2002, 393–94.

59. Brooks 2002, 116–17. Is Wiegman's argument racist or elitist? Because I am familiar with the politics of academe, I think it is neither. Wiegman is sympathetic to the impetus to examine the links between academic feminism and its social-movement counterparts. She simply does not want this to be a requirement of contemporary academic feminism. At the same time, I can also see how arguments such as Wiegman's can easily be recast as such by those who are searching for some way to negotiate the tensions created by their "everyday feminism" and the theoretical feminism in the classroom. The freedom to leave one's social-movement activism at the door is a privilege that does strongly correlate with Whiteness, wealth, and American citizenship.

60. Austin 2002, 157.

61. Hernández and Rehman 2002.

62. Austin 2002, 162.

63. Brooks 2002, 115.

64. Hernández and Rehman 2002, xxii. Kimberly Springer also briefly examines the significance of Black feminism being introduced within college classrooms. Springer queries how the ideas of Black feminism might reach young people who do not have access to the *Village Voice*, a major publication that publishes the work of the women she surveys, or, for that matter, who do not live in New York City (Springer 2002, 1077).

65. Martinez 2002, 146.

66. See, for example, the essays in Bambara 1970.

67. Roth 2004.

68. I am indebted to Whitney Peoples, a graduate student in women's studies at the University of Cincinnati, for the ideas in this paragraph.

69. George 1998; Kitwana 2002; Rose 1994.

70. Springer 2002.

71. Pough 2004.

72. Morgan 1999.

73. For responses to Springer's analysis, see Radford-Hill 2002; Guy-Sheftall 2002.

74. Guy-Sheftall 2002, 1093.

75. Bynoe 2004.

76. Pierce-Baker 1998; West 1999; White 1985.

77. Additional information on *"NO!"* is available by contacting AfroLez Productions, P.O. Box 58085, Philadelphia, Penn. 19102-8085, www.echosoul.com/aishah.htm.

78. Talvi 2003.

79. Latifah 1999, 126–27.

80. Morgan 1999, 36.

81. Jamila 2002, 393–94.

References

Adler, Karen S. 1992. "'Always Leading Our Men in Service and Sacrifice': Amy Jacques Garvey, Feminist Black Nationalist." *Gender and Society* 6, no. 3: 346–75.

Akbar, Na'im. 1991. *Visions for Black Men*. Talahassee, Fla.: Mind Productions.

Alarcón, Norma. 1999. "Chicana Feminism: In the Tracks of 'the' Native Woman." Pp. 63–71 in *Between Woman and Nation: Nationalisms, Transnational Feminisms, and the State*, ed. Caren Kaplan, Norma Alarcón, and Minoo Moallem. Durham, N.C.: Duke University Press.

Alexander, M. Jacqui. 1997. "Erotic Autonomy as a Politics of Decolonization: An Anatomy of Feminist and State Practice in the Bahamas Tourist Industry." Pp. 63–100 in *Feminist Genealogies, Colonial Legacies, Democratic Futures*, ed. M. Jacqui Alexander and Chandra Talpade Mohanty. New York: Routledge.

Alexander, M. Jacqui, and Chandra Talpade Mohanty. 1997. "Introduction: Genealogies, Legacies, Movements." Pp. xiii–xlii in *Feminist Genealogies, Colonial Legacies, Democratic Futures*, ed. M. Jacqui Alexander and Chandra Talpade Mohanty. New York: Routledge.

Amott, Teresa L. 1990. "Black Women and AFDC: Making Entitlement Out of Necessity." Pp. 280–98 in *Women, the State, and Welfare*, ed Linda Gordon. Madison: University of Wisconsin Press.

Amott, Teresa L., and Julie Matthaei. 1991. *Race, Gender, and Work: A Multicultural Economic History of Women in the United States*. Boston: South End Press.

Andersen, Margaret L. 1991. "Feminism and the American Family Ideal." *Journal of Comparative Family Studies* 22, no. 2: 235–46.

Anderson, Benedict. 1983. *Imagined Communities: Reflections on the Origin and Spread of Nationalism*. London: Verso.

Anderson, Elijah. 1990. *Streetwise: Race, Class, and Change in an Urban Community*. Chicago: University of Chicago Press.

Anderson, Talmadge. 1990. *Black Studies: Theory, Method, and Cultural Perspectives*. Pullman: Washington State University Press.

Anderson-Bricker, Kristin. 1999. "'Triple Jeopardy': Black Women and the Growth of Feminist Consciousness in SNCC, 1964–1975." Pp. 49–69 in *Still Lifting, Still Climbing: African American Women's Contemporary Activism*, ed. Kimberly Springer. New York: New York University Press.

Anthias, Floya, and Nira Yuval-Davis. 1992. *Racialized Boundaries: Race, Nation, Gender, Colour and Class and the Anti-Racist Struggle*. New York: Routledge.

Appiah, Kwame A. 1992. *In My Father's House: Africa in the Philosophy of Culture*. New York: Oxford University Press.

Asante, Molefi K. 1987. *The Afrocentric Idea*. Philadelphia: Temple University Press.

———. 1990. *Kemet, Afrocentricity, and Knowledge*. Philadelphia: Temple University Press.

———. 1993. "Racism, Consciousness, and Afrocentricity." Pp. 127–43 in *Lure and Loathing: Essays on Race, Identity, and the Ambivalence of Assimilation*, ed. Gerald Early. New York: Penguin Books.

Asante, Molefi K., and Kariamu W. Asante, eds. 1990. *African Culture: The Rhythms of Unity*. Trenton, N.J.: Africa World Press.

Austin, Paula. 2002. "Femme-Inism: Lessons from My Mother." Pp. 157–69 in *Colonize This! Young Women of Color on Today's Feminism*, ed. Daisy Hernández and Bushra Rehman. New York: Seal Press.

Avery, Byllye Y. 1994. "Breathing Life into Ourselves: The Evolution of the National Black Women's Health Project." Pp. 4–10 in *The Black Women's Health Book: Speaking for Ourselves*, ed. Evelyn C. White. Seattle: Seal Press.

Bacchetta, Paola. 2001. "Extraordinary Alliances in Crisis Situations: Women against Hindu Nationalism in India." Pp. 220–49 in *Feminism and Antiracism: International Struggles for Justice*, ed. France Winddance Twine and Kathleen M. Blee. New York: New York University Press.

Baldwin, James, and Margaret Mead. 1971. *A Rap on Race*. New York: Laurel.

Baldwin, Joseph. 1980. "The Psychology of Oppression." Pp. 95–110 in *Contemporary Black Thought: Alternative Analyses in Social and Behavioral Sciences*, ed. Molefi K. Asante. Beverly Hills, Calif.: Sage Publications.

Balibar, Etienne, and Immanuel Wallerstein. 1991. *Race, Nation, Class: Ambiguous Identities*. New York: Verso.

Bambara, Toni Cade. 1992. *The Salt Eaters*. New York: Vintage.

———. 1996. *Deep Sightings and Rescue Missions: Fiction, Essays, and Conversations*. New York: Pantheon Books.

Bambara, Toni Cade, ed. 1970. *The Black Woman: An Anthology*. New York: Signet.

Bannerji, Himani. 1995. *Thinking Through: Essays on Feminism, Marxism, and Anti-Racism*. Toronto: Women's Press.

Baraka, Imamu A. 1970. "Black Woman." *Black World* 19, no. 9: 7–11.

Barnett, Bernice McNair. 1993. "Invisible Southern Black Women Leaders in the Civil Rights Movement: The Triple Constraints of Gender, Race, and Class." *Gender and Society* 7, no. 2: 162–82.

Battle, Juan, Cathy J. Cohen, Dorian Warren, Gerard Fergerson, and Suzette Audam. 2002. *Say It Loud, I'm Black and I'm Proud: Black Pride Survey 2000*. New York: Policy Institute of the National Gay and Lesbian Task Force.

Bauman, Zygmunt. 1998. *Globalization: The Human Consequences*. New York: Columbia University Press.

Bellah, Robert N. 1992. *The Broken Covenant: American Civil Religion in a Time of Trial*. Chicago: University of Chicago Press.

Benjamin, Medea, and Maisa Mendonca. 1997. *Benedita da Silva: An Afro-Brazilian Woman's Story of Politics and Love*. Oakland, Calif.: Institute for Food and Development Policy, Global Exchange.

Ben-Jochannan, Yosef. 1972. *Black Man of the Nile and His Family (African Foundations of European Civilization and Thought)*. New York: Alkebu-lan Books.

Berry, Mary Frances. 1994. *Black Resistance, White Law: A History of Constitutional Racism in America*. New York: Penguin Press.

Bock, Gisela. 1984. "Racism and Sexism in Nazi Germany: Motherhood, Compulsory Sterilization, and the State." Pp. 27–96 in *When Biology Became Destiny: Women in Weimar and Nazi Germany*, ed. Renate Bridenthal, Atina Grossmann, and Marion Kaplan. New York: Monthly Review Press.

Bogle, Donald. 2001. *Prime Time Blues: African Americans on Network Television*. New York: Farrar, Straus and Giroux.

Bonilla-Silva, Eduardo. 1996. "Rethinking Racism: Toward a Structural Interpretation." *American Sociological Review* 62 (June): 465–80.

———. 2001. *White Supremacy and Racism in the Post-Civil Rights Era*. Boulder, Colo.: Lynne Rienner Publishers.

Brewer, Rose. 1994. "Race, Class, Gender and U.S. State Welfare Policy: The Nexus of Inequality for African American Families." Pp. 115–27 in *Color, Class and Country: Experiences of Gender*, ed. Gay Young and Bette J. Dickerson. London: Zed.

———. 1995. "Gender, Poverty, Culture, and Economy: Theorizing Female-Led Families." Pp. 146–63 in *African American Single Mothers: Understanding Their Lives and Families*, ed. Bette Dickerson. Thousand Oaks, Calif.: Sage.

Bridenthal, Renate, Atina Grossmann, and Marion Kaplan, eds. 1984. *When Biology Became Destiny: Women in Weimar and Nazi Germany*. New York: Monthly Review Press.

Broderick, Francis L. 1974. "W. E. B. Du Bois: History of an Intellectual." Pp. 3–24 in *Black Sociologists: Historical and Contemporary Perspectives*, ed. James E. Blackwell and Morris Janowitz. Chicago: University of Chicago Press.

Brodhead, Frank. 1987. "The African Origins of Western Civilization." *Radical America* (May 21): 29–37.

Brodkin, Karen. 2000. *How Jews Became White Folks and What That Says about Race in America*. New Brunswick, N.J.: Rutgers University Press.

Brooks, Siobhan. 2002. "Black Feminism in Everyday Life: Race, Mental Illness, Poverty and Motherhood." Pp. 99–118 in *Colonize This! Young Women of Color on Today's Feminism*, ed. Daisy Hernández and Bushra Rehman. New York: Seal Press.

Brown, Elaine. 1992. *A Taste of Power: A Black Woman's Story*. New York: Pantheon Books.

Brown, Elsa Barkley. 1994. "Negotiating and Transforming the Public Sphere: African American Political Life in the Transition from Slavery to Freedom." *Public Culture* 7, no. 1: 107–46.

Buker, Eloise. 2003. "Is Women's Studies a Disciplinary or an Interdisciplinary Field of Inquiry?" *NWSA Journal* 15, no. 1: 73–93.

Bynoe, Yvonne. 2004. *Stand and Deliver: Political Activism, Leadership, and Hip Hop Culture*. Brooklyn, N.Y.: Soft Skull Press.

Cabral, Amilcar. 1973. "National Liberation and Culture." Pp. 39–56 in *Return to the Source: Selected Speeches of Amilcar Cabral*, ed. African Information Service. New York: Monthly Review Press.

Calhoun, Craig. 1993. "Nationalism and Ethnicity." *Annual Review of Sociology* 19: 211–39.

Calmore, John O. 2001. "Race-Conscious Voting Rights and the New Demogra-
  phy in a Multiracing America." *North Carolina Law Review* 79, no. 5: 1254–81.
Cannon, Katie G. 1988. *Black Womanist Ethics*. Atlanta: Scholars Press.
Caraway, Nancie. 1991. *Segregated Sisterhood: Racism and the Politics of American
  Feminism*. Knoxville: University of Tennessee Press.
Carbado, Devon W. 1999. "Introduction: Where and When Black Men Enter."
  Pp. 1–17 in *Black Men on Race, Gender, and Sexuality*, ed. Devon W. Carbado.
  New York: New York University Press.
Chambers, Veronica. 1996. *Mama's Girl*. New York: Riverhead Books.
Chang, Grace. 1994. "Undocumented Latinas: The New 'Employable Mothers.'"
  Pp. 259–86 in *Mothering: Ideology, Experience, and Agency*, ed. Evelyn Nakano
  Glenn, Grace Chang, and Rennie Forcey. New York: Routledge.
Childress, Alice. 1986. *Like One of the Family: Conversations from a Domestic's Life*.
  Boston: Beacon Press.
Chow, Rey. 1993. *Writing Diaspora: Tactics of Intervention in Contemporary Cultural
  Studies*. Bloomington: Indiana University Press.
Christian, Barbara. 1988. "The Race for Theory." *Feminist Studies* 14, no. 1: 67–79.
Clarke, Cheryl. 1983. "The Failure to Transform: Homophobia in the Black
  Community." Pp. 197–208 in *Home Girls: A Black Feminist Anthology*, ed.
  Barbara Smith. New York: Kitchen Table Press.
Cleage, Pearl. 1995. "What Can I Say?" Pp. 430–32 in *Words of Fire: An Anthology
  of African American Feminist Thought*, ed. Beverly Guy-Sheftall. New York:
  New Press.
———. 1997. *What Looks Like Crazy on an Ordinary Day*. New York: Avon Books.
———. 2001. *I Wish I Had a Red Dress*. New York: Perennial.
Cleaver, Eldridge. 1968. *Soul on Ice*. New York: McGraw-Hill.
Cohen, Cathy J. 1999. *The Boundaries of Blackness: AIDS and the Breakdown of Black
  Politics*. Chicago: University of Chicago Press.
Cohen, Cathy J., and Tamara Jones. 1999. "Fighting Homophobia versus
  Challenging Heterosexism: 'The Failure to Transform' Revisited." Pp. 80–101
  in *Dangerous Liaisons: Blacks, Gays, and the Struggle for Equality*, ed. Eric Brandt.
  New York: New Press.
Cole, Johnnetta Betsch, and Beverly Guy-Sheftall. 2003. *Gender Talk: The Struggle
  for Women's Equality in African American Communities*. New York: Ballantine.
Collier, Jane, Michelle Z. Rosaldo, and Sylvia Yanagisako. 1992. "Is There a
  Family? New Anthropological Views." Pp. 31–48 in *Rethinking the Family:
  Some Feminist Questions*, ed. Barrie Thorne and Marilyn Yalom. Boston:
  Northeastern University Press.
Collier-Thomas, Bettye, and V. P. Franklin, eds. 2001. *Sisters in the Struggle:
  African American Women in the Civil Rights–Black Power Movement*. New York:
  New York University Press.
Collins, Patricia Hill. 1989. "A Comparison of Two Works on Black Family Life."
  Signs 14, no. 4: 875–84.
———. 1994. "Shifting the Center: Race, Class, and Feminist Theorizing about
  Motherhood." Pp. 45–65 in *Mothering: Ideology, Experience and Agency*, ed.
  Evelyn Nakano Glenn, Grace Chang, and Linda Forcey. New York: Rout-
  ledge.

————. 1998a. *Fighting Words: Black Women and the Search for Justice.* Minneapolis: University of Minnesota Press.

————. 1998b. "It's All in the Family: Intersections of Gender, Race, and Nation." *Hypatia* 13, no. 3: 62–82.

————. 1998c. "The Tie That Binds: Race, Gender and U.S. Violence." *Ethnic and Racial Studies* 21, no. 5: 918–38.

————. 1999. "Producing the Mothers of the Nation: Race, Class and Contemporary U.S. Population Policies." Pp. 118–29 in *Women, Citizenship and Difference,* ed. Nira Yuval-Davis. London: Zed Books.

————. 2000a. *Black Feminist Thought: Knowledge, Consciousness, and the Politics of Empowerment.* New York: Routledge.

————. 2000b. "Gender, Black Feminism, and Black Political Economy." *Annals of the American Academy of Political and Social Science* 568 (March): 41–53.

————. 2001. "Like One of the Family: Race, Ethnicity, and the Paradox of US National Identity." *Ethnic and Racial Studies* 24, no. 1: 3–28.

————. 2004. *Black Sexual Politics: African Americans, Gender, and the New Racism.* New York: Routledge.

Combahee River Collective. 1995. "A Black Feminist Statement." Pp. 232–40 in *Words of Fire: An Anthology of African-American Feminist Thought,* ed. Beverly Guy-Sheftall. New York: New Press.

Cone, James H. 1972. *The Spirituals and the Blues: An Interpretation.* New York: Seabury Press.

Conyers, James H. 1995. *The Evolution of African American Studies.* Lantham, Md.: University Press of America.

Coontz, Stephanie. 1992. *The Way We Never Were: American Families and the Nostalgia Trap.* New York: Basic Books.

Crawford, Vickie, Jacqueline Anne Rouse, and Barbara Woods, eds. 1990. *Women in the Civil Rights Movement: Trailblazers and Torchbearers, 1941–1965.* Bloomington: Indiana University Press.

Crenshaw, Kimberlé W. 1991. "Mapping the Margins: Intersectionality, Identity Politics, and Violence against Women of Color." *Stanford Law Review* 43, no. 6: 1241–99.

————. 1992. "Whose Story Is It Anyway? Feminist and Antiracist Appropriations of Anita Hill." Pp. 402–40 in *Race-ing Justice, En-Gendering Power,* ed. Toni Morrison. New York: Pantheon Books.

————. 1993. "Beyond Racism and Misogyny: Black Feminism and 2 Live Crew." Pp. 111–32 in *Words That Wound: Critical Race Theory, Assaultive Speech, and the First Amendment,* ed. Mari J. Matsuda, Charles R. I. Lawrence, Richard Delgado, and Kimberlé Crenshaw. Boulder, Colo.: Westview Press.

————. 1997. "Color Blindness, History, and the Law." Pp. 280–88 in *The House That Race Built: Black Americans, U.S. Terrain,* ed. Wahneema Lubiano. New York: Pantheon.

Cross, William. 1971. "The Negro to Black Conversion Experience: Toward a Psychology of Black Liberation." *Black World* 20, no. 9: 13–27.

Daniels, Arlene K. 1991. "Careers in Feminism." *Gender and Society* 5, no. 4: 583–607.

Davis, Angela Y. 1974. *Angela Davis: An Autobiography.* New York: Bantam.

————. 1981. *Women, Race, and Class*. New York: Random House.

————. 1994. "Afro Images; Politics, Fashion, and Nostalgia." *Critical Inquiry* 21, no. 2: 37–45.

————. 1997. "Race and Criminalization: Black Americans and the Punishment Industry." Pp. 264–79 in *The House That Race Built: Black Americans, U.S. Terrain*, ed. Wahneema Lubiano. New York: Pantheon.

Dawson, Michael C. 1994. *Behind the Mule: Race and Class in African-American Politics*. Princeton, N.J.: Princeton University Press.

Dent, Gina, ed. 1992. *Black Popular Culture*. Seattle: Bay Press.

Dickerson, Bette J. 1995. "Introduction." Pp. ix–xxx in *African American Single Mothers: Understanding Their Lives and Families*, ed. Bette J. Dickerson. Thousand Oaks, Calif.: Sage.

Dill, Bonnie Thornton. 1988. "Our Mothers' Grief: Racial Ethnic Women and the Maintenance of Families." *Journal of Family History* 13, no. 4: 415–31.

————. 2002. "Work at the Intersections of Race, Gender, Ethnicity, and Other Dimensions of Difference in Higher Education." *Connections: Newsletter of the Consortium on Race, Gender and Ethnicity* (Fall), 5–7.

Diop, Cheikh A. 1974. *The African Origin of Civilization: Myth or Reality*, ed. and trans. Mercer Cook. Westport, Conn.: Lawrence Hill.

Douglas, Kelly Brown. 1999. *Sexuality and the Black Church: A Womanist Perspective*. Maryknoll, N.Y.: Orbis.

Dubey, Madhu. 1994. *Black Women Novelists and the Nationalist Aesthetic*. Bloomington: Indiana University Press.

Du Bois, William E. B. 1969. *The Negro American Family*. Westport, Conn.: Negro Universities Press/Greenwood Press.

Duster, Troy. 1990. *Backdoor to Eugenics*. New York: Routledge.

Dyson, Michael E. 1993. *Reflecting Black: African-American Cultural Criticism*. Minneapolis: University of Minnesota Press.

Emeagwali, Gloria T. 1995. *Women Pay the Price: Structural Adjustment in Africa and the Caribbean*. Trenton, N.J.: Africa World Press.

Enloe, Cynthia. 1990. *Bananas, Beaches, and Bases: Making Feminist Sense of International Politics*. Berkeley: University of California Press.

Entman, Robert M., and Andrew Rojecki. 2000. *The Black Image in the White Mind: Media and Race in America*. Chicago: University of Chicago Press.

Essed, Philomena. 1991. *Understanding Everyday Racism: An Interdisciplinary Theory*. Newbury Park, Calif.: Sage.

Fanon, Frantz. 1963. *The Wretched of the Earth*. New York: Grove Press.

————. 1967. *Black Skin, White Masks*. New York: Grove Press.

Feldstein, Ruth. 2000. *Motherhood in Black and White: Race and Sex in American Liberalism, 1930–1965*. Ithaca, N.Y.: Cornell University Press.

Ferber, Abby L. 1998. *White Man Falling: Race, Gender, and White Supremacy*. Lanham, Md.: Rowman and Littlefield.

Fester, Gertrude. 1998. "Closing the Gap—Activism and Academia in South Africa: Towards a Women's Movement." Pp. 215–37 in *Sisterhood, Feminisms, and Power: From Africa to the Diaspora*, ed. Obioma Nnaemeka. Trenton, N.J.: Africa World Press.

Foucault, Michel. 1980. *Power/Knowledge: Selected Interviews and Other Writings, 1972–1977*, ed. Colin Gordon. New York: Pantheon.

Fox-Genovese, Elizabeth. 1979–80. "Personal Is Not Political Enough." *Marxist Perspectives* (Winter): 94–113.

Franklin, Donna L. 1997. *Ensuring Inequality: The Structural Transformation of the African-American Family*. New York: Oxford University Press.

Franklin, Vincent P. 1992. *Black Self-Determination: A Cultural History of African-American Resistance*. Brooklyn, N.Y.: Lawrence Hill.

Fried, Amy. 1994. " 'It's Hard to Change What We Want to Change': Rape Crisis Centers as Organizations." *Gender and Society* 8, no. 4: 562–83.

Garcia, Alma M. 1997. "The Development of Chicana Feminist Discourse." Pp. 247–68 in *Feminist Nationalism*, ed. Lois A. West. New York: Routledge.

Gates, Henry Louis. 1992. *Loose Canons: Notes on the Culture Wars*. New York: Oxford University Press.

Gayle, Addison. 1971. *The Black Aesthetic*. Garden City, N.Y.: Doubleday.

Geiger, Shirley M. 1995. "African-American Single Mothers: Public Perceptions and Public Policies." Pp. 244–57 in *Black Women in America*, ed. Kim Marie Vaz. Thousand Oaks, Calif.: Sage.

George, Nelson. 1998. *Hip Hop America*. New York: Penguin.

Gilkes, Cheryl Townsend. 1983. "From Slavery to Social Welfare: Racism and the Control of Black Women." Pp. 288–300 in *Class, Race, and Sex: The Dynamics of Control*, ed. Amy Swerdlow and Hanna Lessinger. Boston: G. K. Hall.

———. 2001. *If It Wasn't for the Women: Black Women's Experience and Womanist Culture in Church and Community*. Maryknoll, N.Y.: Orbis.

Gilman, Sander L. 1985. "Black Bodies, White Bodies: Toward an Iconography of Female Sexuality in Late Nineteenth-Century Art, Medicine, and Literature." *Critical Inquiry* 12, no. 1: 205–43.

Gilroy, Paul. 1987. *"There Ain't No Black in the Union Jack": The Cultural Politics of Race and Nation*. Chicago: University of Chicago Press.

———. 1992. "It's a Family Affair: Black Culture and the Trope of Kinship." Pp. 192–207 in Paul Gilroy, *Small Acts: Thoughts on the Politics of Black Culture*. New York: Serpent's Tail.

———. 1993. *The Black Atlantic: Modernity and Double Consciousness*. Cambridge, Mass.: Harvard University Press.

———. 2000. *Against Race: Imagining Political Culture beyond the Color Line*. Cambridge, Mass.: Belknap Press of Harvard University Press.

Glasgow, Douglas G. 1980. *The Black Underclass: Poverty, Unemployment, and Entrapment of Ghetto Youth*. San Francisco: Jossey-Bass.

Glenn, Evelyn Nakano. 1992. "From Servitude to Service Work: Historical Continuities in the Racial Division of Paid Reproductive Labor." *Signs* 18, no. 1: 1–43.

Gluck, Sherna Berger. 1997. "Shifting Sands: The Feminist–Nationalist Connection in the Palestinian Movement." Pp. 101–29 in *Feminist Nationalism*, ed. Lois A. West. New York: Routledge.

Goldberg, David Theo. 1993. *Racist Culture: Philosophy and the Politics of Meaning*. Cambridge, Mass.: Blackwell.

Gordon, Linda. 1994. *Pitied but Not Entitled: Single Mothers and the History of Welfare*. Cambridge: Harvard University Press.

Gossett, Thomas F. 1963. *Race: The History of an Idea in America*. Dallas: Southern Methodist University Press.

Gould, Stephen Jay. 1981. *The Mismeasure of Man*. New York: W. W. Norton.

Graham, Lawrence Otis. 2000. *Our Kind of People: Inside America's Black Upper Class*. New York: HarperPerennial.

Grant, Jacqueline. 1989. *White Women's Christ and Black Women's Jesus: Feminist Christology and Womanist Response*. Atlanta: Scholars Press.

Gray, Herman. 1995. *Watching Race: Television and the Struggle for "Blackness."* Minneapolis: University of Minnesota Press.

Green, Dan. S., and Edwin Driver, eds. 1978. *W. E. B. Du Bois: On Sociology and the Black Community*. Chicago: University of Chicago Press.

Gregory, Steven. 1994. "Race, Identity and Political Activism: The Shifting Contours of the African American Public Sphere." *Public Culture* 7, no. 1: 147–64.

Griffin, Farah Jasmine. 2002. "Conflict and Chorus: Reconsidering Toni Cade Bambara's *The Black Woman: An Anthology*." Pp. 111–29 in *Is It Nation Time? Contemporary Essays on Black Power and Black Nationalism*, ed. Eddie S. Glaude. Chicago: University of Chicago Press.

Guerrero, Marie Anna Jaines. 1997. "Civil Rights versus Sovereignty: Native American Women in Life and Land Struggles." Pp. 101–24 in *Feminist Genealogies, Colonial Legacies, Democratic Futures*. ed. M. Jacqui Alexander and Chandra Talpade Mohanty. New York: Routledge.

Guinier, Lani, and Gerald Torres. 2002. *The Miner's Canary: Enlisting Race, Resisting Power, Transforming Democracy*. Cambridge, Mass.: Harvard University Press.

Gutman, Herbert. 1976. *The Black Family in Slavery and Freedom, 1750–1925*. New York: Random House.

Guy-Sheftall, Beverly. 2002. "Response from a 'Second Waver' to Kimberly Springer's 'Third Wave Black Feminism?'" *Signs* 27, no. 4:1091–94.

Hall, Jacqueline D. 1983. "The Mind That Burns in Each Body: Women, Rape, and Racial Violence." Pp. 329–49 in *Powers of Desire: The Politics of Sexuality*, ed. Ann Snitow, Christine Stansell, and Sharon Thompson. New York: Monthly Review Press.

Haller, Mark H. 1984. *Eugenics: Hereditarian Attitudes in American Thought*. New Brunswick, N.J.: Rutgers University Press.

Hanisch, Carol. 1978. "The Personal Is Political." Pp. 204-5 in *Feminist Revolution*, 2nd ed., ed. Redstockings. New York: Random House.

Harding, Sandra. 1986. *The Science Question in Feminism*. Ithaca, N.Y.: Cornell University Press.

Harris, Trudier. 1984. *Exorcising Blackness: Historical and Literary Lynching and Burning Rituals*. Bloomington: Indiana University Press.

———. 1986. "Introduction." Pp. xi–xxxviii in *Like One of the Family: Conversations from a Domestic's Life*, ed. Alice Childress. Boston: Beacon Press.

Hartouni, Valerie. 1997. "Breached Birth: Anna Johnson and the Reproduction of Raced Bodies." Pp. 85–98 in Valerie Hartouni, *Cultural Conceptions: On*

Reproductive Technologies and the Remaking of Life. Minneapolis: University of Minnesota Press.

Hartsock, Nancy. 1983. The Feminist Standpoint: Developing the Ground for a Specifically Feminist Historical Materialism. Pp. 283–310 in *Discovering Reality*, eds. Sandra Harding and Merrill B. Hintikka. Boston: D. Reidel.

Heng, Geraldine, and Janadas Devan. 1992. "State Fatherhood: The Politics of Nationalism, Sexuality and Race in Singapore." Pp. 343–64 in *Nationalisms and Sexualities*, ed. Andrea Parker, Mary Russo, Doris Sommer, and Patricia Yaeger. New York: Routledge.

Hernández, Daisy, and Pandora L. Leong. 2004. "Feminism's Future: Young Feminists of Color Take the Mic." *In These Times*, Internet ed., April 21. Available at: http://www.inthesetimes.com/site/main/article/feminisms_future (last viewed July 25, 2004).

Hernández, Daisy, and Bushra Rehman, ed. 2002. *Colonize This! Young Women of Color on Today's Feminism*. New York: Seal Press.

Herskovitz, Melville. 1990. *The Myth of the Negro Past*. Boston: Beacon Press.

Higginbotham, Elizabeth, and Lynn Weber. 1992. "Moving Up with Kin and Community: Upward Social Mobility for Black and White Women." *Gender and Society* 6, no. 3: 416–40.

Higginbotham, Evelyn Brooks. 1993. *Righteous Discontent: The Women's Movement in the Black Baptist Church 1880–1920*. Cambridge, Mass.: Harvard University Press.

Hine, Darlene Clark. 1992. "The Black Studies Movement: Afrocentric–Traditionalist–Feminist Paradigms for the Next Stage." *Black Scholar* 22, no. 3: 11–18.

———. 1993. "'In the Kingdom of Culture': Black Women and the Intersection of Race, Gender, and Class." Pp. 337–51 in *Lure and Loathing: Essays on Race, Identity, and the Ambivalence of Assimilation*, ed. Gerald Early. New York: Penguin Books.

Holloway, Joseph, ed. 1990. *Africanisms in American Culture*. Bloomington: Indiana University Press.

Hood, Robert E. 1994. *Begrimed and Black: Christian Traditions on Blacks and Blackness*. Minneapolis: Fortress Press.

Hord, Fred Lee, and Jonathan Scott Lee. 1995. *I Am Because We Are: Readings in Black Philosophy*. Amherst: University of Massachusetts Press.

Huggins, Nathan. 1985. *Afro-American Studies*. New York: Ford Foundation.

Ignatiev, Noel. 1995. *How the Irish Became White*. New York: Routledge.

Ikemoto, Lisa C. 1996. "The InFertile, the Too Fertile, and the Dysfertile." *Hastings Law Journal* 47, no. 4: 1007–61.

Jackson, Peter, and Jan Penrose. 1993. "Introduction: Placing 'Race' and Nation." Pp. 1–23 in *Constructions of Race, Place and Nation*, ed. Peter Jackson and Jan Penrose. Minneapolis: University of Minnesota Press.

James, Stanlie M. 1993. "Mothering: A Possible Black Feminist Link to Social Transformation?" Pp. 44–54 in *Theorizing Black Feminisms: The Visionary Pragmatism of Black Women*, ed. Stanlie M. James and Abena P. A. Busia. New York: Routledge.

Jamila, Shani. 2002. "Can I Get a Witness? Testimony from a Hip Hop Feminist." Pp. 382–94 in *Colonize This! Young Women of Color on Today's Feminism*, ed. Daisy Hernández and Bushra Rehman. New York: Seal Press.

Jarrett, Robin L. 1994. "Living Poor: Family Life among Single Parent, African-American Women." *Social Problems* 41, no. 1: 30–49.

Jhally, Sut, and Justin Lewis. 1992. *Enlightened Racism*. Boulder, Colo.: Westview Press.

Jones, Jacqueline. 1985. *Labor of Love, Labor of Sorrow: Black Women, Work, and the Family from Slavery to the Present*. New York: Basic Books.

Jones, James H. 1993. *Bad Blood: The Tuskegee Syphilis Experiment*. New York: Free Press.

Jones, Lisa. 1994. *Bulletproof Diva: Tales of Race, Sex, and Hair*. New York: Doubleday.

Jones, Yvonne V. 1997. "African-American Cultural Nationalism." Pp. 115–37 in *Cultural Portrayals of African Americans: Creating an Ethnic/Racial Identity*, ed. Janis F. Hutchinson. Westport, Conn.: Bergin and Garvey.

Jordan, June. 1981. *Civil Wars*. Boston: Beacon Press.

Jordan, Winthrop D. 1968. *White over Black: American Attitudes toward the Negro, 1550–1812*. New York: W. W. Norton.

Kaplan, Gisela. 1997. "Feminism and Nationalism: The European Case." Pp. 3–40 in *Feminist Nationalism*, ed. Lois A. West. New York: Routledge.

Karenga, Maulana R. 1978. "Afro-American Nationalism: Beyond Mystification and Misconception." *Black Books Bulletin* (Spring): 7–12.

———. 1982. *Introduction to Black Studies*. Los Angeles: University of Sankore Press.

———. 1995. "The Nguzo Saga (The Seven Principles): Their Meaning and Message." Pp. 276–87 in *Modern Black Nationalism: From Marcus Garvey to Louis Farrakhan*, ed. William L. Van Deburg. New York: New York University Press.

Karenga, Maulana R., ed. 1990. *Reconstructing Kemetic Culture: Papers, Perspectives, Projects*. Los Angeles: University of Sankore Press.

Katz, Michael B. 1989. *The Undeserving Poor: From the War on Poverty to the War on Welfare*. New York: Pantheon.

Katzenstein, Mary F. 1990. "Feminism within American Institutions: Unobtrusive Mobilization in the 1980s." *Signs* 16, no. 1: 27–54.

Kelley, Robin D. G. 1994. *Race Rebels: Culture, Politics, and the Black Working Class*. New York: Free Press.

———. 2002. *Freedom Dreams: The Black Radical Imagination*. Boston: Beacon Press.

Kershaw, Terry. 1992. "Afrocentrism and the Afrocentric Method." *Western Journal of Black Studies* 16(3): 160–68.

Kitwana, Bakari. 2002. *The Hip Hop Generation: Young Blacks and the Crisis in African-American Culture*. New York: Basic Books.

Kuumba, Monica B. 1993. "Perpetuating Neo-Colonialism through Population Control: South Africa and the United States." *Africa Today* 40, no. 3: 79–85.

Latifah, Queen. 1999. *Ladies First: Revelations of a Strong Woman*. New York: Quill.

Lee, Martha F. 1996. *The Nation of Islam: An American Millenarian Movement*. Syracuse, N.Y.: Syracuse University Press.

Lefkowitz, Mary. 1996. *Not Out of Africa: How Afrocentrism Became an Excuse to Teach Myth as History*. New York: Basic Books.

Lemert, Charles. 1995. *Sociology after the Crisis*. Boulder, Colo.: Westview Press.

Lerner, Gerda, ed. 1972. *Black Women in White America: A Documentary History*. New York: Vintage.

Lichterman, Paul. 1995. "Piecing Together Multicultural Community: Cultural Differences in Community Building among Grass-Roots Environmentalists." *Social Problems* 42, no. 4: 513–34.

Lincoln, C. Eric. 1999. *Race, Religion, and the Continuing American Dilemma*. New York: Hill and Wang.

Lorde, Audre. 1984. *Sister Outsider: Essays and Speeches*. Freedom, Calif.: Crossing Press.

Lubiano, Wahneema. 1992. "Black Ladies, Welfare Queens, and State Minstrels: Ideological War by Narrative Means." Pp. 323–63 in *Race-ing Justice, En-Gendering Power*, ed. Toni Morrison. New York: Pantheon Books.

———. 1997. "Black Nationalism and Black Common Sense: Policing Ourselves." Pp. 232–52 in *The House That Race Built: Black Americans, U.S. Terrain*, ed. Wahneema Lubiano. New York: Pantheon.

Lusane, Clarence. 1993. "Rap, Race and Politics." *Race and Class* 35, no. 1: 41–55.

Madhubuti, Haki R. 1990. *Black Men, Obsolete, Single, Dangerous?* Chicago: Third World Press.

Magona, Sindiwe. 1998. *Mother to Mother*. Cape Town: David Philip Publishers.

Mangaliso, Zengie A. 1997. "Gender and Nation-Building in South Africa." Pp. 130–44 in *Feminist Nationalism*, ed. Lois A. West. New York: Routledge.

Marable, Manning. 1993. "Beyond Identity Politics: Towards a Liberation Theory for Multicultural Democracy." *Race and Class* 35, no. 1: 113–30.

Martin, Patricia Y. 1990. "Rethinking Feminist Organizations." *Gender and Society* 4, no. 2: 182–206.

Martinez, Erica G. 2002. "Dutiful Hijas: Dependency, Power and Guilt." Pp. 142–56 in *Colonize This! Young Women of Color on Today's Feminism*, ed. Daisy Hernández and Bushra Rehman. New York: Seal Press.

Massey, Douglas S., and Nancy A. Denton. 1993. *American Apartheid: Segregation and the Making of the Underclass*. Cambridge, Mass.: Harvard University Press.

Matthews, Nancy A. 1989. "Surmounting a Legacy: The Expansion of Racial Diversity in an Anti-Rape Movement." *Gender and Society* 3, no. 4: 518–32.

Mbiti, John. S. 1969. *African Religions and Philosophy*. London: Heinemann.

McClintock, Anne. 1995. *Imperial Leather: Race, Gender, and Sexuality in the Colonial Contest*. New York: Routledge.

McKee, James B. 1993. *Sociology and the Race Problem: The Failure of a Perspective*. Urbana: University of Illinois Press.

McKinnon, Jesse. 2003. *The Black Population in the United States: March 2002*, vol. P-20-541. Washington, D.C.: U.S. Census Bureau.

Memmi, Albert. 2000. *Racism*. Minneapolis: University of Minnesota Press.

Mercer, Kobena. 1994. *Welcome to the Jungle: New Positions in Black Cultural Studies*. New York: Routledge.

Miles, Robert. 1989. *Racism*. New York: Routledge.

Miller, Jerome G. 1996. *Search and Destroy: African-American Males in the Criminal Justice System*. New York: Cambridge University Press.

Mink, Gwendolyn. 1990. "The Lady and the Tramp: Gender, Race, and the Origins of the American Welfare State." Pp. 92–122 in *Women, the State, and Welfare*, ed. Linda Gordon. Madison: University of Wisconsin Press.

Mirza, Heidi Safia, ed. 1997. *Black British Feminism: A Reader*. New York: Routledge.

Mitchell, Henry H., and Nicholas C. Lewter. 1986. *Soul Theology: The Heart of American Black Culture*. San Francisco: Harper and Row.

Moghissi, Haideh. 1999. *Feminism and Islamic Fundamentalism: The Limits of Postmodern Analysis*. London: Zed.

Mohanty, Chandra Talpade. 1997. "Women Workers and Capitalist Scripts: Ideologies of Domination, Common Interests, and the Politics of Solidarity." Pp. 3–29 in *Feminist Genealogies, Colonial Legacies, Democratic Futures*, ed. M. Jacqui Alexander and Chandra Talpade Mohanty. New York: Routledge.

Morgan, Joan. 1999. *When Chickenheads Come Home to Roost: My Life as a Hip-Hop Feminist*. New York: Simon and Schuster.

Moses, Wilson Jeremiah. 1978. *The Golden Age of Black Nationalism, 1850–1925*. New York: Oxford University Press.

Mosse, George L. 1985. *Nationalism and Sexuality: Middle-class Morality and Sexual Norms in Modern Europe*. New York: H. Fertig.

Moynihan, Daniel Patrick. 1965. *The Negro Family: The Case for National Action*. Washington, D.C.: U.S. Government Printing Office.

Myers, Linda J. 1988. *Understanding an Afrocentric World View: Introduction to an Optimal Psychology*. Dubuque, Iowa: Kendall/Hunt.

Naples, Nancy. 1991. " 'Just What Needed to be Done': The Political Practice of Women Community Workers in Low Income Neighborhoods." *Gender and Society* 5, no. 4: 478–94.

Neal, Mark Anthony. 2002. *Soul Babies: Black Popular Culture and the Post-Soul Aesthetic*. New York: Routledge.

Nelson, Barbara. 1990. "The Origins of the Two-Channel Welfare State: Workmen's Compensation and Mothers' Aid." Pp. 92–122 in *Women, the State, and Welfare*, ed. Linda Gordon. Madison: University of Wisconsin Press.

Neubeck, Kenneth J., and Noel A. Cazenave. 2001. *Welfare Racism: Playing the Race Card against America's Poor*. New York: Routledge.

New York Radical Feminists. 1969. "The Politics of the Ego: A Manifesto for New York Radical Feminists." Pp. 442–45 in *Rebirth of Feminism*, ed. Judith Hole and Ellen Levine. New York: Quadrangle.

Nnaemeka, Obioma, ed. 1998. *Sisterhood, Feminisms, and Power: From Africa to the Diaspora*. Trenton, N.J.: Africa World Press.

Nobles, Wade. 1972. "African Philosophy: Foundations for Black Psychology." Pp. 18–32 in *Black Psychology*, ed. Rhett L. Jones. New York: Harper and Row.

Nsiah-Jefferson, Laurie. 1989. "Reproductive Laws, Women of Color, and Low-Income Women." Pp. 23–67 in *Reproductive Laws for the 1990s*, ed. Sherrill Cohen and Nadine Taub. Clifton, N.J.: Humana Press.

Okongwu, Anne. 1993. "Some Conceptual Issues: Female Single-Parent Families in the United States.: Pp. 107–30 in *Where Did All the Men Go? Female-Headed/Female-Supported Households in Cross-Cultural Perspective*, ed. Joan P. Mencher and Anne Okongwu. Boulder, Colo.: Westview Press.

Oliver, Melvin L., and Thomas M. Shapiro. 1995. *Black Wealth/White Wealth: A New Perspective on Racial Inequality*. New York: Routledge.

Omi, Michael, and Howard Winant. 1994. *Racial Formation in the United States: From the 1960s to the 1990s*. New York: Routledge.

Omolade, Barbara. 1994. *The Rising Song of African American Women*. New York: Routledge.

Orfield, Gary, and Carole Ashkinaze. 1991. *The Closing Door: Conservative Policy and Black Opportunity*. Chicago: University of Chicago Press.

Padilla, Genero M. 1989. "Myth and Comparative Cultural Nationalism: The Ideological Uses of Aztlan." Pp. 111–34 in *Aztlan: Essays on the Chicano Homeland*, ed. Rudolfo Anaya and Francisco A. Lomeli. Albuquerque: Academia/El Norte Publications.

Pala, Achola O., ed. 1995. *Connecting across Cultures and Continents: Black Women Speak Out on Identity, Race, and Development*. New York: United Nations Development Fund for Women.

Paris, Peter J. 1995. *The Spirituality of African Peoples: The Search for a Common Moral Discourse*. Minneapolis: Fortress Press.

Patillo-McCoy, Mary. 1998. "Church Culture as a Strategy of Action in the Black Community." *American Sociological Review* 63 (December): 767–84.

———. 1999. *Black Picket Fences: Privilege and Peril among the Black Middle Class*. Chicago: University of Chicago Press.

Pierce-Baker, Charlotte. 1998. *Surviving the Silence: Black Women's Stories of Rape*. New York: W. W. Norton.

Pieterse, Jan N. 2004. "Ethnicities and Multiculturalisms: Politics of Boundaries." Pp. 27–49 in *Nationalism, Ethnicity and Minority Rights*, ed. Stephen May, Tariq Madood, and Judith Squires. London: Cambridge University Press.

Pinar, William F. 2001. *The Gender of Racial Politics and Violence in America: Lynching, Prison Rape, and the Crisis of Masculinity*. New York: Peter Lang.

Pinkney, Alphonso. 1976. *Red, Black, and Green: Black Nationalism in the United States*. London: Cambridge University Press.

Polletta, Francesca, and James M. Jasper. 2001. "Collective Identity and Social Movements." *Annual Review of Sociology* 27: 283–305.

Poster, Winifred R. 1995. "The Challenges and Promises of Class and Racial Diversity in the Women's Movement." *Gender and Society* 9, no. 6: 659–79.

Pough, Gwendolyn D. 2004. *Check It While I Wreck It: Black Womanhood, Hip-Hop Culture, and the Public Sphere*. Boston: Northeastern University Press.

Proctor, Robert N. 1988. *Racial Hygiene: Medicine under the Nazis*. Cambridge, Mass.: Harvard University Press.

Radford-Hill, Sheila. 2000. *Further to Fly: Black Women and the Politics of Empowerment*. Minneapolis: University of Minnesota Press.

———. 2002. "Keepin' It Real: A Generational Commentary on Kimberly Springer's 'Third Wave Black Feminism?'" *Signs* 27, no. 4: 1083–89.

Ransby, Barbara, and Tracye A. Matthews. 1993. "Black Popular Culture and the Transcendence of Patriarchal Illusions." *Race and Class* 35, no. 1: 57–68.

Raymond, Janice. 1993. *Women as Wombs: Reproductive Technologies and the Battle over Women's Freedom*. San Francisco: HarperSanFrancisco.

Reagon, Bernice Johnson. 1987. "African Diaspora Women: The Making of Cultural Workers." Pp. 167–80 in *Women in Africa and the African Diaspora*, ed. Rosalyn Terborg-Penn, Sharon Harley, and Andrea Benton Rushing. Washington, D.C.: Howard University Press.

Rhode, Deborah L. 1995. "Media Images, Feminist Issues." *Signs* 20, no. 3: 685–710.

Richards, Dona. 1980. "European Mythology: The Ideology of 'Progress.'" Pp. 59–79 in *Contemporary Black Thought*, ed. Molefi K. Asante and A. Vandi. Beverly Hills, Calif.: Sage.

———. 1990. "The Implications of African-American Spirituality." Pp. 207–31 in *African Culture: The Rhythms of Unity*, ed. Molefi K. Asante and. K. W. Asante. Trenton, N.J.: Africa World Press.

Roberts, Dorothy E. 1997. *Killing the Black Body: Race, Reproduction, and the Meaning of Liberty*. New York: Pantheon.

Robinson, Dean E. 2001. *Black Nationalism in American Politics and Thought*. New York: Oxford University Press.

Rodriguez, Noelle M. 1988. "Transcending Bureaucracy: Feminist Politics at a Shelter for Battered Women." *Gender and Society* 2, no. 2: 214–27.

Rose, Tricia. 1994. *Black Noise: Rap Music and Black Culture in Contemporary America*. Hanover, N.H.: Wesleyan University Press.

Ross, Loretta J., Sarah L. Brownlee, Dazon Dixon Diallo, Luz Rodriguez, and SisterSong Women of Color Health Project. 2002. "Just Choices: Women of Color, Reproductive Health, and Human Rights." Pp. 147–74 in *Policing the National Body: Race, Gender, and Criminalization*, ed. Jael Silliman and Anannya Bhattacharjee. Cambridge, Mass.: South End Press.

Roth, Benita. 2004. *Separate Roads to Feminism: Black, Chicana, and White Feminist Movements in America's Second Wave*. New York: Cambridge University Press.

Rouse, Carolyn Moxley. 2004. *Engaged Surrender: African American Women and Islam*. Berkeley: University of California Press.

Rowland, Robyn. 1987. "Technology and Motherhood: Reproductive Choice Reconsidered." *Signs* 12, no. 3: 512–28.

Sacks, Karen Brodkin. 1988. "Gender and Grassroots Leadership." Pp. 77–96 in *Women and the Politics of Empowerment*, ed. Ann Bookman and Sandra Morgen. Philadelphia: Temple University Press.

———. 1994. "How Did Jews Become White Folks?" Pp. 78–102 in *Race*, ed. Steven Gregory and Roger Sanjek. New Brunswick, N.J.: Rutgers University Press.

Saegert, Susan. 1989. "Unlikely Leaders, Extreme Circumstances: Older Black Women Building Community Households." *American Journal of Community Psychology* 17, no. 3: 295–317.

Sampaio, Anna. 2002. "Transforming Chicana/o and Latina/o Politics: Globalization and the Formation of Transnational Resistance in the United States and Chiapas." Pp. 47–71 in *Transnational Latina/o Communities: Politics, Processes, and Cultures*, ed. Carlos G. Velez-Ibanez and Anna Sampaio. Boston: Rowman and Littlefield.

San Juan Jr., E. 1992. *Racial Formations/Critical Transformations: Articulations of Power in Ethnic and Racial Studies in the United States*. Atlantic Highlands, N.J.: Humanities Press.

Sarachild, Kathie. 1978. "Consciousness-Raising: A Radical Weapon." Pp. 144–50 in *Feminist Revolution*, 2nd ed., ed. Redstockings. New York: Random House.

Scott, James C. 1985. *Weapons of the Weak: Everyday Forms of Peasant Resistance*. New Haven, Conn.: Yale University Press.

———. 1990. *Domination and the Arts of Resistance: The Hidden Transcripts*. New Haven, Conn.: Yale University Press.

Senghor, Leopold. 1995. "Negritude: A Humanism of the Twentieth Century." Pp. 45–54 in *I Am Because We Are: Readings in Black Philosophy*, ed. Fred L. Hord and Jonathan Scott Lee. Amherst: University of Massachusetts Press.

Serequeberhan,Tsenay, ed. 1991. *African Philosophy: The Essential Readings*. New York: Paragon House.

Shakur, Sanyika. 1993. *Monster: The Autobiography of a L.A. Gang Member*. New York: Atlantic Monthly Press.

Simon, David, and Edward Burns. 1997. *The Corner: A Year in the Life of an Inner-City Neighborhood*. New York: Broadway Books.

Small, Mario Luis, and Katherine Newman. 2001. "Urban Poverty after *The Truly Disadvantaged*: The Rediscovery of the Family, the Neighborhood, and Culture." *Annual Review of Sociology* 27: 23–45.

Smith, Barbara E. 1995. "Crossing the Great Divides: Race, Class and Gender in Southern Women's Organizing, 1979–1991." *Gender and Society* 9, no. 6: 680–96.

Smith, Barbara. 1998. *The Truth That Never Hurts: Writings on Race, Gender, and Freedom*. New Brunswick, N.J.: Rutgers University Press.

Smith, Taigi. 2002. "What Happens When Your Hood Is the Last Stop on the White Flight Express?" Pp. 54–70 in *Colonize This! Young Women of Color on Today's Feminism*, ed. Daisy Hernández and Bushra Rehman. New York: Seal Press.

Smitherman, Geneva. 1977. *Talkin' and Testifyin': The Language of Black America*. Boston: Houghton Mifflin.

———. 1996. "A Womanist Looks at the Million Man March." Pp. 104–07 in *Million Man March/Day of Absence*, ed. Haki R. Madhubuti and Maulana Karenga. Chicago: Third World Press.

Smooth, Wendy G., and Tamelyn Tucker. 1999. "Behind but Not Forgotten: Women and the Behind-the-Scenes Organizing of the Million Man March." Pp. 241–58 in *Still Lifting, Still Climbing: African American Women's Contemporary Activism*, ed. Kimberly Springer. New York: New York University Press.

Sobel, Mechal. 1979. *Trabelin' On: The Slave Journey to an Afro-Baptist Faith*. Princeton, N.J.: Princeton University Press.

Solinger, Rickie. 1992. *Wake Up Little Susie: Single Pregnancy and Race Before Roe vs. Wade*. New York: Routledge.

Souljah, Sister. 1994. *No Disrespect*. New York: Times Books.

———. 1999. *The Coldest Winter Ever*. New York: Pocket Books.

Spivak, Gayatri C. 1993. *Outside in the Teaching Machine*. New York: Routledge.

Springer, Kimberly. 2002. "Third Wave Black Feminism?" *Signs* 27, no. 4: 1059–82.

Springer, Kimberly, ed. 1999. *Still Lifting, Still Climbing: African American Women's Contemporary Activism*. New York: New York University Press.

Squires, Gregory D. 1994. *Capital and Communities in Black and White: The Intersections of Race, Class, and Uneven Development*. Albany: State University of New York Press.

Stanley, Liz, and Sue Wise. 1993. *Breaking Out Again: Feminist Ontology and Epistemology*. New York: Routledge.

Steady, Filomina Chioma. 1993. "Women and Collective Action: Female Models in Transition." Pp. 90–101 in *Theorizing Black Feminisms: The Visionary Pragmatism of Black Women*, ed. Stanlie M. James and Abena P. A. Busia. New York: Routledge.

Sudarkasa, Niara. 1981. "Interpreting the African Heritage in Afro-American Family Organization." Pp. 37–53 in *Black Families*, ed. Harriette P. McAdoo. Beverly Hills, Calif.: Sage.

Sudbury, Julia. 1998. *"Other Kinds of Dreams": Black Women's Organizations and the Politics of Transformation*. New York: Routledge.

Tait, Vanessa. 1999. " 'Workers Just Like Anyone Else': Organizing Workfare Unions in New York City." Pp. 297–324 in *Still Lifting, Still Climbing: African American Women's Contemporary Activism*, ed. Kimberly Springer. New York: New York University Press.

Talvi, Silja A. 2003. "Women on the Edge," *In These Times*, Internet ed., August 15. Available at: http:/www.inthesetimes.com/site/main/article/women_on _the_edge (last viewed July 25, 2004).

Tate, Claudia, ed. 1983. *Black Women Writers at Work*. New York: Continuum.

Taylor, Verta. 1989. "Social Movement Continuity: The Women's Movement in Abeyance." *American Sociological Review* 54: 761–75.

Taylor, Verta, and Leila J. Rupp. 1993. "Women's Culture and Lesbian Feminist Activism: A Reconsideration of Cultural Feminism." *Signs* 19: 32–61.

Taylor, Verta, and N. Whittier. 1992. "Collective Identity in Social Communities: Lesbian Feminist Mobilization." Pp. 104–30 in *Frontiers in Social Movement Theory*, ed. Aldon D. Morris and C. M. Mueller. New Haven, Conn.: Yale University Press.

Terborg-Penn, Rosalyn, Sharon Harley, and Andrea B. Rushing, eds. 1987. *Women in Africa and the African Diaspora*. Washington, D.C.: Howard University Press.

Terrelonge, Pauline. 1984. "Feminist Consciousness and Black Women." Pp. 557–67 in *Women: A Feminist Perspective*, 3rd ed., ed. Jo Freeman. Palo Alto, Calif.: Mayfield.

Thiam, Awa. 1978. *Black Sisters, Speak Out: Feminism and Oppression in Black Africa*. London: Pluto Press.

Thompson, Robert F. 1983. *Flash of the Spirit: African and Afro-American Art and Philosophy*. New York: Vintage.

Thorne, Barrie. 1992. "Feminism and the Family: Two Decades of Thought." Pp. 3–30 in *Rethinking the Family: Some Feminist Questions*, ed. Barrie Thorne and Marilyn Yalom. Boston: Northeastern University Press.

Trebay, Guy. 2000. "Homo Thugz Blow Up the Spot: A Gay Hip-Hop Scene Rises in the Bronx." *Village Voice*, 2–8 February.

Tuan, Mia. 1998. *Forever Foreigners or Honorary Whites? The Asian Ethnic Experience Today*. New Brunswick, N.J.: Rutgers University Press.

Tucker, William H. 1994. *The Science and Politics of Racial Research*. Urbana: University of Illinois Press.

Turner, Patricia A. 1994. *Ceramic Uncles and Celluloid Mammies: Black Images and Their Influence on Culture*. New York: Anchor.

Twine, France Winddance, and Kathleen M. Blee. 2001. *Feminism and Antiracism: International Struggles for Justice*. New York: New York University Press.

"Two Mission Statements—National Black Women's Health Project and African American Women Are for Reproductive Freedom." 1999. Pp. 37–41 in *Still Lifting, Still Climbing: African American Women's Contemporary Activism*, ed. Kimberly Springer. New York: New York University Press.

Van Deburg, William L. 1992. *New Day in Babylon: The Black Power Movement and American Culture, 1965–1975*. Chicago: University of Chicago Press.

———, ed. 1997. *Modern Black Nationalism: From Marcus Garvey to Louis Farrakhan*. New York: New York University Press.

Van Dijk, Teun A. 1993. *Elite Discourse and Racism*. Newbury Park, Calif.: Sage.

Wallace, Michele. 1990. *Invisibility Blues: From Pop to Theory*. New York: Verso.

Waters, Mary. 1996. "Optional Ethnicities: For Whites Only?" Pp. 444–54 in *Origins and Destinies: Immigration, Race and Ethnicity in America*, ed. Silvia Pedraza and Ruben G. Rumbaut. Belmont, Calif.: Wadsworth.

Wells, Julia. 1998. "Maternal Politics in Organizing Black South African Women: The Historical Lessons." Pp. 251–62 in *Sisterhood, Feminisms, and Power: From Africa to the Diaspora*, ed. Obioma Nnaemeka. Trenton, N.J.: Africa World Press.

Welsing, Frances C. 1991. *The Isis Papers: The Keys to the Colors*. Chicago: Third World Press.

West, Cornel. 1993. *Race Matters*. Boston: Beacon Press.

West, Lois A. 1997a. *Feminist Nationalism*. New York: Routledge.

———. 1997b. "Introduction: Feminism Constructs Nationalism." Pp. xi–xxxvi in *Feminist Nationalism*, ed. Lois A. West. New York: Routledge.

West, Traci C. 1999. *Wounds of the Spirit: Black Women, Violence, and Resistance Ethics*. New York: New York University Press.

White, Deborah Gray. 1999. *Too Heavy a Load: Black Women in Defense of Themselves 1894–1994*. New York: W. W. Norton.

White, E. Frances. 1990. "Africa on My Mind: Gender, Counter Discourse and African-American Nationalism." *Journal of Women's History* 2, no. 1: 73–97.

White, Evelyn C. 1985. *Chain, Chain, Change: For Black Women Dealing with Physical and Emotional Abuse*. Seattle: Seal Press.

White, Joseph L., and Thomas A. Parham. 1990. *The Psychology of Blacks: An African-American Perspective*, 2nd ed. Englewood Cliffs, N.J.: Prentice-Hall.

Wiegman, Robyn. 2002. "Academic Feminism against Itself." *NWSA Journal* 14, no. 2: 18–37.

Williams, Brackett F. 1995. "Classification Systems Revisited: Kinship, Caste, Race, and Nationality as the Flow of Blood and the Spread of Rights." Pp. 201–36 in *Naturalizing Power: Essays in Feminist Cultural Analysis*, ed. Sylvia Yanagisako and Carol Delaney. New York: Routledge.

Williams, Patricia. 1995. *The Rooster's Egg*. Cambridge, Mass.: Harvard University Press.

Wilson, William Julius. 1978. *The Declining Significance of Race*. Chicago: University of Chicago Press.

———. 1987. *The Truly Disadvantaged: The Inner City, the Underclass, and Public Policy*. Chicago: University of Chicago Press.

————. 1996. *When Work Disappears: The World of the New Urban Poor*. New York: Knopf.

Winant, Howard. 1994. *Racial Conditions: Politics, Theory, Comparisons*. Minneapolis: University of Minnesota Press.

————. 2001. *The World Is a Ghetto: Race and Democracy since World War II*. New York: Basic Books.

Young, Robert J. C. 1995. *Colonial Desire: Hybridity in Theory, Culture and Race*. New York: Routledge.

Yuval-Davis, Nira. 1997. *Gender and Nation*. Thousand Oaks, Calif.: Sage.

Zinn, Maxine B. 1992. "Family, Race, and Poverty in the Eighties." Pp. 71–90 in *Rethinking the Family: Some Feminist Questions*, ed. Barrie Thorne and Marilyn Yalom. Boston: Northeastern University Press.

Zook, Kristal B. 1992. "Reconstructions of Nationalist Thought in Black Music and Culture." Pp. 255–66 in *Rockin' the Boat: Mass Music and Mass Movements*, ed. Reebee Garofalo. Boston: South End Press.

Index